REVELATION

BELIEF

A Theological Commentary
on the Bible

GENERAL EDITORS

Amy Plantinga Pauw
William C. Placher[†]

REVELATION

AMOS YONG

WJK WESTMINSTER
JOHN KNOX PRESS
LOUISVILLE · KENTUCKY

First edition
Published by Westminster John Knox Press
Louisville, Kentucky

21 22 23 24 25 26 27 28 29 30—10 9 8 7 6 5 4 3 2 1

Book design by Drew Stevens
Cover design by Lisa Buckley
Cover illustration: © David Chapman/Design Pics/Corbis

Library of Congress Cataloging-in-Publication Data
Names: Yong, Amos, author.
Title: Revelation / Amos Yong.
Other titles: Belief (Series)
Description: First edition. | Louisville, Kentucky : Westminster John Knox
  Press, 2021. | Series: Belief: a theological commentary on the Bible |
  Includes bibliographical references and index. | Summary: "In this
  volume of the Belief series, Amos Yong analyzes the message of
  Revelation to its earliest readers and speaks to its ongoing meaning for
  believers today"-- Provided by publisher.
Identifiers: LCCN 2021026136 (print) | LCCN 2021026137 (ebook) | ISBN
  9780664232481 (hardback) | ISBN 9781646981991 (ebook)
Subjects: LCSH: Bible. Revelation--Commentaries.
Classification: LCC BS2825.53 .Y66 2021 (print) | LCC BS2825.53 (ebook) |
  DDC 228/.07--dc23
LC record available at https://lccn.loc.gov/2021026136
LC ebook record available at https://lccn.loc.gov/2021026137

Most Westminster John Knox Press books are available at special quantity discounts when purchased in bulk by corporations, organizations, and special-interest groups. For more information, please e-mail SpecialSales@wjkbooks.com.

To

Rich and Helena Coffelt
Ben and Debbie Cabitac
Siang Yang and Angela Tan

Contents

Publisher's Note

William C. Placher worked with Amy Plantinga Pauw as a general editor for this series until his untimely death in November 2008. Bill brought great energy and vision to the series and was instrumental in defining and articulating its distinctive approach and in securing theologians to write for it. Bill's own commentary for the series was the last thing he wrote, and Westminster John Knox Press dedicates the entire series to his memory with affection and gratitude.

William C. Placher, LaFollette Distinguished Professor in Humanities at Wabash College, spent thirty-four years as one of Wabash College's most popular teachers. A summa cum laude graduate of Wabash in 1970, he earned his master's degree in philosophy in 1974 and his PhD in 1975, both from Yale University. In 2002 the American Academy of Religion honored him with the Excellence in Teaching Award. Placher was also the author of thirteen books, including *A History of Christian Theology, The Triune God, The Domestication of Transcendence, Jesus the Savior, Narratives of a Vulnerable God,* and *Unapologetic Theology.* He also edited the volume *Essentials of Christian Theology,* which was named as one of 2004's most outstanding books by both *The Christian Century* and *Christianity Today* magazines.

Series Introduction

Belief: A Theological Commentary on the Bible is a series from Westminster John Knox Press featuring biblical commentaries written by theologians. The writers of this series share Karl Barth's concern that, insofar as their usefulness to pastors goes, most modern commentaries are "no commentary at all, but merely the first step toward a commentary." Historical-critical approaches to Scripture rule out some readings and commend others, but such methods only begin to help theological reflection and the preaching of the Word. By themselves, they do not convey the powerful sense of God's merciful presence that calls Christians to repentance and praise; they do not bring the church fully forward in the life of discipleship. It is to such tasks that theologians are called.

For several generations, however, professional theologians in North America and Europe have not been writing commentaries on the Christian Scriptures. The specialization of professional disciplines and the expectations of theological academies about the kind of writing that theologians should do, as well as many of the directions in which contemporary theology itself has gone, have contributed to this dearth of theological commentaries. This is a relatively new phenomenon; until the last century or two, the church's great theologians also routinely saw themselves as biblical interpreters. The gap between the fields is a loss for both the church and the discipline of theology itself. By inviting forty contemporary theologians to wrestle deeply with particular texts of Scripture, the editors of this series hope not only to provide new theological resources for the church but also to encourage all theologians to pay more attention to Scripture and the life of the church in their writings.

We are grateful to the Louisville Institute, which provided funding for a consultation in June 2007. We invited theologians, pastors, and biblical scholars to join us in a conversation about what this series could contribute to the life of the church. The time was provocative, and the results were rich. Much of the series' shape owes to the insights of these skilled and faithful interpreters, who sought to describe a way to write a commentary that served the theological needs of the church and its pastors with relevance, historical accuracy, and theological depth. The passion of these participants guided us in creating this series and lives on in the volumes.

As theologians, the authors will be interested much less in the matters of form, authorship, historical setting, social context, and philology—the very issues that are often of primary concern to critical biblical scholars. Instead, this series' authors will seek to explain the theological importance of the texts for the church today, using biblical scholarship as needed for such explication but without any attempt to cover all of the topics of the usual modern biblical commentary. This thirty-six-volume series will provide passage-by-passage commentary on all the books of the Protestant biblical canon, with more extensive attention given to passages of particular theological significance.

The authors' chief dialogue will be with the church's creeds, practices, and hymns; with the history of faithful interpretation and use of the Scriptures; with the categories and concepts of theology; and with contemporary culture in both "high" and popular forms. Each volume will begin with a discussion of *why* the church needs this book and why we need it *now*, in order to ground all of the commentary in contemporary relevance. Throughout each volume, text boxes will highlight the voices of ancient and modern interpreters from the global communities of faith, and occasional essays will allow deeper reflection on the key theological concepts of these biblical books.

The authors of this commentary series are theologians of the church who embrace a variety of confessional and theological perspectives. The group of authors assembled for this series represents more diversity of race, ethnicity, and gender than most other commentary series. They approach the larger Christian tradition with a critical respect, seeking to reclaim its riches and at the same time to acknowledge its shortcomings. The authors also aim to make available to readers a wide range of contemporary theological voices from many parts of the world. While it does recover an older genre of writing, this series is not an attempt to retrieve some idealized past. These commentaries have learned from tradition, but they are most importantly commentaries for today. The authors share the conviction that their work will be more contemporary, more faithful, and more radical, to the extent that it is more biblical, honestly wrestling with the texts of the Scriptures.

William C. Placher
Amy Plantinga Pauw

Preface

Why would anyone want to write a(nother) commentary on the book of Revelation, and what would she or he say? More particularly, how would an Asian American Pentecostal Christian read this book at the turn of the third decade of the twenty-first century? And more precisely, why risk a somewhat respectable reputation as a theologian and missiologist, but certainly not as a biblical scholar by any even gracious stretch of the imagination, by daring to comment on the Apocalypse, long known as *the* book on the so-called *end times*, when even Jesus did not seem to know about these "times or periods that the Father has set by his own authority" (Acts 1:7)? And on the other side of these questions, I have wondered that if I ever finished this book (which I have been thinking seriously about since the summer of 2015), would I have anything else to say after that? Think of it: Would it not be that completing a commentary on arguably the most difficult book of the Bible, which concerns the goal and end of *all things,* mean that any other words would be superfluous?

Well, my introductory chapter tries to provide some of the reasons why I thought, and still believe, this might be a good idea; although in the end, you, my readers, will be the ones who decide if the risk I took was worth the effort. But in the meanwhile, let me thank Belief series editor Amy Plantinga Pauw for the invitation to write this theological commentary, even as I express gratitude to whoever it was who originally agreed to do so but had to withdraw and opened up a slot for me as a second choice. However this commentary is received, I have learned a great deal in this process and am grateful for how my study of Revelation has pushed me to think about important theological and missiological matters.

I am grateful to Fuller Theological Seminary for a sabbatical leave during the spring term of 2019 during which much of the first draft of this book was completed. If I had waited another year and written this book after the emergence of the coronavirus, this commentary may have made much more of the various racial, economic-political, and environmental crises catalyzed by the global plague. On the other hand, that may well also have dated the theological takeaways of the book as the world inevitably, even if also gradually, adapts to a post-pandemic reality. Yet the increase in North America especially of anti-Asian and anti-Asian American sentiment brought on by foistering the origins of the virus on the Chinese, along with the spike of discrimination against and harassment of those of Asian descent, unfortunately confirms the relevance of the Asian American interpretive optic adopted in the following pages. In attending to the penultimate revisions of the copyedited manuscript received from the publisher in the spring of 2021, I have resisted the urge to rewrite the commentary to address these matters, but I have inserted a handful of footnotes at the end of the "Further Reflections" sections of especially pertinent passages.

Thanks to Alice Song, Gail Frederick, and others in the Hubbard Library for facilitating my access to books and articles over the years. My friend Frank D. Macchia, who himself has commented theologically on Revelation, gave me helpful feedback on an earlier version of my introductory chapter, which was encouraging at that time. U-Wen Low and Jon Newton read the full manuscript, and both sent editorial comments and many helpful suggestions to improve the manuscript, with the former especially pressing me to be more consistent with my Asian American hermeneutical lens. Amy Pauw and Don McKim also sent encouraging words following the first full draft and ensured that I followed the series template, while an anonymous reviewer also read the manuscript very carefully and helped me clarify and improve the book. My graduate assistants Nok Kam and Jeremy Bone both were helpful in my research for this volume. Yosam Manafa, another graduate assistant, helped with creating a full bibliography for the book. Daniel Braden was a copyeditor extraordinaire, and his attentiveness to details improved the volume enormously. David Dobson, Michele Blum, Natalie Smith, Julie Tonini, and others at Westminster John Knox have been fantastic to work with throughout these years.

My wife, Alma, has been the bedrock of my life and work. We celebrated thirty-two years of marriage in the middle of my making revisions on one of the drafts of the manuscript, which gave me the needed impetus to finish it, and a year later we celebrated our thirty-third-year anniversary, after which I returned to complete the final revisions in response to the reviewer's comments. I am continuously amazed by her steadfastness and delighted afresh each passing year by her companionship. Her love, care, and presence bless me beyond words.

This book is dedicated to three couples, two who have been precious friends since Alma and I met them at Bethany College of the Assemblies of God (which closed in 2009) in the mid-1980s. We reconnected with Rich Coffelt when we first arrived at Regent University in 2005, and he was finishing his Doctor of Ministry degree there at the school of divinity. He introduced us to Helena (who was not a Bethany student), they welcomed us to the Virginia Beach area, and our families bonded. We have missed them since they moved back to Northern California to take a pastorate in Castroville a few years before we came to Southern California to Fuller. Over the last ten plus years Rich and Helena have been faithful in their congregation but have come to be widely recognized as ministers and pastors for the wider community within which they live and serve. We cherish our memories together and always look forward to their visits south or anticipate opportunities to connect in our visits north.

Ben and Debbie Cabitac were part of the ministry team that Alma led at Bethany from 1984–1985 (which was also the venue where I first laid eyes on Alma!). Ben and Debbie have since served faithfully as pastors in both Northern and Southern California, including the last almost decade at Bethel Church in Glendale, a city next to Pasadena. We have been blessed to fellowship with them more regularly since arriving at Fuller—except since the spring of 2020 when most of us have been isolated under COVID-19 circumstances—and have shared life events involving the gradual emancipation of our adult children (three each). Bethel Church has always also served a Spanish-speaking congregation on their premises, and recently Ben has been invited to serve as minister also to that community; so he is now practicing preaching in Spanish regularly, and his two congregations have worked more closely together than ever before.

I met Siang Yang Tan when I first arrived at Fuller Seminary in the fall of 2014 where, as a member of the School of Psychology, he welcomed me to the seminary faculty. Having taught at Fuller since the mid 1980s, Siang Yang and his wife, Angela, have also pastored First Evangelical Church in Glendale for the last two-plus decades. Amid his bivocational commitments—shepherding this large and vibrant trilingual ecclesial community (with weekly services in English, Cantonese, and Mandarin) while being engaged teaching and mentoring as a full professor, publishing important and renowned works in pastoral ministry and counseling, and retaining his clinical practice as our School of Psychology professors often do—he found time to take me to lunch every few months. Over curry laksa and char kway teow, we shared our lives and prayed together. Siang Yang retired from the Seminary last year but will continue to serve the church locally and globally through his writing, preaching, and teaching.

These ministry couples are our heroes because there is no vocation more challenging than the shepherding of local congregations in very different and diverse parts of California that they have been faithfully persistent during a period of history that has seen, in many respects, the marginalization of the church in North America. The book of Revelation repeatedly urges "anyone who has an ear listen to what the Spirit is saying to the churches" (Rev. 2:7 passim). The Coffelts, Cabitacs, and Tans have shown us what that means in pastoral, congregational, and wider community contexts, even as they have embraced us on our common journey of faith that waits for when "the kingdom of the world has become the kingdom of our Lord and of his Messiah" (Rev. 11:15).

* * * * *

Note to the reader: It is highly recommended that this theological commentary be read with the text of the book of Revelation close at hand. May working through the former not replace reading the latter but instead motivate deeper engagement with this final book of the Bible. All parenthetical citations of chapter and verse are also to the book of Revelation unless otherwise referenced.

Introduction
Why Revelation? Why Now?

This initial chapter takes up the three elements of its title in reverse order. We begin by situating our theological reading of the book of Revelation—also known as the Apocalypse, from the Greek *apokalypsis,* which is the first word of the Greek text and can be translated as "disclosure" or "unveiling"—at this moment in history, which will provide the guidelines and constraints for how we will approach the book. Then, the middle section will elaborate on the major theological aspects of this final book of the Christian canon that frame the rationale and motivation for engaging in this commentarial task. Finally, we turn toward some introductory matters related to this biblical book, briefly taking up questions regarding authorship, date, genre, and more, but do so with an eye toward implications for our own theological engagement. In each case, I also situate more precisely my own Asian American Pentecost[1] approach to this portion of Scripture.

---

1. I say "Pentecost" purposively although I am also a lifelong member of modern pentecostal denominations and continue to retain ministerial credentials with such; but while I therefore recognize that I read Revelation from my perspective and experience of the modern pentecostal movement, I am more conscious and intentional in this commentary to highlight the Day of Pentecost as a hermeneutical frame. I say more about this throughout this introductory chapter, but see also my essay "Unveiling Interpretation after Pentecost: Revelation, Pentecostal Reading, and Christian Hermeneutics of Scripture—A Review Essay," *Journal of Theological Interpretation* 11:1 (2017): 139–55.

To the Seven Churches in Asia: An Asian (American) Reading after Pentecost

At first glance, to suggest an Asian American reading of Revelation seems quite parochial.[2] Unless we American readers (presumably many who pick up this book) shed our American exceptionalism and realize not only that the continent of Asia holds 60 percent of the world's current population but also that the Asian diaspora has brought them to every place on the globe, including to the United States. Now of course, Asian America is a political construct related to the consideration of migrants who realized that together they could exert more social and political influence in this country than when categorized according to countries of national origin (e.g., China, India, or, as in my case, a first-generation immigrant from Malaysia). But to be frank, Asia itself is not much more than a geographical construct. There is little the binds East Asians and South Asians together, not to mention those spread out across Central Asia. Not even the landmass holds Asia together, since Southeast Asia includes the Indonesian archipelago and the Philippine islands out east.[3]

If Asian Americans are effectively multiply constituted, so also is every other of these geographically considered Asian regions. Whereas East Asia includes China, Mongolia, North and South Korea, and Japan, West Asia includes modern-day Turkey, countries in the Arabian Peninsula, and those in the regions of the South Caucasus (e.g., Georgia, Armenia, and others) and the Fertile Crescent (from Iraq to Israel). Surely any Asian American experience is vastly different from any East or West Asian one. Yet, any Asian American perspective begs to be further specified relative both to the country of origin and to the distinctive North American regional contexts that forms it (for instance, mine is a Malaysian Chinese experience

2. Mainstream scholarship would ignore or dismiss such readings, e.g., Nyugễn văn Thanh, "Revelation from the Margins: A Vietnamese American Perspective," in Uriah Y. Kim and Seung Ai Yang, eds., *T&T Clark Handbook of Asian American Biblical Hermeneutics* (New York: Bloomsbury, 2019), 439–49.

3. I grapple with the notion of Asianness (and Americanness) in the first few chapters of my book, *The Future of Evangelical Theology: Soundings from the Asian American Diaspora* (Downers Grove: IVP Academic, 2014).

currently in Southern California but with prior sojourn in the Pacific Northwest, the Northeast, the Upper Midwest, and the Eastern seaboard) in very similar ways to how any continental Asian perspective can and should be further specified relative to both historical and contemporary realities that inform it.

The Apocalypse, it is clear, is written "to the seven churches that are in Asia" (Rev. 1:4a). Since the second millennium BCE, the Greeks had understood Asia to refer to the landmasses east of Europe, yet also distinct from Africa, and by the first century, it was known as that segment off the Aegean coast (what is now part of the western Turkish peninsula) populated by Greeks, indigenous groups, and also those from the Jewish diaspora.[4] The reality is that large portions of the New Testament derive from or address Asian communities—e.g., think of the Pauline Letters to Ephesians, Colossians, Timothy, and Titus; of James and 1 Peter, written to diaspora Jews across the Asian region; of the Fourth Gospel and the Johannine letters, traditionally situated at Ephesus—so much so that it is generally uncontroversial to claim that Christianity has Asian origins, if not being, at least originally, an Asian religion. The inception of the Christian community, dated from the perspective of the Day of Pentecost event in Jerusalem not too long after the life and ministry of Jesus, is also indicated as including Jews and proselytes from around the Mediterranean world—"from every nation under heaven," Luke puts it (Acts 2:5)—including, specifically mentioned, also from Asia (Acts 2:9b).

I will later say more about each of the seven churches and consider why only these seven are addressed. Yet if Revelation may in light of its intended recipients be understood as an Asian document, it is equally comprehensible as involving and engaging with multiple Asian experiences, at least as many as the number of churches to which it was composed. Revelation hence evinces and concerns a plurality of Asian realities, not just one, even while we may nevertheless talk about these under a single (Asian) rubric. This is actually consistent also with the Day of Pentecost narrative that insists that Christian witness proceeds not in one but in many

4. David E. Aune, *Revelation 1–5*, Word Biblical Commentary 52A (Nashville: Thomas Nelson, 1997), 29.

languages, including, by extension, those of the Asian region (see Acts 2:5–11). The point here, then, is not only a political and geographical one but also a theological one, leaping off such a Day of Pentecost hermeneutical horizon that is cast over the entirety of the early Christian experience: that consciously adopting an Asian and Pentecost-related standpoint in reading Revelation cautions against any monovalent understanding and prompts instead recognition that such an approach necessarily involves diverse perspectives and considerations.[5]

The plurivocality of Pentecost, however, extends not only synchronically across the Mediterranean and West Asian world but also diachronically back into the Semitic history of ancient Israel. Pentecost was an ancient Hebrew festival, and its ongoing celebration was an extension and development of that memory. If the Day of Pentecost event empowered resourcing of the messianic message from the earlier covenant with Israel, so also does the book of Revelation heavily depend on and demonstrate a creative reappropriation of the Old Testament canon, not least the prophets.[6] Although our efforts will not be devoted to identifying every allusion—over five hundred by various counts![7]—to the Hebrew Scriptures, the point is to note that the many tongues of Pentecost both draw from a multiplicity of ancient sources and enable a variety of witnesses and testimonies. Our reading of Revelation will attend to these many voices as relevant for current theological purposes.

Yet my Asian American background also invites recognition and embrace of a more specific positionality, one that is rather conducive to reading the book of Revelation more on its own terms, to the degree that such may even be possible two thousand years later. I am referring to what many in my community call the *perpetual foreigner* experience, the sense that because of our racial phenotype, skin

---

5. For more on my Pentecost hermeneutic—not quite pentecostal in the sense of the modern churches that go by that name but, I would grant, informed surely by my own lifetime participant in the Assemblies of God and various other pentecostal and charismatic movements—see my book *The Hermeneutical Spirit: Theological Interpretation and the Scriptural Imagination for the 21st Century* (Eugene, OR: Cascade Books, 2017).

6. See G. K. Beale, *John's Use of the Old Testament in Revelation*, Library of New Testament Studies 166 (1998; reprint, London and New York: Bloomsbury T&T Clark, 2015).

7. Steve Moyise, *The Old Testament in the Book of Revelation* (1995; reprint, New York and London: Bloomsbury T&T Clark, 2015), 16.

color, and sometimes also because of our linguistic accents, we are presumed when in the United States to be foreigners to this nation, even while we are assumed when in our Asian countries of origin to be aliens from there also.[8] The result is a somewhat liminal identity, always betwixt-and-between, continually seeking home but never quite able to secure that sensibility.[9] Even if we were to desire to belong in one or the other space—in *any* space, honestly speaking— we never feel fully at ease. While the notion of perpetual foreigner has been developed theoretically most extensively vis-à-vis Asian American history,[10] many other ethnic groups resonate with that description even as minoritized communities also empathize with aspects of that experience under majority or dominant cultures. In other words, while my own Asian American location informs my use of the perpetual minority trope, I do not believe its effectiveness is limited only to those from such contexts.[11]

Further, as I hope to show, something like the perpetual foreigner experience is inherent in the early Christian milieu. While surviving as perpetual foreigners sometimes breeds resentment, inevitably those so located learn to draw resources from both or multiple sites to develop hybridic identities that enable at least persistence and endurance. This is found in early Christian documents, including both apostles like Paul who took advantage of their Roman citizenship for evangelistic and missiological purposes (e.g., Acts 16:37–39; 22:22–29; 25:9–12) and messianists (the early followers of Jesus) who drew encouragement from their Hebrew ancestors

8. I have written some on the perpetual foreigner experience elsewhere, e.g., "American Political Theology in a Post-al Age: A Perpetual Foreigner and Pentecostal Stance," in Miguel A. De La Torre, ed., *Faith and Resistance in the Age of Trump* (Maryknoll, NY: Orbis Books, 2017), 107–14.

9. See Peter C. Phan, "Betwixt and Between: Doing Theology with Memory and Imagination," in Peter C. Phan and Jung Young Lee, eds., *Journeys at the Margin: Toward an Autobiographical Theology in American-Asian Perspective* (Maryknoll, NY: Orbis, 1999), 113–33; also, Sang Hyun Lee, *From a Liminal Place: An Asian American Theology* (Minneapolis: Fortress, 2010); and Russell Jeung, *At Home in Exile: Finding Jesus among My Ancestors and Refugee Neighbors* (Grand Rapids: Zondervan, 2016).

10. E.g., Frank H. Wu, *Yellow: Race in America Beyond Black and White* (New York: Basic Books, 2003), ch. 2.

11. For instance, African American scholars, like Lynne St. Clair Darden, *Scripturalizing Revelation: An African American Postcolonial Reading of Empire* (Atlanta: SBL Press, 2015), talk about the "strangeness of home" (ch. 3 of her book); see also a perspective informed by resistance to apartheid: Allan A. Boesak, *Comfort and Protest: Reflections on the Apocalypse of John of Patmos from a South African Perspective* (Philadelphia: The Westminster Press, 1987).

who navigated covenantal promises regarding the land of Canaan on the one hand but also found their values oriented toward Yahwistic commitments on the other hand. As the author of the Letter to the Hebrews put it, the ancient exemplars of faith "confessed that they were strangers and foreigners on the earth, for people who speak in this way make it clear that they are seeking a homeland. If they had been thinking of the land that they had left behind, they would have had opportunity to return. But as it is, they desire a better country, that is, a heavenly one" (Heb. 11:13b–6a). These early followers of Jesus found themselves citizens of imperial Rome but also anticipating the divine rule revealed in Jesus. Might delving deeper into such hybridic experiences in dialogue with these early disciples enable us to transcend the binary options that we often find ourselves trapped in even as we may be also more open to adopting a transcendent (heavenly) perspective required for prophetic stances in our socio-historical and political lives?[12]

Rather than bemoan marginality, then, as a perpetual foreigner, I proffer that being the perpetual foreigner is both closer to and more conducive to fostering an empathetic disposition with the author and perhaps also the original audience of the Apocalypse.[13] Not only does it appear that the author wrote this book while exiled and perhaps imprisoned (1:9), but the book's readers or hearers—it was intended to be read aloud to the community (1:3a)—were repeatedly both commended for and urged to persist in patient endurance (2:2, 3, 19; 3:10, 13:10; 14:12), even while anticipating an "hour of trial that is coming on the whole world" (13:10), and admonished to be faithful through persecution and even impending death (e.g., 6:9–11; 7:9–14; 12:11; 13:7; 16:6; 17:6; 18:24; 20:4).[14] John of Patmos surely found himself existing in this liminal site, being

---

12. See my "From Every Tribe, Language, People, and Nation: Diaspora, Hybridity, and the Coming Reign of God," in Chandler H. Im and Amos Yong, eds., *Global Diasporas and Mission*, Regnum Edinburgh Centenary Series 23 (Oxford: Regnum Books International, 2014), 253–61.

13. Deploying Korean American theologian Jung Young Lee's *Marginality: The Key to Multicultural Theology* (Minneapolis: Fortress, 1985), which urges that life on the (any) border opens up on both directions, Nyugễn, "Revelation from the Margins," reads both John and Jesus as marginal and hybridic figures *par excellence*, and the seven churches as marginalized groups within the Roman Empire.

14. John E. Hurtgen, *Anti-Language in the Apocalypse of John* (Lewiston, NY: Mellen Biblical Press, 1993), 3, does not refer to my *perpetual foreigner* notion but deploys sociolinguistic

under Roman rule on the one hand even as he castigated its imperial designs in terms of the biblical Babylon and then urged his audience of (seven) churches to be wary of, if not attempt to live outside as a counter- or alternative social body to, a state engulfed by beastly mechanisms. Even if there is scholarly debate about the existence and extent of persecution of Christians during the time in which this document was written (which we will return to below), the literary and rhetorical point remains: that members of these seven churches in Asia were at best at the edges of the existing sociopolitical order and at worst de facto outcasts, persecuted for their faith and faithfulness. As such, adopting a socially peripheral perspective, one perhaps drawn from the perpetual foreigner horizons of Asian America (which by no means needs to be the only source), provides a more conducive point of entry to the world of Revelation.

Put otherwise, any reading of the Apocalypse from a position of sociopolitical power and privilege may be misleading. We shall see that the author castigates, and predicts the final destruction of, the worldly powers of his day and age. This would have been the Roman Empire, close to the height of its strength and expansiveness in the first century.[15] Intriguingly, in the twenty-first century, with the center of gravity for Christianity having shifted from the Christian Euro-American West to the non-Christian global South, there are more Christians reading this book from Asia, Africa, and Latin America than ever, and many of these do so either at the sociopolitical margins or in contexts where Christianity is either subordinated to other dominant religions or problematically situated vis-à-vis the existing political powers. And wherever such readings are occurring in countries or regions of the world that were colonized by Western

---

analysis to identify how John's apocalyptic language displays "all kinds of verbal play that a group employs to register its opposition to a dominant group in the culture."

15. In his study of first century Jewish apocalypses, Richard A. Horsley, *Revolt of the Scribes: Resistance and Apocalyptic Origins* (Minneapolis: Fortress, 2010), 193 and 201, concludes: "the contents and principal concerns of the Second Temple Judean texts customarily classified as 'apocalyptic' indicates that they are all responses to imperial rule"; and: "Far from looking for the end of the world, they [the authors of these texts] were looking for the end of empire. And far from living under the shadow of an anticipated cosmic dissolution, they looked for the renewal of the earth on which a humane societal life could be renewed." Let us see as we move forward if and how close our seer from Patmos comes to fitting in with other apocalyptically minded authors and communities of his (and our) time in countering imperial rule.

> ... the genre of apocalyptic in its very structure is the quintessential
> expression of local opposition to the Greek kingdoms and the Roman empire.
> It might be said that without such powers, there would not have been
> apocalypses. . . . In short, the apocalypse served as a genre of local resistance
> and non-translatability aimed at the imperium of foreign powers.
>
> Mark S. Smith, *God in Translation: Deities in Cross-Cultural Discourse in the Biblical World* (2008; reprint,
> Grand Rapids and Cambridge, UK: William B. Eerdmans Publishing Company, 2010), 290–91.

nations during the early modern period, they continue to struggle
with the colonial legacies and in that respect comprehend their faith
within the shadow of alien and oppressive (economically at least)
foreign powers. Unless something like a perpetual foreigner men-
tality is sought out, it will be challenging to hear the message of
Revelation; and any approach to the book from a position of socioeconomic privilege will in turn expose us directly to the harshest of
the author's polemical and uncompromising rhetoric.

The Theology of Revelation: Toward a Pentecost Praxis for the Twenty-First Century

The preceding overview of *how* we will be approaching the book of
Revelation today—from an Asian American (e.g., perpetual foreigner) Pentecostal perspective—here connects with and is extended
in discussion of the *why*: because the Apocalypse resounds meaningfully for our time when read theologically in light of the New Testament Day of Pentecost event. I grant that my own discovery of what
I call a Pentecost hermeneutic grounded in this central salvation historical event recorded in Acts 2 was routed through the emergence of
a self-conscious interpretative standpoint developed by scholars connected with the modern Pentecostal movement. Now into its second
century (if the origins are dated to the time of the Azusa Street revival
in the early twentieth century), the burgeoning Pentecostal academia
has forged its own hermeneutical self-understanding and has begun
to apply it to reading the book of Revelation.[16] My own approach is

---

16. Leading the way are R. Hollis Gause, *Revelation: God's Stamp of Sovereignty on History*

surely rooted in my upbringing in the movement and engagement for almost three decades with the Society for Pentecostal Studies. Yet I read theologically for the church ecumenical and catholic (universal) and do so intentionally from what I consider a more radical Pentecost perspective, one grounded at the core of the New Testament itself. More precisely, I suggest that Christian faith itself proceeds not just after Easter—after incarnation, death, resurrection, and ascension— but after Pentecost: after the outpouring of the holy spirit by the resurrected Jesus from the right hand of the Father.[17] If Christian faith and life itself comes through the working of the spirit, then Christian theological reflection is also pneumatologically funded.[18] The New Testament witness itself proceeds from out of the Pentecost event.

Yet what does such a Pentecost reading of the Apocalypse entail and why is such relevant for us at the beginning of the third millennium? Let me respond to this along four interlocking and interwoven theological trajectories: the pneumatological, the christological,

---

(Cleveland, TN: Pathway Press, 1998); Robby Waddell, *The Spirit of the Book of Revelation*, Journal of Pentecostal Theology Supplement Series 30 (Blandford Forum, UK: Deo, 2006); Rebecca Skaggs and Priscilla C. Benham, *Revelation*, Pentecostal Commentary Series (Blandford Forum, UK: Deo Publishing, 2009); John Christopher Thomas, *The Apocalypse: A Literary and Theological Commentary* (Cleveland, TN: CPT Press, 2012); Melissa L. Archer, *'I Was in the Spirit on the Lord's Day': A Pentecostal Engagement with Worship in the Apocalypse* (Cleveland, TN: CPT Press, 2015); and David R. Johnson, *Pneumatic Discernment in the Apocalypse: An Intertextual and Pentecostal Exploration* (Cleveland, TN: CPT Press, 2018). Other pentecostal New Testament scholars who have provided readings of Revelation but not foregrounded their ecclesial positionality include Craig S. Keener, *Revelation*, The NIV Application Commentary (Grand Rapids: Zondervan, 2000); Gordon D. Fee, *Revelation*, New Covenant Commentary Series (Eugene, OR: Cascade Books, 2011); John Christopher Thomas and Frank D. Macchia, *Revelation*, The Two Horizons New Testament Commentary (Grand Rapids and Cambridge, UK: Eerdmans, 2016); and Jon K. Newton, *The Revelation Worldview: Apocalyptic Thinking in a Postmodern World* (Eugene, OR: Wipf & Stock, 2015).

17. Intriguingly, Revelation does not mention the *Holy Spirit* explicitly. Further, the book's rich pneumatology anticipates but is not equivalent to the Trinitarian theology codified at the Council of Nicaea (325), which is presumed in our contemporary theological understandings of Father, Son, and Spirit. For these and other reasons (see also the further explanation in ch. 1 below), I do not capitalize *holy spirit* or any references to the divine *spirit* unless quoting other sources. The goal is to call attention to the continuities between the New Testament materials, Revelation included, and later understandings, but also be careful about presuming that John's perspective is the same as our own Nicene-formulations. See also John R. Levison, *Filled with the Spirit* (Grand Rapids: Eerdmans, 2009), for other cautions against reading Nicene trinitarianism back into our biblical theological interpretation.

18. See my *Learning Theology: Tracking the Spirit of Christian Faith* (Louisville, KY: Westminster John Knox Press, 2018).

the eschatological, and the practical or missional (or missiological). We shall see that these theological themes work together to chart our reading of Revelation.

First, to read Revelation after Pentecost is to attend to this book as one that not only speaks *about* the divine spirit but also addresses its readers *in* and *through* that same spirit.[19] Here we are talking less about what the Apocalypse tells us about the spirit of God (and there is much *information* about the pneumatological that can be gleaned),[20] and more about what it itself continually reminds its readers and hearers: "Let anyone who has an ear listen to what the Spirit is saying to the churches" (2:7a and passim). Such is effectively an injunction toward what the New Testament elsewhere calls life in the spirit, and is consistent with the visions of the book being spiritually given to John—e.g., when he was "in the spirit" (1:10; also 4:2; 17:3; 21:10)—and its message mediated in or as "the spirit of prophecy" (19:10b).[21] In other words, to appreciate the words of John, readers will need to be attentive to the manifold and pluriform witness the divine spirit is calling for or inviting toward (see 22:17). Just as Day of Pentecost is not only about the outpouring of the spirit but about the many tongues the spirit seeks to enable and redeem in the followers of Jesus as Messiah, so also is Revelation focused not on what the divine *pneuma* is doing but on what that breath seeks to accomplish in the hearers and readers of these visions that come "from every tribe and language and people and nation" (5:9b).

Second, note that any Pentecost reading, as already indicated, centers not on the divine spirit but on the living Messiah, the one anointed by that divine breath. The principal and predominant figure of the Apocalypse is, after all, Jesus Christ, both as object and

---

19. See also the discussion of John's pneumatic perspective in Ronald Herms, "Invoking the Spirit and Narrative Intent in John's Apocalypse," in Kevin L. Spawn and Archie T. Wright, eds., *Spirit and Scripture: Exploring a Pneumatic Hermeneutic* (London and New York: T&T Clark, 2012), 99–114.

20. An excellent summary of the pneumatology of the Apocalypse is Richard Bauckham, *The Theology of the Book of Revelation* (Cambridge: Cambridge University Press, 2003), ch. 5; see also Hee Youl Lee, *A Dynamic Reading of the Holy Spirit in Revelation* (Eugene, OR: Wipf & Stock, 2014).

21. Richard Bauckham, *The Climax of Prophecy: Studies in the Book of Revelation* (1993; reprint, London and New York: T&T Clark, 2005), ch. 1, suggests that the fourfold formula of John being "in the spirit" serves to structure his visions into four parts.

subject. The first words of the book thus announce, "The revelation of Jesus Christ, which God gave him to show his servants what must soon take place . . ." (1:1a), even as in the closing segment, John has the protagonist himself say, "It is I, Jesus, who sent my angel to you with this testimony for the churches . . ." (22:16a). Jesus the anointed one thus is uncovered and lifted up throughout the book on the one hand even as he also unveils himself through angelic and human messengers on the other hand. In short, reading Revelation after Pentecost introduces us to Jesus the Messiah anointed by the divine breath who also invites us to follow in his same steps by the power of the same divine wind that

> The pneumatological perspective on Revelation lends meaning to the all-containing vision. "Although quantitatively the Spirit is seldom mentioned, his deeds in Revelation are qualitatively active: so much so that Revelation was realized *in coram Spiritu.*"
>
> Kobus de Smidt "Hermeneutical Perspectives on the Spirit in the Book of Revelation," *Journal of Pentecostal Theology* 7 (1999): 27–47, at 44.

enabled his own testimony and witness.[22] This christological focus ensures that we are oriented around what John himself identified as being most important: the lamb who is also the lion at the right hand of the throne of God.[23]

Third, then, note that Pentecost carried forward the eschatological redemption initiated in the life and ministry of Jesus the christened Messiah. Luke records Peter, drawing from the prophet Joel, explain the events of the festive event thus: "*In the last days* it will be, God declares, that I will pour out my Spirit upon all flesh . . ." (Acts 2:17a, emphasis added; cf. Joel 2:28a). If Jesus the anointed one heralded the coming reign of the Lord (Luke 4:18–19), then the outpoured spirit of God further instantiated and realized the divine

---

22. The hermeneutical key must also be christological because of the need to discipline the fantasticness of the interpretations of the book; see Judith Kovacs and Christopher Rowland, *Revelation*, Blackwell Bible Commentaries series (Malden, MA: Blackwell, 2004), 247–50.

23. Christological readings of the Apocalypse have been led by Mennonite/Anabaptist scholars like Mark Bredin, *Jesus, Revolutionary of Peace: A Nonviolent Christology in the Book of Revelation* (Waynesboro, GA: Paternoster, 2003), and Loren L. Johns, *The Lamb Christology of the Apocalypse of John*, Wissenschaftliche Untersuchungen zum Neuen Testament 2.167 (Tübingen: Mohr Siebeck, 2003). My own approach is spirit-christological, to be developed in the rest of this book.

rule. Now it is important here to clearly recognize that reading Revelation eschatologically has had both a long and illustrious history, one which has intensified in the last two hundred years, especially among those who approach the book with hermeneutical and theological perspectives guided by dividing up salvation history into several dispensations in which God deals with humanity variously and distinctly. If the former more historically traditional approaches have given way to a variety of millennial interpretations of the book—e.g., how to understand the one thousand years referred to in Revelation 20:4, in particular whether such is to be comprehended more or less literally, more spiritually, or more figuratively and symbolically— Dispensationalist readings have spawned a range of eschatological interpretations revolving around whether the Parousia will occur before or after the millennium, or, at a further level of differentiation, whether such will happen before, during, or after the so-called "great tribulation" (2:22; 7:14, KJV) that precedes the millennium.[24] Our Pentecost reading, outlined above and to be developed in the rest of this book, however, relies neither on a literal understanding of the millennium (although such is not necessarily rejected either) nor on views that insist that much of Revelation 4–22 pertain to the future unfolding in linear, sequential, and chronological ways suggested especially by Dispensationalist schemes of interpretation. Instead, in accordance with the Lukan witness, the eschatological involves *both* the *now-and-the-not-yet*, the present and the future, together.[25] As such, amid much out-of-control speculation in many Christian circles about the *end times*, our approach will be robustly eschatological but missiological and pastoral rather than conjectural: hope for the full salvation to come empowers our present endurance and witness in the divine spirit. Such eschatological confidence means that the ends of which the prophet sees and writes about concern not just those in that final generation but also empower the seven

---

24. These various positions are debated in C. Marvin Pate, ed., *Four Views on the Book of Revelation* (Grand Rapids: Zondervan, 1998). Because of the prominence of interpretations of Revelation that distinguish between tribulation, millennium, and other events or periods as distinct "dispensations" of divine interation with the world, I will capitalize *Dispensationalism* and its forms when so-referring in the rest of this book.

25. See ch. 2 of my *Renewing Christian Theology: Systematics for a Global Christianity*, images and commentary by Jonathan A. Anderson (Waco, TX: Baylor University Press, 2014).

churches in first-century Asia Minor, and every generation since who attend to these words, to live faithfully and hopefully in a world that is passing away.

Finally, then, if the eschatological involves and relates time and history to the thereafter and eternity, then we return full circle to the Pentecost message, one in which witness is borne through the divine spirit to the ends of the earth (Acts 1:8). If the Pentecost wind empowered witness in many tongues, even to the point of death (as in Stephen in Acts 7), so also does the Apocalypse feature both the testimony of Jesus himself (1:2, 9; 19:10; 22:20) and the testimonies of his followers to him (12:17), even to the point of death (2:13; 6:9; 11:7; 12:11; 17:6; 20:4). We also need to distinguish that although the Pentecost witness included the establishment, growth, and expansion of the church in local communities to the ends of the earth, this evangelistic and missiological component, especially as more traditionally comprehended, is secondary at best in the Apocalypse. Yet the bearing and giving of witness is at the heart of each of these books.[26] Our own missional-missiological reading, then, will focus on the illocutionary dimensions of Revelation's rhetoric: what kinds of emotions, dispositions, and actions does John wish to prompt in the telling of his visions? The gerunds—verbs with -*ing* endings that function also as nouns—appearing in many of the chapter subtitles call attention to this performative aspect of our theological approach: What ought we to do in light of what the divine spirit is saying and doing? The question here is less the what and how of mission and evangelism, especially as defined by colonial modernity, than the embodiment and practice of faithful messianic discipleship relevant for our late and even postmodern time.[27] More precisely, as the Apocalypse will itself insist to us, the question has to do with faithful witness in the many tongues of those who experience reality as perpetual foreigners in an otherwise pluralistic and

---

26. See also vănThanh Nguyễn, "The Final Testimony of *Missio Dei*: A Missiological Reading of Revelation," in Dale T. Irvin and Peter C. Phan, eds., *Christian Mission, Contextual Theology, Prophetic Dialogue: Essays in Honor of Stephen B. Bevans, SVD* (Maryknoll: Orbis Books, 2018), 3–16.

27. I apply such a missiological (and pneumatological) hermeneutic to Revelation in my *Mission after Pentecost: The Witness of the Spirit from Genesis to Revelation*, Mission in Global Community (Grand Rapids: Baker Academic, 2019), §§8.4–8.5.

idolatrous cosmopolis.[28] Each chapter of our commentary after the two devoted to Revelation 1, then, will conclude with some "further reflections" that invite contemporary readers to consider the performative dimensions of faithful apocalyptic discipleship relevant for our present contexts and occasions.

Introductory Matters: Reading in the Spirit

In this final section of the introduction, I wish to comment briefly on the history behind the text of Revelation, clarify what kind of document it is, and draw out the implications of its symbolic language. Throughout, however, the goal is to invite readers of this theological commentary further into its Pentecost and pneumatological approach. What does it mean to read Revelation in the spirit, and how might this be accomplished?

Traditional considerations of introductory matters related to authorship, date, circumstances of writing, and original audience are important for providing context for reading ancient texts. In the case of the Apocalypse, we are told both at the beginning and the end that the author's name is John (1:1, 4, 9; 22:8), although which John this is—given how many are associated with the early Christian and apostolic periods—or even whether he was a Jewish-Christian (from Palestine) or a Gentile-Christian is not easily decided, even among scholars.[29] Nevertheless, John, taken as indicative of he or those (editors and others) responsible for the final form of the text as we have it, may well have drawn from visionary and other experiences spanning decades. Not only might the command to measure the temple (11:1) presume that the Roman sack

---

28. Whereas my *In the Days of Caesar: Pentecostalism and Political Theology* (Grand Rapids and Cambridge, UK: Eerdmans, 2010) was developed in conversation primarily with Luke (the Gospel and Acts), here we chart an apocalyptically informed public theological witness.

29. My *Renewing Christian Theology*, §12.1, discusses up to a half dozen possible persons going by the name John within the first generation or two of Jesus' life and ministry. Robert K. MacKenzie, *The Author of the Apocalypse: A Review of the Prevailing Hypotheses of Jewish-Christian Authorship*, Mellen Biblical Press Series 51 (Lewiston, NY: Mellen Biblical Press, 1997), examines evidence over the last century of Revelation scholarship about John being Jewish-Christian and suggests that such is rather thin and that there is at least as much evidence he was a Gentile Christian whose prophetic biblicisms provide just as good an explanation for the unusual Greek syntax of the book.

of Jerusalem (and temple) in 70 CE had not yet occurred when that vision was received, but opaque references to the mortal wound and yet survival of one of the dragon's heads (13:3, 12, 14; 17:10) has been taken as alluding to or based on the legend that the Emperor Nero, although supposedly having committed suicide in 68 CE, was believed to be still living or would soon be returning to continue his infamous persecution of Christians. On the other hand, the letters to the seven churches of Asia suggests a later date, as they evidence a further development of early Christian communities beyond what is described in the book of Acts as having happened by the end of the sixth decade CE and depict emergence of sociopolitical conditions that allow for the kind of exile characterizing John's self-described situation as "your brother who shares with you in Jesus the persecution and the kingdom and the patient endurance, was on the island called Patmos because of the word of God and the testimony of Jesus" (1:9).

The question of whether and to what degree John and his fellow addressees were the subjects of political persecution is an open and complicated one, with arguments that such persecution was real or at least perceived to be real as well as counterarguments that John wished to "otherize" those he deemed to be opponents of his message and thus portrayed these as evil, oppressive, and dangerous.[30] These are not necessarily exclusive of each other. For the moment we might conclude that if Irenaeus, who served as bishop of Lyon (modern France today) during the latter half of the second century, is close to the truth in dating John's Revelation "toward the end of [Emperor] Domitian's reign"—which would have been in the early to mid-nineties[31]—then we might grant that portions, if not the bulk, of the twenty-two chapters that we have may have originated in the late sixties when the Neronic persecution was more intense and worrisome, and then the final form of the book as we know it

---

30. Leonard L. Thompson, *The Book of Revelation: Apocalypse and Empire* (Oxford: Oxford University Press, 1990), argues that the traditional assumption of extensive persecution of Christians is historically untenable, although Adela Yarbro Collins's, *Crisis and Catharsis: The Power of the Apocalypse* (Philadelphia: Westminster Press, 1984), is also potent in arguing that whatever the historical realities, the original audience of the Apocalypse certainly perceived that they were the targets of an antagonistic Roman state (which is discussed more later in this commentary).

31. Domitian was Roman emperor from 81–96; see Irenaeus, *Against Heresies* 5.30.3.

gradually came together over three decades or so during periods when other issues, particularly teachings in the churches that John deemed to be false and contrary to his own views, were more at the fore.[32]

More important than determining the precise *Sitz im Leben*, or sociohistorical context, of this Revelation is discerning its form. Revelation has been labeled as part of apocalyptic literature, no doubt due to its title but also given both its contents about a sectarian community anticipating the end of a hostile world as they knew it and its medium as a series of visions delivered by angels (many of them!) to a seer via ecstatic journeys—"in the spirit," it will be recalled—transcending the phenomenal world. Both are surely features of apocalypses preceding and following the latter half of the first century. Yet the author also identified what he wrote as a prophecy (1:3a; 22:7, 10)—even as he considered himself a prophet and to be numbered among them (22:6, 9)—and commended it as an expansive circular letter to be read among the churches with conventional epistolary greetings and farewell (1:4, 11; 22:21). Approaching Revelation as an epistle concerns the destination of this book for the Asian churches and opens up considerations of how local particularity interfaces with ecclesial catholicity (to which we return in excursus A below), while reading it as a prophecy invites adoption of both apocalyptic and prophetic perspectives together, especially as we see these overlap among some of the Old Testament writings. Receiving Revelation as a prophetic text, however, means recognizing that the author is less interested in foretelling the future than he is in forthtelling the word of Jesus through his spirit in calling the book's readers and hearers to repentance and faithfulness. Attentive

---

32. Aune, *Revelation 1–5*, cx–cxxxiv, overviews both the major source-critical theories of Revelation's text and proposes his own speculative hypothesis of the book's two major stages or phases of composition, even as J. [Josephine] Massyngberde Ford, *Revelation: A New Translation with Introduction and Commentary*, The Anchor Bible 38 (Garden City, NY: Doubleday & Company, 1975), 28–45, 50–56, hypothesizes an early date for the majority of the text (under the authorship of John the Baptist and his disciples) and a much later Christian redaction (of the prologue and letters to the seven churches, among other sections) that is distinct from but not inconsistent with Aune and other theories of production extending over decades of the first century; one does not need to agree with each and every detail of Aune's or Ford's reconstructions to appreciate how the final form of the text might have evolved and then, for our theological purposes, retrieve such as addressing multiple first-century audiences, contexts, and equally dynamic reading communities.

to and recognizing this distinction, then, we do not need to choose; rather, to receive prophetic disclosure through the divine spirit is to be invited into a transcendent viewpoint, one that reveals and illuminates the meaning of Jesus Christ and the God "who is and who was and who is to come" (1:4; cf. 1:8).

Recognizing this threefold temporal characterization of this central figure of the Apocalypse might invite reading the book also according to such a template, especially given that John is told to "write what you have seen, what is, and what is to take place after this" (1:19). Readers across the last two millennia then have been divided into how to take, and then interpret, the book. Four general camps have emerged: *preterists* prioritize the first century "what is" context and seek to grasp how the book was understood by its original audience; *historicists* emphasize the "what is to take place after this" but do so historically, especially in relationship to the unfolding history of the Christian church over the centuries; *futurists* also zero in on "what is to take place after this" but hold that much of the book, specifically chapters 4–22, concern the end of history and therefore remain ahead of "us" readers across historical time (Dispensationalists are futurists who believe that most of Revelation remains ahead of us living in the early part of the twenty-first century); finally, *idealists* are those looking for transcendent truths that may be applicable regardless of how one feels about the issues raised by those advocating the other perspectives.[33] Our own (Asian American) Pentecost approach is fundamentally theological, and in that sense characterizable as idealist, although we are also devoted to understanding the text in its original context—the preterist commitment—as much as possible since our conviction is that the latter both constrains and is generative of theological interpretation in every generation.

Revelation as an apocalyptic prophecy requires that twenty-first-century readers put on hold as much as possible their own prejudgments about such texts. Our literal approach, in particular to what the future holds—about which we are understandably both fascinated and anxious—is or ought to be tempered by John's announcement

---

33. See Steve Gregg, ed., *Revelation: Four Views—A Parallel Commentary* (Nashville: Thomas Nelson, 1997), for how these approaches engage with the text of the Apocalypse.

that the "revelation of Jesus Christ" is being "made . . . known" (*esēmanen* from the Greek *sēmeion* or sign) angelically (1:1), which means also "by means of symbols."[34] John invites, in other words, a symbolic hermeneutic, an approach to his apocalyptic prophecy that is attentive to the many ways in which symbolic language operates,[35] much of which is quite different from the linearity and discursivity presumed by us "enlightened" moderns. Sometimes the symbols are explained, but mostly they are not, which means that because this is a symbolically rich text, we will have to see how the various symbols function in order to discern their meaning. Hence, we will be cross-referencing quite a bit across the Apocalypse, particularly in order to trace symbolic representations and how their interconnections within the seer's account might be illuminative.

I would like to characterize John's pneumatic and symbolic imagination also as thoroughly embodied rather than only and abstractly intellective and cognitive. Let's parse out what might seem paradoxical—a pneumatic-and-embodied-hermeneutic[36]—along three lines: the visual, the audial, and the affective.

First, John's being "in the spirit" enables a visionary seeing. Thirty-five times throughout Revelation, John tells us "I saw." It is important to distinguish at this point that seeing is not quite the same as reading. Reading is a discursive task that moves from words to ideas in order to develop the ideas sequentially across the process of engaging a text. Seeing, on the other hand, involves both simultaneity and imagination, the latter involving the capacity to fill in the blanks around what is occluded visually. More important, seeing is an act that processes imaginatively and imagistically, meaning, among other things, being attentive to polyvalence rather than expecting single meanings, inferentially guided rather than having

---

34. Grant R. Osborne, *Revelation*, Baker Exegetical Commentary on the New Testament (Grand Rapids: Baker Academic, 2002), 55; see also Beale, *John's Use of the Old Testament in Revelation*, ch. 4, esp. 295–98, for more on John's use of *esēmanen* to frame his prophecy.

35. Richard Shiningthunder Francis, *The Apocalypse of Love: Mystical Symbolism in Revelation* (n.p.: Bookman Publishing, 2004).

36. Again, modernity assumes a binary between the material and the spiritual; a Pentecost approach precedes such modern bifurcation—see Yong, *Spirit of Love: A Trinitarian Theology of Grace* (Waco, TX: Baylor University Press, 2012).

explicit instructions, dependent on dynamic, dramatic, and narrative movements as opposed to being propositionally dominant.[37]

Second, and extending from the first, John's Revelation involves sound as much as sight. John not only sees, but he also hears, especially voices. Of the forty-six times that the verb *to hear* occurs in the book, more than two dozen of those apply to John's hearing (not to mention the about three dozen references to voices in the book, only some of which are related to the instances John tells about his own hearing).[38] Our seer also seeks to be clear: "Blessed is the one who reads aloud the words of the prophecy, and blessed are those who hear and who keep what is written in it" (1:3)—so that he expects both the resonating of his prophecy, read in its entirety perhaps in one sitting (it is suggested), and that most who encounter these visions will do so audibly. If seeing nevertheless allows still some semblance of subject-object detachment, hearing collapses that gap since sound reverberates in our bodies in and through distances.[39] Somehow, then, visionary encounters in the spirit enable unconventional

> The imagination of the reader is stimulated by this wide-ranging and wild narrative, in which action, images, actors, sights, and sounds converge. … At any moment the reader expects the narrative to come to a conclusion, but instead meets a "deceptive cadence."
>
> Edith M. Humphrey, *And I Turned to See the Voice: The Rhetoric of Vision in the New Testament* (Grand Rapids: Baker Academic, 2007), 198–99.

---

37. For more on such an imagistic hermeneutic, see M. Eugene Boring, *Revelation*, Interpretation: A Bible Commentary for Teaching and Preaching (Louisville, KY: John Knox, 1989), esp. 53–59. On this point, Austin Farrer, *A Rebirth of Images: The Making of St. John's Apocalypse* (1949; reprint, Albany: State University of New York Press, 1986), is a whirlwind of imagistic and symbolic reasoning about Revelation, which even if true (which is unconfirmable due to the speculative nature of the argument) would not be comprehensible by most (because of the complexity of Farrer's interpretation of John's symbols). Ingolf Dalferth, "The Stuff of Revelation: Austin Farrer's Doctrine of Inspired Images," in Ann Loades and Michael McLain, eds., *Hermeneutics, the Bible and Literary Criticism* (New York: Palgrave Macmillan, 1992), 71–95, is correct to respond that readers of Revelation (not to mention of Farrer) would need to be just as inspired by the divine spirit to be edified by the angelic message (certainly to comprehend *A Rebirth of Images*).
38. Kayle B. de Waal, *An Aural-Performance Analysis of Revelation 1 and 11*, Studies in Biblical Literature 163 (New York: Peter Lang, 2015), 63.
39. See my discussion in "Orality and the Sound of the Spirit: Intoning an Acoustemological Pneumatology," part 2 of a longer essay in *The Living Pulpit* (May 2015), http://www.pulpit.org/2015/05/.

seeing and hearing, as when John tells us: "I turned to see whose voice it was that spoke to me" (1:12). If creational space-time sensory capacities see things/forms and hear voices, as distinct perceptions, prophetic visions *see voices*. The point is that engaging the Apocalypse invites suspension, to whatever degree possible, of our normal perceptual capacities so that we can appreciate the unveiling and disclosure of Jesus Christ and his message.[40]

This means, last but not least, hearing and reading Revelation affectively. The affective is not entirely disconnected from the cognitive; rather, the opposite is the case: our intellectual considerations derive from and emerge out of underlying emotional and embodied perceptions and experience. Hence, we must *feel* John's visions *before* they are processed cognitively. As Robin Whitaker shows, "The full version of the adage 'seeing is believing' is actually 'seeing is believing, but feeling's the truth.'"[41] And to feel the Apocalypse is to be touched—emotionally in fear or anticipation, affectively in hope or aspiration—and to be moved in our heart of hearts, so to speak.[42] Note that Luke tells us also that the divine spirit is poured out at Pentecost not on immaterial souls but "on all flesh,"[43] on the carnal bodies of men and women, young and old, slave and free (Acts 2:17–18), precisely so that those to whom the divine spirit is given can see, hear, and feel the reality of that breath.[44] Revelation, in

---

40. See Sean Michael Ryan, *Hearing at the Boundaries of Vision: Education Informing Cosmology in Revelation 9*, Library of New Testament Studies 448 (London and New York: T&T Clark, 2012), chs. 2–3.

41. Robyn J. Whitaker, *Ekphrasis, Vision, and Persuasion in the Book of Revelation*, Wissenschaftliche Untersuchungen zum Neuen Testament 2.410 (Tübingen: Mohr Siebeck, 2015), 221; *ekphrasis* (in the title of this book) has to do with vivid descriptions. For more on the emotional and pathic dimensions of John's text, see David A. deSilva, *Seeing Things John's Way: The Rhetoric of the Book of Revelation* (Louisville, KY: Westminster John Knox, 2009), esp. chs. 7–8.

42. See Alexander E. Stewart, "*Ekphrasis*, Fear, and Motivation in the Apocalypse of John," *Bulletin of Biblical Research* 27:2 (2017): 227–40.

43. I use "souls" conventionally throughout the book to refer to human persons but not assuming the veracity of popular beliefs in a tripartite anthropology (of bodies, spirits, and souls); for my own emergent anthropology, see Yong, *The Spirit of Creation: Modern Science and Divine Action in the Pentecostal-Charismatic Imagination*, Pentecostal Manifestos 4 (Grand Rapids and Cambridge, UK: Eerdmans, 2011), ch. 5.

44. See Yong, "The Spirit Poured Out: A (Pentecostal) Perspective after Pentecost," in Guido Vergauwen, o.p., and Andreas Steinbruber, eds., *Veni, Sancte Spiritus! Theologiesche Beiträge zue Sendung des Geistes/Contributions théologiques à la mission de l'Esprit/Theological Contributions to the Mission of the Spirit* (Münster: Aschendorff-Verlag, 2018), 198–210; also,

short, is not just about information (related to the mind) but about transformation (of the heart),[45] so that its hearers and readers can be those who live differently—who "keep what is written" (1:3b)—as material and historical creatures yet in light of spiritual and heavenly realities.[46]

Come, holy spirit, as we reread this book.

David Trementozzi, *Salvation in the Flesh: Understanding How Embodiment Shapes Christian Faith* (Eugene, OR: Wipf & Stock, 2018).

45. This is also the conclusion of scholars who have attempted to provide a visual exegesis, so to speak, of the book; see Natasha O'Hear and Anthony O'Hear, *Picturing the Apocalypse: The Book of Revelation in the Arts over Two Millennia* (Oxford: Oxford University Press, 2015), 293.

46. David L. Barr, "Beyond Genre: The Expectations of Apocalypse," in David L. Barr, ed., *The Reality of Apocalypse: Rhetoric and Politics in the Book of Revelation*, SBL Symposium Series 39 (Atlanta: Society of Biblical Literature, 2006), 71–89, is correct that this is how John anticipated that the seven churches (and beyond) would receive his visions; the question is whether or not we can approach Revelation with similar expectations.

Outline of the Book

Every commentary will include the author's own efforts to outline the book. The following provides a sketch of how I approach the Apocalypse, which correlates, generally, with the divisions of the chapters in the following pages. Informed readers will observe in the following my own interaction with and response to various scholarly proposals regarding the structure of the book, including but not limited to how there is a prologue and epilogue, how the first half's author addressing seven churches anticipates the latter part of the book's seven visions and concluding authorial discourse, and how the central sections compare and contrast the majesty and glory of God with the judgment and wrath of God. Further rationale is given in the course of the commentary, but also especially in the four excurses.

I. Prologue ~ 1:1–9

II. Author's first words and the seven churches ~ 1:10–3:22
   A. The unveiling of Jesus Christ ~ 1:10–20
   B. Letters to the churches ~ 2:1–3:22
      i. In Ephesus ~ 2:1–7
      ii. In Smyrna ~ 2:8–11
      iii. In Pergamum ~ 2:12–17
      iv. In Thyatira ~ 2:18–29
      v. In Sardis ~ 3:1–6
      vi. In Philadelphia ~ 3:7–13
      vii. In Laodicea ~ 3:14–22

III. The Majesty and glory of God ~ 4:1–11:19
   A. The heavenly setting ~ 4:1–5:14
      i. The throne ~ 4:1–11
      ii. The Lamb ~ 5:1–14
   B. The seven seals ~ 6:1–8:5
      i. Celebration: Seal interlude ~ 7:1–17
   C. The seven trumpets ~ 8:6–11:14
      i. Prophetic interlude ~ 10:1–11:14
   D. The final celebration (anticipated) ~ 11:15–19

IV. The Justice and wrath of God ~12:1–19:10
   A. The earthly setting ~ 12:1–13:18
      i. The dragon ~ 12:1–18
      ii. The beasts out of the sea and out of the earth ~ 13:1–18
   B. The seven angelic messages–signs ~ 14:1–20
      i. On Mt. Zion: Song of the Lamb prelude ~ 14:1–5
   C. The seven bowls and judgment of Babylon ~ 15:1–18:24
      i. In the heavenly temple: Song of Moses prelude ~ 15:1–8
   D. Hallelujah! Celebration of justice ~ 19:1–10

V. Seven final visions and the author's last words ~ 19:11–22:17
   A. Visions of the final judgment and salvation ~ 19:11–22:5
      i. The rider on the white horse ~ 19:11–16
      ii. Angelic announcement ~ 19:17–18
      iii. The final battle ~ 19:19–21
      iv. The judgment of the dragon ~ 20:1–3
      v. Millennial and final judgments ~ 20:4–10
      vi. The judgment of the dead ~ 20:11–15
      vii. The new heaven and the new earth ~ 21:1–8
         a. The new Jerusalem ~ 21:9–22:5
   B. The last words of Jesus Christ ~ 22:6–17

VI. Epilogue ~ 22:18–21

1:1–9

Apocalypse: Then and Now

Because 1:1–9 is the opening prologue to the entire book of Revelation, I want to attend to matters the author himself identifies—
namely, the from, through, and to of this Apocalypse—before
turning to the *why* and especially its theological implications. Our
goal here is to provide a preliminary answer in dialogue with John's
own introduction to the question of the relevance of this mysterious book for Christian discipleship at the beginning of the third
millennium.

This is a revelation of and from Jesus Christ, given to him by God
(1:1). More precisely, greetings are invoked "from him who is and
who was and who is to come, and from the seven spirits who are
before his throne, and from Jesus Christ . . ." (1:4–5a). There is a
proto-trinitarian ring to this threefold salutation, even if we would
do well to resist moving too quickly to that conclusion, especially if
that also means rereading back the later (Nicene) tradition into the
Apocalypse. For instance, because John also sees "the seven angels
who stand before God" (8:2), some commentators believe that in
Revelation, the seven spirits are better understood "as the seven principal angels of God."[1] Revelation is unique in referring to the seven
spirits, and the number seven's notion of fullness and completeness
is consistent with seeing this vis-à-vis what the broader New Testament tradition calls the holy spirit. However, John never refers to the
holy spirit as such, even as the seven messianic spirits in the Old Testament background (Isa. 11:2) are also described as being of God

---

1. E.g., David E. Aune, *Revelation 1–5*, Word Biblical Commentary 52A (Nashville: Thomas
Nelson, 1997), 34.

(Rev. 3:1), portrayed as "seven flaming torches[burning] in front of the throne" (4:5), and related to the eyes of the Lamb that are "sent out into all the earth" (5:6).

I take it that Nicene Trinitarianism is much too clean and neat to be able to account for the complexity of the biblical witness, including these references to the seven spirits in the Apocalypse.[2] The triune character of John's greetings suggests that what the later tradition understands as the holy spirit is in John's cosmology intelligible in terms of seven spirits, and these overlap with, rather than exclude, angelic realities. So, although I treat the seven spirits and the divine spirit practically synonymously in the rest of this theological commentary, the point is that the spiritual realm in the seer's imagination is cosmologically varied, and these seven spirits caution us to envision a complex, rather than simple, Christian monotheism.[3] Two referential guidelines for the rest of this commentary thus emerge from this discussion. First, I will not capitalize divine spirit, which will be used regularly since its semantic range includes what most Christians understand by the holy spirit on the one hand but yet its ambiguity is a reminder that for John, the spiritual and divine realm is intertwined with the created and ecclesial domains. Second, I will periodically deploy spirits in the plural when discussing Revelation's pneumatology in order to remind us that John's is a pluralistic—not pluri-theistic!—rather than singular perspective of the divine breath and wind. Catherine Keller rightly thus notes about John's pneumatology, "In order therefore to release the radically democratic, plurivocal, and sustainable potencies of the present we may need to retrieve a relation to select premodern traditions of spirit."[4]

How else then is the God from whom this revelation derives described? God is the one who is, was, and is to come, and is also

---

2. See also the introductory chapter to my *Mission after Pentecost: The Witness of the Spirit from Genesis to Revelation,* Mission in Global Community (Grand Rapids: Baker Academic, 2019) for more on sorting out how the ecumenical and theological tradition post-Nicaea ought to relate to our biblical theologies (and pneumatologies).

3. See also Bogdan G. Bucur, "Hierarchy, Prophecy, and the Angelomorphic Spirit: A Contribution to the Study of the Book of Revelation's *Wirkungsgeschichte,*" *Journal of Biblical Literature* 127:1 (2008): 173–94.

4. Catherine Keller, *Apocalypse Now and Then: A Feminist Guide to the End of the World* (1996; reprint, Minneapolis: Fortress Press, 2005), 288.

"the Alpha and the Omega" and "the Almighty" (1:4, 8). It is precisely this trans-temporal and omnipotent deity who can provide glimpses to his servants about "what must soon take place" (1:1). Regardless of what may happen, the destiny of God's servants is secure because their future is also not just in the divine hands but is part of that divine life and identity. Put otherwise, God is transcendent over the vicissitudes of time, but time itself, both in its dynamic character and in its temporalized terms of the present dividing the past and future, is taken up into the nature of divinity.

And the identity and character of this God is manifest and revealed in the "Son of God," Jesus Christ (2:18). Elsewhere in Revelation, Jesus is also referred to as "the Alpha and Omega" (22:13a)—so that his identity and that of God is equated—even as these opening remarks identify him as one who "*is coming* with the clouds" (1:7a, emphasis added). Yet Jesus is not only on the future horizon, but he is also multiply characterized: according to this status as "the faithful witness, the firstborn of the dead, and the ruler of the kings of the earth"; according to what he has done, as he "who loves us and freed us from our sins by his blood, and made us to be a kingdom, priests serving his God and Father"; and according to being worthy of worship, as one who "to [whom] be glory and dominion forever and ever" (1:5–6). If the Father is Almighty and has supreme authority (2:28), the Son is ruler over kings; if the Father is on the throne (3:21), the Son has accomplished the salvation from sins that enables those so redeemed to serve in and according to the authority of the divine reign. Will those so delivered live into their promised potential as priests in the kingdom of God (cf. 5:10, 12:10)?

Before delving further into this question regarding the addressees of these visions, we turn quickly to those *through* whom they are circulated: an angel and John himself (1:1b). Angels are not only innumerable when manifest in Revelation but they also appear innumerably (dozens of times). For our purposes, the opening verse emphasizes the double mediation of these apocalyptic visions: through an angelic mediator and then through the human agent, John the prophet, both of whom reappear, as if reiterated, at the close of the book (22:8). The former alerts us to the heavenly character of these messages and anticipates the plethora of angelic manifestations to follow; the latter, John the human agent, confirms that this disclosure unfolds through a visionary conduit, one involving symbolic elements requiring semiotic or interpretive elaboration. If the Gospel accounts reveal God in and through the human life of Jesus of Nazareth, then this revelatory apocalypse unveils the divine figure of Jesus Christ in and through intermediaries divine (angelic) and human (John).

What we know otherwise about John can be briefly summarized from what he self-discloses in his book. He is a servant or slave of God and Jesus Christ (1:1b), and "was [past tense] on the island called Patmos because of the word of God and the testimony of Jesus" (1:9). Since a number of other instances when John refers to the testimony of or to Jesus occur in the context of persecution (e.g., 12:17; 20:4), some find it plausible that John himself was exiled to Patmos as punishment for his religious beliefs and practices, especially as these had political ramifications.[5] Whether or not this can be confirmed beyond any shadow of historical doubt, or whether or not the Apocalypse was finalized after John was released from exile (as the aorist tense related to the Patmos reference might suggest), is less material than that we appreciate his own self-perception as a visionary prophet. Most important, whenever we might get carried away by the extravagance of the visions that John recorded, we must not forget that ultimately he is attempting to convey "the word of God and to the testimony of Jesus Christ" (1:2), nothing more, nothing less.

And who was this revelation intended for, first and foremost? As already indicated, the seven Asian churches. More precisely, however, the title of the book indicates that the recipients of this epistolary prophecy be no less than "servants" of God and Jesus Christ (1:1). Thus, they were to read aloud, hear, and keep these words (1:3). From this perspective, however, the seer also cast a wide net of possible hearers and readers: "Blessed is the one who reads aloud the words of the prophecy, and blessed are those who hear and who keep what is written in it" (1:3). In other words, the blessing surely was intended for those among the seven churches (on which more

---

5. E.g., Allan A. Boesak, *Comfort and Protest: Reflections on the Apocalypse of John of Patmos from a South African Perspective* (Philadelphia: The Westminster Press, 1987), 25–27.

in a moment)—as are the six other words of blessing, or macarisms (from the ancient Greek term for beatitudes or sayings praising or wishing and promoting happiness), that are found in the rest of the book (14:13; 16:15; 19:9; 20:6; 22:7, 14)—but beyond that, those who find themselves within the echoes of its reading are invited to listen and obey, and those who respond as such are promised divine blessing.

Why does the seer bless the book's readers, hearers, and keepers? The prophet's introductory comments present two interrelated reasons: because the visions concern "what must soon take place" and because "the time is near" (1:1, 3b). Let me elaborate on each.

The first relates to the concerns about what will happen next. Human creatures with only much better hindsight and minimal foresight want especially the latter in order to anticipate and prepare for what is coming. The book of Revelation thus presents itself as providing some kind of roadmap for the future. If its readers and hearers can decipher the trajectories imaged, they will be in a better position to navigate the coming unknowns. This was presented to the members of the seven churches in order to engage their attention. It has surely been successful in drawing ongoing attention to any and all who wish a more detailed forecast of their times, and especially of the time when Jesus will be returning in and with the clouds.[6]

Part of the challenge of seeing John's perspective involves understanding what he means by "soon" (*en tachei*, "quickly"). The rest of the New Testament evinces widespread convictions about the impending return of Jesus, but there are also indicators that this belief had eroded over time and was not very compelling to unbelievers (e.g., 2 Pet. 3:3–4). If "soon" means imminent and it has been almost two thousand years since Revelation was written, then how reliable is its message? Yet, as will be argued in this book, although John's language might imply that he is interested in unfolding future events in a predictive sense, his deeper and more foundational

---

6. For histories of readings of this book, see Arthur W. Wainwright, *Mysterious Apocalypse: Interpreting the Book of Revelation* (1993; reprint, Eugene, OR: Wipf & Stock, 2001), and Judith Kovacs and Christopher Rowland, *Revelation*, Blackwell Bible Commentaries series (Malden, MA: Blackwell, 2004).

motivations are pastoral, intending to shape his readers' and hearers' actions in the present. In other words, John's prophecy is fundamentally theological and eschatological, yes, with one eye on what will (soon) come to pass but, more important, with the other eye on how we are postured in the present toward the unknown but anticipated future. We will need to read with both eyes, to use the preceding metaphor, as we work our way through the text: one attentive to the urgency of John's message and the other to the pastoral care that message communicates.

John's message, and the eschatological message of the New Testament more generally, becomes distorted when we interpret the future coming in ways disconnected from the incarnational and pentecostal realization, already, of the divine reign. Recall that in Lukan perspective, the "last days" refer not only to the end of the world but also to the salvific events inaugurated in the life, death, and resurrection of Jesus and in his giving of the divine spirit to the world. From that perspective, then, the Greek *en tachei* refers less to the speed or nearness of historical and experiential time than to the quality of theological time: the Pentecost time of the divine spirit's outpouring that carries forward the reign of God announced in the anointed Messiah, even as this same temporal dispensation eagerly awaits, and works for, the full consummation of God's salvific work. This does not undermine the apostolic belief in the imminent Parousia of Jesus since even Jesus himself, Luke records, responds to the disciples' question about when the final restoration of Israel would be achieved: "It is not for you to know the times or periods that the Father has set by his own authority . . ." (Acts 1:7). The return of Jesus can continue to be expected at any time as any later generation, ours included, is patient in heralding and in that sense witnessing to its (partially realized) promise. From this perspective, then, John expected that "the final tribulation, defeat of evil, and establishment of the kingdom . . . would begin in his own generation, and, indeed, that it had already begun to happen."[7]

This helps us also understand John's claim that "the time is near"

---

7. G. K. Beale, *The Book of Revelation: A Commentary on the Greek Text*, The New International Greek Testament Commentary (1999; reprint, Grand Rapids: Eerdmans, and Carlisle, UK: Paternoster, 2013), 182.

(1:3). Remember that this nearness of time is intertwined by the promised blessing for those who read, hear, and obey: precisely *because* (*gar*) *"the time* is near" (*ho kairos engys*). The biblical *kairos*, of course, refers not to historical but to theological time: the time of salvation history, understood for us incarnationally and pentecostally. So here again, those who encounter the apocalyptic visions are admonished that the time of contrition and salvation is near indeed. *Now* is that moment when the words of Revelation could resound in our hearing or come across our sight, and whenever that is the case, readers and hearers are given time—the opportunity—to listen and respond. This occasion will not last indefinitely, which highlights its urgent character.

As we begin our consideration of John's visions, then, the question is posed: What kind of hearers and readers will we be of this apocalyptic prophecy? How will we respond to its images and voices? What are we prepared to do, if anything, in light of its commendations? We might be drawn to this book for many of the same reasons its countless interpreters have grappled with its words and symbols: because we wish to know what the future holds and how to traverse its turbulences. The book of Revelation will surely illuminate what is to come, although perhaps not in ways that we are expecting. The question is how we will then respond to the future that is actually unveiled, and to the Jesus that is revealed as ahead of us but also present in our midst by his (seven) spirit(s).

1:10–20

The Revelation of Jesus Christ: Encouragement to the Churches in the Spirit

The prologue to the Apocalypse has already announced the book's concerns, which is the disclosure of Jesus Christ. This next passage then moves right into the heart of this revelation, but situates the "one like the Son of Man" (1:13) amid the seven churches as a prelude to addressing them. We will initially engage with the revealed Son of Man affectively, as did John, and then explore further how this affective revelation to these seven churches nevertheless is also for the church universal. Being in the spirit, as was John, prepares and encourages us to encounter the living Christ not just with our heads but also in our hearts and through our bodies, and as a (new and) collective people of God gathered under his Messiah.

Much has been made of this initial revelation of Jesus, so we limit ourselves to three sets of observations. First, note that there is a brief depiction of this "one like the Son of Man" and then there is the figure's own self-identification. The former appears to have been shaped, at least in part, by the prophecies of Daniel,[1] in particular visions of "one like a human being" (Dan. 7:13–14; also 10:5–6) that have also been incorporated in the "Son of Man" references in the four Gospels. The latter, the one-who-looks-like the Son of Man's self-description, clearly accentuates his divine qualities: "I am the first and the last, and the living one. I was dead, and see, I am alive forever and ever; and I have the keys of Death and of Hades" (1:17b–18). If the Almighty is the Alpha and the Omega (1:8a),

---

1. For John's Danielic allusions, of which there are many, see G. K. Beale, *The Use of Daniel in Jewish Apocalyptic Literature and in the Revelation of St. John* (Lanham, MD: University Press of America, 1984).

then Jesus Christ is the first and the last, both with trans-temporal identities that include the future and all of its unknowns. Yet while the Almighty lives "for ever and ever" (4:9–10; 10:6), Jesus does so only as interrupted, temporarily, by death. For this reason, he holds "the keys of Death and of Hades," not the Almighty.

Second, then, while the "Son of Man" language appears only once more in Revelation—and there (14:14), not clearly referring to Jesus but possibly to another angelic being (see comments on 14:6–20 later)—what is striking is that his portrayal in this initial vision is directly pertinent to the varied messages to the seven churches. The first and the last, who was dead and is now alive, is exactly who greets the church in Smyrna (2:8), even as the one who has the keys of Death and Hades also offers the Philadelphians a key (of David) that can open and shut doors for and on their behalf (3:7–8). With regard to his appearance, the one wearing "a long robe" both extends to those in Sardis (white) robes (3:5) and admonishes those in Laodicea to put on (white) robes (3:18), even as the same eyes of flaming fire and feet of burnished bronze encounters those in Thyatira (2:18). Unfortunately for the church in Pergamum, it is the sharp two-edged sword—with the mouth owning the sword and the words from that mouth—that meets them (2:12). Clearly, this "one like the Son of Man" is both the one walking among the seven lampstands, which he explains as referring to the seven churches (1:20b), and also seeks to speak directly to each one (being introduced to the Ephesians precisely in this way; 2:1).

We will return momentarily to further consider the seven churches, but for now, observe, third, that John's reaction shows that even if he is intellectually dazzled by the revelation, what wells up within him is the tremendousness of *fear*, to the point—almost like Daniel!—falling before the vision "as though dead" (1:17; cf. Dan. 10:8–9). "Do not be afraid . . . [but] write . . ." (1:17b, 19a), is the verbal response, but the "one like the Son of Man" also touches John with his right hand and thus authoritatively (1:17a).[2] John is both

---

2. It is rightly said: "one can love God but must fear him," even if Jung's wider psychoanalytic reading of Revelation is contestable; see C. G. Jung, *Answer to Job*, trans. R. F. C. Hull, 2nd ed. (1969; reprint, Princeton: Princeton University Press / Bollingen Foundation, 1973), quotation from 89.

comforted and commissioned, in his dread and distress, to bear witness to all he envisions. We will return to discuss *how* John receives this commissioning at the end of this section.

Much has been written about the seven churches,[3] but our two questions here are interrelated: *why seven*, and *why these seven*? Taking up the latter first: there has been much speculation, especially since we know of other important cities in Asia, such as Colossae and Troas (Paul stayed seven days in Troas: Acts 20:6; cf. 2 Cor. 2:12; 2 Tim. 4:13), that are excluded from mention. Some of the reasons given for these seven include that they are important capital cities in West Asia (except Philadelphia, which was nevertheless also one of the larger cities), each therefore a center of postal districts along a major route "which forms a sort of inner circle round the [Asian] Province,"[4] and also a site of provincial and local expressions of the imperial cult and devoted to the civil religion of the Roman Empire and especially to the worship of its emperors as expressions of divine authority.[5] The postal theory aligns with the instructions given to John, that he both write down his visions in a book "and send it to the seven churches" (1:11a), while the observations about the prominence of the imperial cult at these locations is consistent with the

> ... it is the spirit of God itself, which blows through the weak mortal frame and again demands man's *fear* of the unfathomable Godhead.
>
> C. G. Jung, *Answer to Job*, 82, italics orig.

---

3. For starters, see Colin J. Hemer, *The Letters to the Seven Churches of Asia in Their Local Setting*, Journal for the Study of the New Testament Supplement Series 11 (Sheffield: JSOT Press, 1986).

4. W. M. Ramsay, *The Letters to the Seven Churches of Asia and Their Place in the Plan of the Apocalypse* (London: Hodder & Stoughton, 1904; reprint, Grand Rapids: Baker Book House, 1963), 191.

5. Roland H. Worth Jr., *The Seven Cities of the Apocalypse and Greco-Asian Culture* (Mahwah, NJ: Paulist Press, 1999), ch. 5, and B. J. Oropeza, *Apostasy in the New Testament Communities*, vol. 3: *Churches under Siege of Persecution and Assimilation: The General Epistles and Revelation* (Eugene, OR: Cascade, 2012), 182–222; see also J. Nelson Kraybill, *Imperial Cult and Commerce in John's Apocalypse*, Journal for the Study of the New Testament Supplement Series 132 (Sheffield: Sheffield Academic Press, 1996); and Steven J. Friesen, *Imperial Cults and the Apocalypse of John: Reading Revelation in the Ruins* (Oxford: Oxford University Press, 2001).

polemic in the rest of the Apocalypse against the Roman regime and what is stands for (and against: Jesus as Lord, rather than Caesar).

Without taking anything away from the witnesses borne through exactly these seven churches (the subject of sections 2:1–7 and 2:8–11 below), it has also been long observed that the actual number seems arbitrary until we notice that in the ancient Jewish world seven is the number of completion, and seven also structures the Apocalypse variously. There are not only seven churches but also seven seals, seven trumpets, and seven bowls (with their seven angels; 15:7). (Some have argued also that there are seven unnumbered visions in two other segments of the book; see excursuses C and D later.) We have already noted the seven spirits and the seven angels, but beyond these there are also seven thunders (10:3–4) and seven heads, mountains, and kings (Rev. 17). William Ramsay's comment from a century ago remains apropos, then: "the Seven Churches make up the complete Church of the Province Asia, because each of them stands in place of a group of Churches, and the Church of the Province Asia in its turn stands in place of the Universal Church of Christ."[6]

Remember that the revealed Son of Man is initially situated among (probably an allusion to the prophet Zechariah) "seven golden lampstands . . . in the midst of [them]" (1:12b–13a; cf. Zech. 4:2). Then John also sees that there are seven stars in the right hand of this divine figure, and the latter explains both of these symbolic sevens thus: "As for the mystery of the seven stars that you saw in my right hand, and the seven golden lampstands: the seven stars are the angels of the seven churches, and the seven lampstands are the seven churches" (1:20). Herein, the divine figure's revelation is not for its or John's own sake, but for the purpose of addressing the (seven) churches. At the conclusion of each message, there is a pneumatological refrain (perhaps also extending from the same Zechariah text that says the rebuilding of the temple, symbolized by the lampstands, will happen only by the divine spirit): "Let anyone who has an ear listen to what the Spirit is saying to the churches" (Rev. 2:7a, 11a, 17a, 29; 3:6, 13, 22).[7] Notice then that each message, while

---

6. Ramsay, *The Letters to the Seven Churches of Asia*, 197.
7. Zech. 4:6b reads, "Not by might, nor by power, but by my spirit, says the LORD of hosts";

addressed to a specific congregation, is nevertheless commended to all the others. In short, the "one like the Son of Man" walks (2:1) among the churches and holds them—each congregation individually but the togetherness of all congregations as his Church also—in his right hand. Perhaps part of the mystery concerns how each star and lampstand is uniquely individual on the one hand yet part of the complete body of Christ and people of God on the other hand. It is certainly the case—and this we need to keep in mind moving forward in the rest of this book—that the entirety of how the seven stars relate to the seven churches is part of the larger mystery of how the heavenly and the earthly are intertwined, and hence the Apocalypse remains the mystery par excellence even if it ultimately attempts to uncover the interwovenness of the spiritual and the material worlds.

Theologically, note that the revelation of the "one like the Son of Man" comes to John when he "was in the spirit on the Lord's day" (1:10). Technically, *en pneumati*, being anarthrous—which means without the definite article *the*—should be more accurately, if less elegantly, translated to convey that this occurred when John was "in spirit" (the anarthrous is consistent across the other three references to John being "in spirit": 4:2; 17:3; 21:10). Not that it is inappropriate to say that John was "in the divine spirit," although this is implied; but it is equally warranted, if not also insisted upon, that ecstatic and extraordinary interaction with divinity involves one's own dispositional orientation toward and embrace of a spiritual posture and practice. Deciding on whether "the Lord's day" refers to the first or seventh day of the week therefore misses the point: it's the regularized practice of devotional piety that cultivates spiritual openness and makes possible spiritual encounter. Thus, John's preliminary vision is an invitation to each of us to enter into that spiritual practice—to be "in spirit"—precisely so that we can receive the encouragement of the divine spirit, which is the revelation of the Christ.

Cullen Tanner, "Climbing the Lampstand-Witness-Trees: Revelation's Use of Zechariah 4 in Light of Speech Act Theory," *Journal of Pentecostal Theology* 20 (2011): 81–92, at 91, thus discusses John's "Spirit-led ecclesiology" as Zechariah-inspired.

Excursus A
The Seven Churches (Chapters 2–3)

Our goal here is to make observations about both the broad structure and the literary characteristics of the seven letters so we can focus on the content of the letters themselves in our discussion of Revelation 2–3 next. We will lay out the overall structure and then make relevant remarks about the individual parts, observing when patterns are broken only if we believe there are theological ramifications.

Broadly speaking, the seven letters have been recognized as organized concentrically. For instance, the first and the seventh churches are in danger, while the second and the sixth are only commended and not censured; then, these leave the three in the middle as in between these outer "extremes."[1] We might note that the fourth letter is also the longest, and that church perhaps with the deepest internal divisions, thus doubly a church in the middle. According to this outline, then, the concentric structure of the seven letters would thus be as follows:

A – Ephesus: in danger
   B – Smyrna: not censured
      C – Pergamum: in the middle
         D – Thyatira: internally divided
      C′ – Sardis: in the middle
   B′ – Philadelphia: not censured
A′ – Laodicea: in danger

There are three basic parts to these letters—the introduction, the main message, and the conclusion—each with multiple components, which are not always in the same order. The introduction includes both the address and a brief indicator of who the addressor is. We have already commented on the addressor: various aspects of the description and the self-identification of the "one like the Son of Man" are carried forward in the letters to the seven churches, effectively reminding them of the one unveiled in John's initial vision (1:10–20). This is the case except for the final letter when Jesus' identity draws from and connects to the prologue instead (cf. 1:5a and 3:14b). In any case, the point is that the letters each contain "the words of" Jesus Christ himself, the subject and object of the revelation.

Intriguingly, however, the letters in each case begin with, "to the angel of

---

1. Robert W. Wall, *Revelation*, New International Biblical Commentary series (Peabody, MA: Hendrickson, 1991), 68–69.

the church in . . . ," followed by the name of the city. We have already been told that Jesus holds the seven stars/angels in his right hand and stands among the seven lampstands/churches (1:20). The perennial question has been how to understand the angelic references here. Angels (and demonic figures, as we shall see) are more or less standard features of apocalyptic treatises, and the modern imagination either dismisses them, or pre- or postmodern sensibilities may literalize them as supernatural beings in ways unfair to John's symbolic worldview. The interpretive options are multiple, although for our purposes, three basic possibilities suffice to be identified: (1) these are nonmaterial beings, each assigned to that specific congregation;[2] (2) these are symbolic referents to the leaders (bishops?) of each of these congregations; (3) these are general symbols standing in for the churches themselves. On the one hand these specific church-angels do not reappear in the rest of the Apocalypse, and there are no other parallels in early Christian or first-century Jewish literature; but on the other hand, the first option seems constrained by the fact that the angelic-ecclesial correlation suggests that the former, usually deemed good, are tarred by unacceptable behavior of the latter, identified and rebuked in five of the seven cases by Jesus.[3] How can angels be "on the point of death" (3:2a) or said to be 'wretched, pitiable, poor, blind, and naked" to the extent that Jesus threatens to spit them forth (3:16–17), for instance, much less exhorted to repent, unless either angelic realities are much more fluid and dynamic than we have classically understood or that they are much more interwoven with earthly historicities and materialities than we have been willing to grant?

Since the latter two conditions are not mutually exclusive, my own inclination is to recognize that associating the stars/angels and lampstands/churches in this way is consistent with the overarching message of Revelation that emphasizes the interrelationship between the heavenly and the earthly, the divine and the human, the spiritual and the material/historical. If John's being "in spirit" enables visualization of the heavenlies and apprehension of the earthly, then the letters to the seven angels/churches also demonstrate how the spiritual and the material/historical are interdependent. More to the point, the intertwining of the heavenly and the earthly means that the battle for the soul, identity, and behavior of the church catholic—and its churches in terms of specific congregations and communities—is one that involves spiritual

---

2. Within this option, broadly defined, are those who believe the seven angels, also identified as seven stars, correlate with actual cosmic phenomena: for instance the seven suns of the Ursa Minor or the Pleiades cluster; for more on astrological readings of Revelation, see Bruce J. Malina, *On the Genre and Message of Revelation: Star Visions and Sky Journeys* (Peabody, MA: Hendrickson, 1995), and Jacques Chevalier, *A Postmodern Revelation: Signs of Astrology and the Apocalypse* (Toronto and Buffalo: University of Toronto Press, 1997).

3. See Aune, *Revelation 1–5*, 108–12.

realities and even principalities and powers.[4] So, we are properly forewarned that the call to ecclesial faithfulness plunges us into the thickets of a spiritual, but not a hyper-spiritualized, battle, one that will need to be fended here on earth. To overcome, then, means less that we are secured in the heavenly hereafter but that we continue to realize in the now that which was heralded by Jesus in his life and ministry and further instantiated in and through his outpouring of the divine spirit.

The middle and largest portions of each of these epistles can also be divided into two components: praise or blame sayings on the one side and admonishments and warnings on the other. The former conjunction highlights that churches in most cases receive both praise and blame (Ephesus, Pergamum, Thyatira, and Sardis) but in three cases either one (praise only: Smyrna and Philadelphia) or the other (blame only: Laodicea). Read collectively for the church catholic, however, these letters show that congregations exist historically, and even in the present, across the praise/blame spectrum. Theological self-examination ought to prompt the question of what is deserved.

Each church, with the exception of the two blameless churches, is also admonished in the sense of called to repent and warned of things to come. In most cases, the warnings relate to impending judgment and doom commensurate with the castigated behaviors, although in the case of Smyrna the forewarning is *not* linked to punishment following nonrepentance (2:10a), and for the Philadelphians, the promise is that they will be preserved "from the hour of trial that is coming on the whole world to test the inhabitants of the earth" (3:11b). Commentators have sought to identify the historical specifics behind each of these correlations—between praise/blame and admonition/warning—with more or less degrees of plausibility. Our own commentary will not generally seek such historical connections unless they are deemed theologically relevant.

These addresses to the seven churches end with so-called victor sayings (which conclude the first three letters) and invitations to heed what the divine spirit is saying to each of the churches (which are in the final position in the last four letters). Reflective of the coherence of this first section of letters with the last set of visions in chapters 19–22 is that at least one of the promises— for some churches, there are multiple assurances—to those who persevere

---

4. See T. Scott Daniels, *Seven Deadly Spirits: The Message of Revelation's Letters for Today's Church* (Grand Rapids: Baker Academic, 2009), esp. 15–32; for my own consideration of the principalities and powers and spiritual—in John the seer's terms: angelic—dimensions of concrete sociohistorical realities, see my *In the Days of Caesar: Pentecostalism and Political Theology* (Grand Rapids and Cambridge, UK: Eerdmans, 2010), ch. 4.

Churches	Promise to the one who overcomes or conquers	Fulfillment
Ephesus	eating of the tree of life (2:7)	22:2, 14, 19
Smyrna	deliverance from the second death (2:11b)	20:6
Pergamum	a new name, unknown except to the recipient (2:17b)	19:12
Thyatira	authority to rule nations with iron rod, "morning star" (2:26b–28)	19:15; 20:4; 22:16
Sardis	white robe, names not blotted out of book of life (3:5)	19:8, 14; 20:15; 21:27; 22:14
Philadelphia	Jesus' new name written, of new Jerusalem's also (3:12b)	21:2, 10; 22:4
Laodicea	a place on the throne (3:21)	20:4

victoriously in every case anticipate eschatological fulfillments at the end, whether in Christ or for the church.[5]

We will later discuss (excursus D) how the final set of visions link with these opening letters. For now, however, it is important only to note that the promises to each specific congregation are also catholic in extent: intended for all who persevere in faithfulness to the risen Christ.

The final element, then, is the already referred to refrain, identical across the seven letters: "Let anyone who has an ear listen to what the Spirit is saying to the churches." The divine spirit in and through whom the visions are experienced—John being "in spirit," we recall—is the same wind that breathes through this prophecy to the churches. Particular congregations can and should learn from each other. By inter-congregational dialogue, each learns to hear the witness of the spirit of Jesus, and attentive listening presumably effects

---

The notion of hearing was given primacy over the concept of seeing in Revelation. Hearing leads to obedience.

Kayle B. de Waal, *An Aural-Performance Analysis of Revelation 1 and 11*, Studies in Biblical Literature 163 (New York: Peter Lang, 2015), 129.

---

5. Detailed in Mark Wilson, *The Victor Sayings in the Book of Revelation* (Eugene, OR: Wipf & Stock, 2007), ch. 5.

obedience and faithfulness. Across the next seven sections we will draw more intentionally upon the Asian (American) experience in our own theological considerations of the seven churches, but we see this not as implying there is a one-to-one correspondence between current experiences and each of the seven churches but as mapping onto the basic thrust of the message of Revelation 2–3 in ways that bring the particularity of these first-century (and twenty-first century) congregations into conversation with the church catholic then (and today). Can the present church in America and across many continents, nations, cultures, tribes, and languages receive the testimony of the divine breath for discipleship in the present time?

2:1–7

Ephesus: (No) Rest for the Weary?
Renewing Our First Love

At least some of the words spoken to the angel of the church in Ephesus will resonate with many contemporary Christians, and from that perspective this letter invites us to otherwise press into what might be uncomfortable questions regarding what faithfulness might mean. We will quickly sketch the basic context and message before spending the bulk of our effort probing into what we might call "the Ephesian condition" in order to assess its theological relevance two millennia later. What kind of faithfulness enables participation in the divine paradise, might be the overarching question. Will the results surprise or empower our own trek?

We know more about the city of Ephesus from Scripture than any of the other six addressed in Revelation,[1] not only because there is a Pauline letter written to that church but also because Luke tells us something about what happened during the apostle Paul's two-year-plus mission there (Acts 19, esp. vv. 6–10). Paul also wrote what we now call the First Corinthian letter from Ephesus (1 Cor. 16:8) even as his colleague, Timothy, labored in that city perhaps also with Paul for a time but certainly as representative of Paul in his absence (1 Tim. 1:3; 2 Tim. 1:18). It may well have been that others of the seven Asian congregations were established out of the beachhead at Ephesus, since Luke tells us the Pauline impact extended "in almost the whole of Asia" (Acts 19:26).

From these first verses of Revelation 2, the church at Ephesus seems to have gotten off to a relatively good start. But even by the

---

1. See also Paul Trebilco, *The Early Christians in Ephesus from Paul to Ignatius* (2004; reprint, Grand Rapids: Eerdmans, 2007).

time the Timothean letters were written—whether authentic to Paul or in a later period—certain issues had emerged with regard to the leadership of the congregation, the role (and behavior) of women, and the general problem of godlessness. Surely, toward the end of the first century when most scholars believe the Johannine epistles were written, and assuming their Ephesian regional provenance as tradition situates them, there were incipient signs of gnostic teachings that had influenced that community in the direction of subordinating historical and material aspects of their faith and practice to spiritual concepts and knowledge-based ideas. What is prominent in the Pastorals and Johannine missives may also be discernible in Revelation, and if the latter was finalized during the latter period of Emperor Domitian's reign (81–96 CE), by then also the cult of Caesar Augustus that was established in Ephesus in the late 80s and dedicated in 89 CE would have been in full swing as a major provincial center of imperial worship.[2] Against this backdrop, what does the one "who holds the seven stars in his right hand, who walks among the seven golden lampstands" (2:1) observe and raise for the congregants there and for others who are eager to "listen to what the Spirit is saying to the churches" (2:7a)?

The Ephesians are commended for their persistent efforts and deeds for the sake of Jesus' name, for their patient and persistent endurance, and for their intolerance of evildoers (2:2–3) in particular groups that falsely claimed apostleship and that were called Nicolaitans. We do not know much about the Nicolaitans—there is some evidence in the postapostolic tradition connecting them to Nicolas of Antioch referred to by Luke (Acts 6:5b), but this is undecisive for our purposes[3]—except that there were some in Pergamum, unlike at Ephesus, who had embraced some of their teachings and in that context, there is some indication that this involved idolatrous and sexually immoral practices (2:14–15; see section 2:12–17 later). The Ephesians, however, are praised because they "hate the works of the Nicolaitans" (2:6). Perhaps that leaves some room for

---

2. See Steven J. Friesen, *Twice Neokoros: Ephesus, Asia and the Cult of the Flavian Imperial Family* (Leiden: Brill, 1993).

3. See also Kenneth A. Fox, "The Nicolaitans, Nicolaus and the Early Church," *Studies in Religion/Sciences Religieuses* 23:4 (1994): 485–96.

contemporary ecclesial practice that involves loving people who are sinners but naming, resisting, and not participating in their sinful actions. The added caution, of course, is not to reduce people to one trait, which categorical naming like the "Nicolaitans" tends to do, while recognizing that apocalyptic discourse generally is not hesitant about reifying and essentializing collective identities.

Yet even with all of the approbations, there is one important point of reproof: that the Ephesian congregants "have abandoned the love you had at first"; because of this, they are called upon to "Remember then from what you have fallen; repent, and do the works you did at first. If not, I will come to you and remove your lampstand from its place, unless you repent" (2:4b–5a). For many who have striven for faithfulness, exactly what the Ephesians were acclaimed for, we might perhaps be sympathetic. Those who had exerted extended effort to be devoted and dedicated, despite challenging circumstances and perhaps even opposition (if the experiences of the other churches similarly pertained at this site), then we can understand that while many endured through their weariness (as Jesus himself recognized), some may not have had the needed stamina. Or put another way, those who were persevering in and through their fatigue and exhaustion may perhaps be forgiven for lacking in some zeal, at least if that is what losing their first love and not continuing in doing what they did at first means.

FURTHER REFLECTIONS
The Call to Repentance

If we wondered more exactly what was entailed in losing their first love or what sorts of works might constitute a renewal of that love, the message to the Ephesians in particular and the book of Revelation more broadly only hints at rather than specifies.[4] The call for repentance may have been as simple as reminding the Ephesians

---

4. I provide a more general discussion of *love* in Revelation elsewhere: "'To Him Who Loves Us and Freed Us from Our Sins by His Blood . . .': A Pentecostal Unveiling of Apocalyptic Love," in Blaine Charette and Robby Waddell, eds., *Spirit and Story: Pentecostal Readings of Scripture—Essays in Honor of John Christopher Thomas* (Sheffield: Sheffield Phoenix Press, 2020), 117–34.

that the greatest commandments involved love of God and neighbor, although that conclusion is presumptuous with little support in this letter. It may be then that the teaching to the Johannine community, long associated with the church at Ephesus, points in a helpful direction: "I give you a new commandment, that you love one another. Just as I have loved you, you also should love one another. By this everyone will know that you are my disciples, if you have love for one another" (John 13:34–35). The Fourth Gospel here clearly connects love with witness: the world—"everyone," pointedly—will know of messianic discipleship through the demonstration of mutual love. We have already seen that this concern for bearing appropriate witness was also surely central to the message of the Apocalypse, in which case, it might be apposite to consider that the renewal of the first love includes the kinds of loving behaviors and actions that amount to bearing truthful and faithful testimony to the (perhaps hostile) world. Whereas the citizens or inhabitants of Ephesus had long worshiped Artemis (cf. Acts 19:28) and now more recently also participated in the imperial cult, it is not inconceivable that this second-generation congregation was no longer as fervent or intentional in their witness in this Asian city and its broader Asian context.[5]

From this perspective, then, the invitation to repentance and to retrieving their first love involves the passion with which their initial embrace of Jesus led also to bearing witness to his name. That said, it is also understandable from this same point of view that the weariness that may set in especially over a period of years or decades of attempting to bear witness amid an adverse environment, one in which messianists were expelled from their communities (cf. John 9:22; 12:42; 16:2) or otherwise assailed (as hinted at in Revelation), would very gradually undermine the will to bear loving and relevant testimony. The current of complacency is even more enchanting in contexts where Christian life and practice is unhindered but where assimilation into a culture of affluence and comfort are not only possible but realized—like as in suburban, middle, and upper-middle-class neighborhoods in metropolitan urban areas of

---

5. See also Beale, *The Book of Revelation*, 230–31, for such a reading.

contemporary (Westernized) democratic societies—since in these cases, our energies are caught up in climbing the socioeconomic ladder of upward mobility. Americans of all types, not least those of Asian descent (like myself), desire this "American dream," and to the degree that increasing numbers are attaining this ideal or ever seeking to maximize their participation in it, to that same extent our love of this world will overshadow if not douse our first love. There may be some indication in the rest of this book that these Asian Christians, including those at Ephesus, may also have been tempted in similar directions (to which we will surely then return), but the point here is thus: inattentiveness to such progression and barring the kind of remorse that recognizes how the first love has grown cold, the possibility of witness gradually diminishes to the point that the lamp is extinguished and the lampstand itself disappears (2:4b).

Separation from the socioeconomic life of the ancient city is the only way that the believer can remain untainted (Rev. 18:4–5) and not share the fate that awaits the rest of humankind . . . . Since its price [of "patient endurance and suffering"] may include socioeconomic withdrawal from the life of the cities, love among the elect expressed as solidarity and mutual support must have played a more prominent role than the sparse references in Revelation itself might suggest.

Pheme Perkins, "Apocalyptic Sectarianism and Love Commands: The Johannine Epistles and Revelation," in Willard M. Swartley, ed., *The Love of Enemy and Nonretaliation in the New Testament* (Louisville, KY: Westminster/John Knox Press, 1992), 287–96, quotes from 292–93 and 294.

The theological question posed by the divine spirit to anyone reading or listening in is a simple one, refracted through this Ephesian congregation: amid all of our striving in, for, and toward faithfulness, has our routinization muffled a love that bears witness to the world? This is in some respects a straightforward and uncomplicated query. Can we become steadfast even in our patient endurance and rejection of false teachings but yet lose our capacity to love others as part and parcel of our bearing up for the sake of Jesus' name? To respond through repentance—now expected in an ongoing sense befitting the patience with which our discipleship is already proceeding—is to retain access to the divine life: "To every-one who conquers, I will give permission to eat from the tree of life that is in the paradise of God" (2:7b). Otherwise, we will have slowly but surely either become too comfortable in this world or sluggishly succumb to our acclimatized lassitude to even notice that there is a tree of life that can transform our terrestrial habitation into a trans-earthly paradise.

2:8–11

Smyrna: Pressured on Every Side?
Living in the Light of Death

As we progress through these letters, certain recurrent themes will emerge—to be expected even when we name particularities of specific ecclesial sites but consider them together vis-à-vis the church catholic—so our focus will be on the points of differentiation. In order to see some implications for contemporary Christian faith and practice, we will zero in on the persecution that the Smyrnaean church suffered, or were expected to suffer, at the hand of their opponents. If Ephesian endurance seems to have persisted over time against relatively light external pressures, not so with the Smyrnaeans. What does it mean to, and how can we, be faithful when stressed from every side, especially and including to the point of death?

Unlike Ephesus, we know very little about Smyrna from Scripture,[1] no more than what we read here in Revelation 2. Its origins date back to the late second millennium BCE, although it was destroyed in the sixth century then rebuilt during the time of Alexander the Great, and it flourished to the point of vying with Ephesus "for the title of 'first in Asia'" by John's time.[2] These historical tidbits may be suggestive of why Jesus introduces himself to the Smyrnaeans as "the first

---

1. There is St. Ignatius's "Letter to the Smyrnaeans" that many believe derives from early in the second century (and therefore perhaps not long after Revelation if Ignatius's dating of that book is accurate) and another "Letter of the Smyrnaens" regarding the martyrdom of Polycarp (69–155) from the later, second part of the second century, among other postapostolic writings related to this city. See also the dated but no less monumental achievement of Cecil John Cadoux, *Ancient Smyrna: A History of the City from the Earliest Times to 324 A.D.* (Oxford: Basil Blackwell, 1938), esp. ch. 9, that includes discussion of John's Apocalypse, Ignatius, and, more expansively, Polycarp.
2. Frederick J. Murphy, *Fallen Is Babylon: The Revelation to John*, The New Testament in Context (Harrisburg, PA: Trinity Press International, 1998), 119.

and the last [and the one] who was dead and came to life" (2:8b) and promised that overcomers would not be snared by the second death (2:11b).[3]

Socially and politically, one commentary characterizes Smyrna with practically a handful of words that helpfully contextualizes the words spoken to this messianic community: "emperor worship, wealth, and a large Jewish population."[4] Smyrnaean poverty is likely to be a more or less literal description, not only because this is an ostracized community but also because such a characterization is not inconsistent with an early Asian Christianity that in other canonical writings is described in exilic and diasporic terms (e.g., 1 Pet. 1:1).[5] On the other hand, given their faithfulness—this congregation is one of two that are blameless among the seven—they are extolled as rich despite their impoverished condition (2:9a), surely wealthy not in material but in spiritual terms.

Smyrnaean poverty no doubt constituted only part of their afflicted condition, albeit surely one that exacerbated the distress suffered from other directions. No doubt the major source of anguish derives from their being slandered by members of the Jewish community, a form of vilification so vile that these adversaries are named as not being authentic Jews but in fact part of "a synagogue of Satan" (2:9b). Nowhere else is this specific label used except in the letter to the church in Philadelphia where, again, they are spoken of as lying Jews (3:9). We may not be able to definitively confirm whether this refers literally to a synagogical community that has spawned a hatred for messianic followers or figuratively to Christian heretics who may be retaining certain Jewish teachings, but thankfully this does not have to be decided upon. The safest route is to recognize that this is a description of those who not only refuse to accept Jesus' messiahship but also oppose and persecute those who do.[6] Why they are so motivated is immaterial since they are clearly led, and deluded,

---

3. Pierre Prigent, *Commentary on the Apocalypse of St. John*, trans. Wendy Pradels (Tübingen: Mohr Siebeck, 2001), 164.
4. Rebecca Skaggs and Priscilla C. Benham, *Revelation*, Pentecostal Commentary Series (Blandford Forum, UK: Deo Publishing, 2009), 36.
5. I discuss the Petrine community in more detail in my essay, "Diasporic Discipleship from West Asia through Southeast Asia and Beyond: A Dialogue with 1 Peter," *Asia Journal of Theology* 32:2 (October 2018): 3–21.
6. Worth, Jr., *The Seven Cities of the Apocalypse and Greco-Asian Culture*, 84–88.

by the satan. Here and especially later in Revelation, the satan is synonymous with the devil (e.g., 20:2), both terms understood as referring to the "deceiver of the whole world" (12:9),[7] and that is consistent with the libelous words of those opposing the Smyrnaean servants of Jesus. But if the most direct enemies of the Christians were Jews, then their wealth guarantees their political influence so that, if in fact messianists were to be imprisoned—as such is said to be impending (2:10)—the Roman police would need to be mobilized. And the latter would not care unless state interests were also threatened, for example, if these poor Jesus-followers were to refuse to pay homage to Caesar at the local imperial cult.

Hence, the Smyrnaeans were besieged from every side, it seems: economically vis-à-vis their social and material situation, spiritually from the satan and the devil, circumstantially in the face of imprisonment, and perhaps ultimately confronting death. It does not help that their trial of incarceration is limited only to "ten days" (2:10) since this is less a reference to 240 hours (24 hours per day multiplied by ten) as moderns count time but is symbolic, as elsewhere in the book, of negativity—e.g., a tenth of Jerusalem falls to a great earthquake (11:13), and there is a beast with ten horns (13:1; 17:3)[8]—so that the other side of imprisonment would not be release and freedom but demise and martyrdom. In short, yes, the Smyrnaeans are said to be spiritually opulent, but their earthly reality is at least troublesome and at worst seriously dire.

What, then, is said to such a community pressured from every side? They also are told (2:10), as was John, not to fear what was to come, even travail; further, they are urged to beware of the devil's mechanisms, even those with physical consequences (being thrown in prison); and last but not least, they are encouraged to "be faithful" even to the point of death. For contemporary Christians who

---

7. Besides being the great deceiver, "the satan," from Job in the Old Testament onward, means "the accuser," and so I will retain the definite article in order to remind ourselves that this word names as much a function as a person—the latter grants the satan too much positivity—and not capitalize it except in direct quotations; there will be occasion to further warrant this position as we make our way through the commentary, particularly beginning with excursus C and the second part of this book.

8. Murphy, *Fallen Is Babylon*, 124. Much has also been made of the ten days Daniel and his friends asked for, and were tested regarding, their preferred diet rather than eating the Babylonian royal menus (Dan. 1:12–15), but the theological implications of this allusion are minimal for our purposes.

live in modern, democratic, and developed cultures, these words to the church in Smyrna are likely to be uncompelling at best or suspicious at worst. First, rather than doing something concrete about poverty, like create jobs or provide training and education, the poor are commended for their faithful piety and devoted commitment; religion and religiosity here functioning as the opium of the people, a Marxist would complain. Second, and building on the first, such a posture not only spiritualizes the situation but also the problem: it's the satan, or the devil, that is the root cause, so be even more fervent and even more vigilant, with the result that we allow for, if not ourselves also perpetuate, the unjust status quo where the poor get poorer and the rich get richer. Third, tarring the Jewish synagogue as belonging to the satan in hindsight—after two millennia—contributes to if not catalyzes anti-Jewish sentiment, effectively demonizing Jews; such anti-Semitism has now been part of the long and tragic history of Christian-Jewish relations. If all this were not enough, we promise those who endure silently (in prayer, of course) an otherworldly reward, one that arrives after this life; it's supposed to be more compelling and motivational, surely, since the promise is that others, including one's oppressors it would be presumed, would be harmed by the second death, but not so those who suffered martyrdom in this life (the first death).

FURTHER REFLECTIONS
Being Faithful unto Death

To adopt such a perspective, it may not need to be said, is to read against rather than with John and his ecclesial communities, including the one located at Smyrna. It undoubtedly ignores the truth that many Christians historically, and even a good number in the current global milieu, live out their faith in similar economic and sociopolitical contexts.[9] Our own Asian (American) "perpetual foreigner" positionality identifies with Christians who often, as minority groups around the world (not only across Asia but elsewhere), are persecuted for their faith, and recognizes such are in need of realistic

---

9. See Daniel Philpott and Timothy Samuel Shah, eds., *Under Caesar's Sword: How Christians Respond to Persecution*, Law and Christianity (Cambridge: Cambridge University Press, 2018).

reassurance. For many of them, regime changes are not coming any time soon, and in this respect they find themselves in much the same situation that West Asian Christians found themselves in at the end of the first century: a long way before the end of the Roman Empire. When poverty is no less easily addressed because "getting a job" is not so achievable as in those parts of the world where such is taken for granted, in those circumstances, it is the human spirit that needs to be fortified. If internment and even death is anticipated before freedom of worship is attained, then how to prepare for fatality at the hands of others becomes a priority. Yet on one point we ought to be clear: if John was from a Jewish background and his visions are incomprehensible apart from that milieu, indebted as they are to the Old Testament writings, any notion that Revelation is anti-Semitic must be dismissed, even as we must also be vigilant against deploying this book, or any other part of the New Testament, in attacking the Jews.[10]

All of this pertains even if it could be demonstrated, as recent scholarship is inclined to conclude, that Domitian's reign was much less consistently inimical toward Christians than the book of Revelation seems to suggest, since the fact is that at least in some contexts and at some times, the early followers of Jesus did encounter persecution for their faith and that today, many continue to experience such challenges. For those who orient themselves steadfastly toward the one who is not only first but also last and who has experienced death in between, theirs will be the crown of life. This may be for some a Pascal's wager for what happens after the first death, but for the life of faith it makes all the difference in how we look the first death in the eye and continue to live in an overcoming manner. Those of us who do not adequately prepare for death will not live well. Others, like the Smyrnaeans of old, can say that we have lived well if in fact we are prepared to die in hope. Can we put on the crown of life in the here and now? Only if we hear what the divine spirit is saying to the churches and are prepared to be faithful until death.

---

10. For more against reading John as anti-Semitic, see Craig S. Keener, *Revelation*, The NIV Application Commentary (Grand Rapids: Zondervan, 2000), 118–19; cf. Philip L. Mayo, *"Those Who Call Themselves Jews": The Church and Judaism in the Apocalypse of John* (Eugene, OR: Pickwick, 2006).

2:12–17

Pergamum: Divided Within? Disambiguating the Faith

If the problem for the Ephesians seemed mostly spiritual (the loss of their first love) and that of the Smyrnaeans mostly external (persecution by antagonists), the church in Pergamum appears to experience real oppositional challenges both within and from without. Having to grapple on multiple fronts introduces tensions very different from those confronted by even extremely beleaguered communities (like the church in Smyrna) since now negotiating skirmishes *within* have to be calibrated with attacks coming from outside. At the same time, perhaps it is the case that for most Christians throughout history and in the majority of contexts, such is the norm rather than the exception. How might considerations of these Pergamum saints illuminate our own struggles in the present?

Let us begin with the first realization announced to the angel of the church: "I know where you are living, where Satan's throne is" (2:13a). Whereas the Smyrnaeans had to deal only with (not to minimize the magnitude of that ordeal) synagogically circumscribed representations of the satan, the entire ecclesial community of Pergamum is said to be located within the satan's domain. The satan, which symbolizes and personifies the ultimate deceiver and the duplicities that captivate human creatures, not only rules Pergamum (signified by its throne) but also pervades Pergamum: it "lives," Jesus specifies, "among you," meaning amid even those who are faithful in the Pergamum church (2:13b). Although some have correlated the throne reference with "the conical hill covered with heathen temples and altars which lay behind the city"[1]—replete as the city was with great religious monuments, including those to Zeus, Demeter, Athena, Dionysius, Orpheus, and Asclepius (a healing deity symbolized by a serpent), among others[2]—and even granting that Pergamum was the first Asiatic municipality to have had a provincial cult established (to Emperor Augustus in 29 CE), the symbolism's potency is communicated in the vision via reference to the martyrdom of Antipas. Emulating his Lord, Antipas is "my witness, my faithful one" (2:13)—remember Jesus is also initially introduced as "the faithful witness" (1:5)—who persisted amid the shadow of death cast by the satan's throne, and his brothers and sisters in that community are also commended as holding fast to Jesus' name and not denying their faith in that same suffocating atmosphere.

But facing the wrath of the satan was not actually even the most worrisome matter confronting this group of believers. Rather, there are deeper problems—"a few things," Jesus says (2:14a)—inside of the community, two of which are specified: first, that "you have some there who hold to the teaching of Balaam, who taught Balak to put a stumbling block before the people of Israel, so that they would eat food sacrificed to idols and practice fornication"; and second, "you also have some who hold to the teaching of the Nicolaitans" (2:14–15). The latter we have already been introduced to, especially that their works were despised and rejected by the Ephesians (2:6). From this letter, we know not much more, except that those in Pergamum were neither as discerning nor as resolute as their brothers and sisters in Ephesus since Nicolaitan teaching is embraced. But, if Nicolaitanism was distinct from Balaamism, the other major problem, the latter might illuminate, at least in part, the former, because both are linked not just sequentially but also verbally by the word, "also" (2:15a). To be sure, what exactly the doctrines of Balaamism were is difficult to say beyond what is specified here, but the pagan festivals and imperial (provincial) cult in the city would have

---

1. J. [Josephine] Massyngberde Ford, *Revelation: A New Translation with Introduction and Commentary*, The Anchor Bible 38 (Garden City, NY: Doubleday & Company, 1975), 399.
2. Mitchell G. Reddish, "Hearing the Apocalypse in Pergamum," *Perspectives in Religious Studies* 41:1 (2014): 3–12, esp. 3–5, considers how the congregants at this location would have heard the reading of their letter given their historical context.

involved religious prostitution and thus invited fornication as well as have had an abundance of food offerings available for consumption. Further, the involvement of the trade guilds in these festivities and rites would have made it difficult for Christians to avoid, at least in terms of those whose livelihood depended on their participation in the wider marketplace.[3] These two activities—eating the food offered to idols and sexual immorality—are attributed to the teachings of Balaam, a reference to the story in the Torah (see Num. 24–25; 31) and are consistent with how he had become, by the time of the New Testament, a representative villain that entices the people of God back toward their pagan way of life (see also 2 Pet. 2:15; Jude 11).[4] Whether or not they are to be taken literally—and we see the same issues delineated as problems for the church in Thyatira (2:20b) and thus say more about them in a moment—is less of an issue than the symbolic threat they represent: that these teachings, perpetrated by those inside the ecclesial community of Pergamum, are "a stumbling block before" the faithful, and if the saints of God are not observant, they will be ensnared.

Thus, the call to repent (2:16a), risking otherwise the judgment of the sword that protrudes from the mouth uttering the words of the letter (2:12b; cf. 1:16a). The word of God, to which we are to testify, is also the judge of our lives and activities (cf. 19:15, 21). For those who either turn from their Balaamism and Nicolaitanism or who hold fast in the face of these incitements, they are given "hidden manna" and "a white stone" on which "is written a new name that no one knows except the one who receives it" (2:17b). Hidden manna (only here in Revelation) looks back to the food that sustained the ancient Hebrews during their forty-year sojourn through the Sinaitic wilderness, and it counters the seductiveness of ingesting the food sacrificed to idols offered by the Balaamite faction of the church. The white stone is a gift of the clean stone, symbolized by the whiteness that throughout the Apocalypse is associated with Jesus (1:14; 2:4–5; 4:4; 6:12; 7:9, 13–14; 14:14; 19:11, 14; 20:11; except 6:2). In part for this reason, and also because later Jesus promises *his* name to the Philadelphians

---

3. Keener, *Revelation*, 124–25; cf. Skaggs and Benham, *Revelation*, 40.
4. For more on Balaam, including some of the reception history of this story in the Bible, see my *Mission after Pentecost*, §1.6.

(3:12b), it seems odd that no one knows what the new name written on the white stone is "except the one who receives it."[5]

FURTHER REFLECTIONS
Allegiance to the Name of Jesus

I wish to pause here to recap that the focus of Jesus' word to those in Pergamum rests on their being seduced by false teachings and practices, not on whatever oppressive forces might be gathered against them, potentially even threatening their freedoms, if not their lives. Yet from a contemporary and especially Western perspective, in particular one informed by a long, even if fairly novel and recent, exploratory history of the separation of church and state or distinction between church and the wider public square, we tend to think of doctrinal deviations as private matters distinguishing between varied—from orthodox to heterodox—opinions argued between "insiders." The case of the church at Pergamum suggests, however, that there can be teachings within the church that either justify or motivate participation in, if not reception of, the religiosity of the wider civil, social, economic, and political spheres. In these cases, the various camps of teachings within the church map not just onto broader arenas and domains but also chart various trajectories of interface outward in these directions. Balaam and the Nicolaitans, then, could surely name other teachers and groups rivaling John's authority—some have inferred these as prophetic personalities with their followers[6]—that reflect those within these

> Elisabeth Schüssler Fiorenza suggests that the seven churches may have advocated for "peaceful co-existence with the pagan society," even via participation in Roman civil religion.
>
> Elisabeth Schüssler Fiorenza, *The Book of Revelation: Justice and Judgment*, 2nd ed. (Minneapolis: Fortress, 1998), 117.

---

5. For more on this name being that of Jesus, see John Christopher Thomas, *The Apocalypse: A Literary and Theological Commentary* (Cleveland, TN: CPT Press, 2012), 142.
6. See Paul B. Duff, *Who Rides the Beast? Prophetic Rivalry and the Rhetoric of Crisis in the Churches of the Apocalypse* (Oxford: Oxford University Press, 2001).

Asiatic congregations who may have wished to be less sectarian in relationship to the broader society.

Sometimes when I think of Asian American congregations in the twenty-first century, I see struggles amid ambiguities internal to these communities. There are older immigrant generations with some transnational commitments (to older traditions) or who are wedded to more traditionalistic stances representative of the Christendom forms of Christian faith that welcomed them a generation plus ago, and then there is the second generation grappling with lures in multiple wider social and ecclesial directions. These various voices don't need to be equated with false prophets, but sometimes amid the politicking of contemporary church discussion and debate, especially the younger generations are seen as yearning for acceptance in the wider world and thereby accused of departing from the orthodoxies of the elders. Herein manifests different aspects of what might be understood as a crisis of leadership that oftentimes degenerates because of mistrust into charges of heterodoxy as well. From this perspective, John insists on allegiance only to the name of Jesus, and the *fornication* he refers to can be comprehended both figuratively with regard to participation in the imperial cult or other idolatrous activities and "as a symbol that refers to no specific act but rather the whole enterprise of assimilation into the pagan world."[7]

In this same line of thinking, then, we have to ask pointedly the question that John sees in binary terms (for or against Jesus). Multiple possibilities for relating Christ and culture, as was famously typologized by H. Richard Niebuhr two generations ago, do *not* exist in the book of Revelation.[8] Hence, while these apocalyptic visions are designed to enable clear discernment of how to identify and reject bewitching pathways (like those of Balaamism and Nicolaitanism), how these are to be embodied and realized in Asia Minor and other places where the church is in, even though it is not supposed to be of, the world is perhaps more complicated. One wonders if the ambiguity of not knowing what the new name says among anyone else who also receives a white stone signifies

7. Duff, *Who Rides the Beast?*, 56.
8. H. Richard Niebuhr, *Christ and Culture* (New York: Harper, 1951).

in some respects this epistemic conundrum: We can live out our faith only according to the dictates of our own consciences. But in some cases, we may never be able to know on this side of death whether our choices are the right ones, especially if they contrast with those others make who find themselves in a similar or identical situation and do not agree with our assessments. There may be no comforting response to this enigma if resolution is sought based on the modernist quest for certainty, but perhaps that is where the letters to the seven churches encourage us to see that we are not alone even when we might feel like it, since we get to listen in on, and perhaps draw inspiration from, what the divine spirit is saying to others and how they also are responding.

Thyatira: Beguiled by the "Deep Things of Satan"? Discerning Faith on the (Gendered) Margins

If Thyatira is "the least known, least important and least remarkable" of the seven cities,[1] we shall see also that perhaps it addresses the smallest group of faithful servants of Jesus. Further, this is not only the longest but also, in my view, the most problematic letter in terms of its gendered character. Yet Jesus specifically and additionally highlights, beyond the divine spirit sayings that appear in all seven letters, that the message for this congregation is both relevant to and intended for "all the churches" (2:23a). As the pivot around which the seven letters turn, what ought the church catholic take away from this Asian congregation's fortunes as convergent in its message?

Note first that there are two groups demarcated by Jesus: (1) those whose works are marked by "love, faith, service, and patient endurance" and whose "last works are greater than the first" (2:19), and (2) those who "tolerate that woman Jezebel, who calls herself a prophet and is teaching and beguiling my servants to practice fornication and to eat food sacrificed to idols" (2:20). Further observe, though, that the ones who "do not hold [Jezebel's] teaching" are identified later also as "the rest of you," which in the Greek (*loipos*) is more accurately translated as "the remnant of you," suggesting that they are the smaller segment.[2] These are the ones multiply burdened, in some part due to their minority status within the Thyatiran congregation.

---

1. Hemer, *The Letters to the Seven Churches of Asia*, 106. Luke tells us that Lydia was from Thyatira (Acts 16:14) but in the context of Paul's mission to Philippi. Thyatira is otherwise not mentioned in the New Testament outside of Revelation.
2. Leslie N. Pollard, "The Function of Λοιπος in the Letter to Thyatira," *Andrews University Seminary Studies* 46:1 (2008): 45–63.

The majority group followed Jezebel, the self-identifying prophet, perhaps parallel with if not related to the self-identifying apostles in the Ephesian context (2:2b), having succumbed to her leadership of practicing fornication and eating ritually prepared meals offered at local temples and cults, precisely the problem wrought by the Balaamites (and Nicolaitans) at Pergamum (2:14–15). More questionably, Jezebel is past the point of possible repentance (2:21a), expectably so since her doctrines and practices are either known as, or so associated by John, with the "deep things of Satan" (2:24). Not found elsewhere in early Christian literature, it is again difficult to know with certainty how to take this satanic reference. Perhaps this is in contrast to the depths of the love of Christ found in the Pauline letter to the Ephesians (Eph. 2:18–19) or to the "depths of God" Paul referred to elsewhere (1 Cor. 2:10), and if so, might have also denoted the strain of incipient Gnosticism taking hold among these churches in Asia Minor, more clearly rejected in the Johannine epistles. At the least, for the Thyatirans it is only Jesus who "searches hearts and minds" and hence knows what is otherwise hidden and able to "give to each . . . as [his or her] works deserve" (2:23b).[3] Regardless, the connection is an extremely damning one: not only are the deep things of God inaccessible to these Jezebelians, but they, and she, will be "throw[n] on a bed . . . into great distress . . . and [Jesus] will strike her children dead"! (2:22–23).

There is a question about whether Jezebel refers to an actual (so-called) prophetess or is used symbolically in this letter to represent the party or group that John is opposing.[4] The name draws on a well-known Old Testament figure, queen to Ahab, a seventh-century king of Israel, who sought to preserve the established sociopolitical status quo for selfish reasons at the expense of justice for the poor and did so in opposition to the prophets of YHWH (1 Kgs. 16–2 Kgs. 9).[5] Not only do some of the Thyatiran congregation tolerate Jezebel (2:20a) but they are also said to "commit adultery with her"

---

3. Stephen S. Smalley, *The Revelation to John: A Commentary on the Greek Text of the Apocalypse* (Downers Grove, IL: InterVarsity Press, 2005), 74.
4. See Ford, *Revelation*, 406; cf. Warren Carter, "Accommodating 'Jezebel' and Withdrawing John: Negotiating Empire in Revelation Then and Now," *Interpretation* 63:1 (2009): 32–47.
5. See also Patricia Dutcher-Walls, *Jezebel: Portraits of a Queen* (Collegeville, MN: Liturgical Press / Michael Glazier, 2004).

(2:22a). With regard to the committing adultery, one would think such is meant figuratively rather than literally. Thus, she is threatened to be cast "on a bed" (2:22a), widely regarded as a euphemism commensurate with the impurities with which she is charged. But her followers will be similarly cast into distress and their children struck dead (2:22b–23a), with the last hazard clearly making a theological rather than literal point, one consistent with the scriptural worldview of considering the fate of children, for good or ill, tied in with the actions of their ancestors.

Now while our theological interpretation is predicated on understanding these divine threats as clothed in figurative language,[6] part of the challenge in reading Revelation is that we will presume the violence, divinely incited, manifest across the text authorizes our own androcentric notions of justice and practices of its enactment. These intuitions are further exacerbated by the gendered characterization in this text.[7] Jezebel prefigures another female figure in the Apocalypse, that of Babylon the "great whore" (17:1),[8] thus inviting further consideration of the symbolic potency of this representation, but along the way, raising the important point regarding how negative gender stereotypes in the ancient world seem to be uncritically deployed by this visionary writer. The problem, particularly from feminist perspectives, is that Revelation seems to perpetuate negative images of women connected to promiscuity, idolatry, danger, and death, with Jezebel being the archetypal case indeed, particularly as tied in explicitly with the depths of the satan.[9]

To their credit, the faithful Thyatirans were a trace that, unlike the much larger group of more tolerant compatriots, have stayed at arm's length from—resisted, even—the teachings of Jezebel. Perhaps

---

6. So that, e.g., being "throw[n] on a bed" is to be prostrated with punishment and the "great distress" emphasizes the severity of the judgment (see Smalley, *The Revelation to John*, 74–75).

7. See Olivia Stewart Lester, "Jezebel: A Study in Prophecy, Divine Violence, and Gender," in Adela Yarbro Collins, ed., *New Perspectives on the Book of Revelation*, Bibliotheca Ephemeridum Theologicarum Lovaniensium CCXCI (Leuven: Peeters, 2017), 509–21.

8. Pollard, "The Function of Λοιπος in the Letter to Thyatira," 56, identifies ten parallels between Jezebel portraits in the Thyatiran letter with the great whore in Rev. 17–18.

9. See Pamela Thimmes, "'Teaching and Beguiling My Servants': The Letter to Thyatira (Rev. 2.18–29)," in Amy-Jill Levine, with Maria Mayo Robbins, ed., *A Feminist Companion to the Apocalypse of John*, Feminist Companion to the New Testament and Early Christian Writings 13 (London and New York: T&T Clark, 2009), 69–87; cf. Tina Pippin, *Death and Desire: The Rhetoric of Gender in the Apocalypse of John* (Louisville, KY: Westminster John Knox, 1992).

Part of the hermeneutical challenge in the Apocalypse is that "the major symbols are mother, prostitute and bride. These are all relational terms with the male at the center. The normative person is male. The hero is male. Women are defined in terms of their sexual and reproductive roles."

Adele Yarbro Collins, "Feminine Symbolism in the Book of Revelation," in Amy-Jill Levine, *A Feminist Companion to the Apocalypse of John*, 130.

---

those more successful in defiance were those whose "last works are greater than the first" (2:19b), and such are encouraged only to "hold fast to what you have until I come" (2:19b). Now if the Ephesians were castigated for their having neglected their first love and works (2:4–5), the faithful Thyatirans were nevertheless not able to keep the spirit of laxity from overcoming some in their fold. Herein we find the posture, one which manifests ongoing embodiment of prior commitments (former works and loves), held forth as ideal for the church catholic, but we also see multifaceted contextual applicability and results.[10] If returning to the first love and works is recommended for one body of believers, then maintenance and even extension of such—the Thyatiran "last works" are said to be *"greater than the first"* (emphasis added)—are no guarantee that a local messianic community as a whole will not fall into sin. Nevertheless, the Thyatiran faithful are urged only to "hold fast" and continue to "do my works to the end" (2:25–26).[11]

To those who persist in their endurance, Jesus promises: "I will give authority over the nations; to rule them with an iron rod, as when clay pots are shattered—even as I also received authority from my Father. To the one who conquers I will also give the morning star" (2:26b–28). We find out later that Jesus himself is that morning star (22:16), but the more important reference is to

10. Similarly, if the expectation to renounce consumption of food sacrificed to idols is consonant with what the Jerusalem Council advocated (Acts 15:29), both are more rigorous than the freedom of conscience Paul allowed with the Corinthians (1 Cor. 8:8–13), another indication that there may be catholic teachings but these are instantiated variously (and not always consistently) across local contexts with varying results.
11. This is characterized as a relatively small "burden" that is put or lain on the Thyatirans (2:24b), which verb in the Greek, *ballō*, would have starkly contrasted for the original hearers and readers of the letter with the way it was used just moments before regarding what was being put on or imposed on Jezebel, effectively "throwing her" down (2:22a) in judgment.

the minoritized Thyatirans finding themselves having authority over nations (or ethnicities—from the Greek *ethnōn*).[12] Taking off from one of the royal (Davidic) psalms wherein YHWH promises that his son would govern and rule the nations/ethnicities with a rod of iron (Ps. 2:7–9), here also the Son of God (2:18)—the only time in Revelation that Jesus is identified as such—not only will bestow the authority of the Father over the nations on those who hold fast, but also will give these non-accommodationistic Thyatirans, through a rod of discipline that also becomes a staff of guidance, the capacity to shepherd the nations to renewal and redemption (2:25, 27, 28a).[13]

FURTHER REFLECTIONS
Listening to the Spirit amid Shifting Margins

There are two distinct but related elements of this passage to reflect on from our Asian American and perpetual foreigner location. First, the satanization (or demonization) of a female figure is surely a perennial issue for women who have been unfairly characterized in male-dominated societies, not least traditionally conservative if not also fundamentalistic (North American evangelical) subcultures. The reality is aggravated in such ecclesial communities when they welcome and absorb patriarchal immigrant cultures along the way, not least those from Confucian and East Asian contexts that now find mutually reinforcing crosscultural rationale

12. Throughout Revelation, the Greek *ethnos* and its derivatives are translated *nations*; the language is slippery not only in the first century but also two thousand years later. The problem is twofold: that, on the one hand, a twenty-first century rendition of *nations* thinks in terms of the modern nation-state and such is far from John's perspective in his visions; and, on the other hand, the modern notion of *ethnicity* has become much more racialized and is thus much less multidimensional than first-century understandings of *ethnos* that include notions of territoriality, kinship, government, shared history, social customs, religious commitments, and cultural practices. Precisely for these reasons, it would be important for us to keep this ethnic dimension of "the nations" in mind throughout our reading of Revelation, and we shall periodically insert *ethnicity* or *ethnicities* alongside the references to *nations* in order to be reminded of this more inclusive and complicated first-century apocalyptic understanding.

13. See Jon Morales, *Christ, Shepherd of the Nations: The Nations as Narrative Character and Audience in John's Apocalypse,* Library of New Testament Studies 377 (New York and London: Bloomsbury, 2018), ch. 3.

for the subordination of women.[14] It is quite right to point out that John is an equal-opportunity vilifier of both genders, even as our visionary cannot be blamed for the cultural repertoire available in his place and time that allowed such gendered imagery to be used as effectively as it was in his book. On the other hand, to recognize that gendered thinking comes from historical and political constructs is the first step toward situating this apocalyptic use of gendered symbols in ways that enable our efforts to eventually transcend the correlational binary of male/female // good/evil.[15] We will return to this matter later (see Excursus D), but for now, we need to be attentive to how this text (and all sacred writings) communicate through the particularity of their symbols even as we are alert to the ways in which they may also perpetuate unhelpful (at best) and destructive (at worst) assumptions, especially as these might impact women and other historically marginalized and oppressed groups.

Further, identification with minority or majority cultures are fraught enterprises; Asian Americans may be a minority demographic from a numerical perspective but may be part of the majority from the perspective of the dominant evangelical subculture that presumes a "Christian America." Additionally, any diminutive community of Jesus followers who renew their first love and works can lead to greater exaltation and responsibility, partiality realizable in the present age, and increase in socioeconomic upward mobility and growth of cultural capital. Hence, those on the socio-ecclesial margins can move to the center at some point and, if so, that would simply rearrange the actors but leave intact the existing structures of power (for instance replacing patriarchy with matriarchy). Instead, the paradoxical message of Revelation is that the one with the two-edged sword and rod of iron will also be revealed as the slain Lamb, so that the perpetual foreigner stance can also anticipate when their own exercise of divinely authorized judgment will be in, through, and alongside unexpected and previously sidelined

14. See my essay, "Yin-Yang and the Spirit Poured Out on All Flesh: An Evangelical Egalitarian East-West Dialogue on Gender and Race," *Priscilla Papers* 34:3 (2020): 21–26.
15. As urged in the epilogue of Elisabeth Schüssler Fiorenza, *The Book of Revelation: Justice and Judgment*, 2nd ed. (Minneapolis: Fortress, 1998), esp. 206–26.

means and modalities. The key is not to be deceived by what may sometimes be the majority or the minority sociopolitical locations, but to attend as best as we can to the spirit of him who alone searches and knows the depths of our minds and hearts. Listening to the spirit of his voice, we might yet be able to overcome the deceitfulness of what otherwise sounds like prophetic messages.

3:1–6

Sardis: Can the Dead Live?
Awakening by the (Seven) Spirit(s)

Like at Thyatira, there appears at Sardis to be also not much more than a remnant, a small core group of "a few persons" (3:4a), who had persisted and continued to walk with Jesus. Is this letter one of "preaching to the choir," to use a contemporary colloquialism, to a group that will continue to sing even if the rest of the congregation has already checked out, so to speak? Yet amid such "choir speak," the broader congregation is nevertheless addressed (as choirs are supposed to do in any case), so how should we understand this discourse within this wider circle? More precisely, if John is usually quite set in dividing up these communities into the faithful and the unfaithful, the question here is whether the latter can indeed wake up or if they are dead and set in their sin. Is the ongoing breathing of the divine (seven) spirit(s) a key for how we (Asian American) Pentecostal and other Christians might benefit from this letter for our current purposes?

This is not the shortest letter (the one to Smyrna is), but it is, rivalling with the one to Laodicea, one of the most brutally indictive: "you have a name of being alive, but you are dead" (3:1b). If there are a few "who have not soiled their clothes" (3:4a), then the rest would appear to have clean outfits, but they are filthy in actuality, even if these Sardians may choose to ignore such or have become even incapable of noticing the difference between being sanitary and dirty. These congregants might be going about doing this and that or maintaining the form of piety, but Jesus charges: "I have not found your works perfect in the sight of my God" (3:2b). Regardless of the works performed, they have not amounted to much, if anything, before God.

These so-called efforts were clearly of the sort that did not bring forward what they had initially received, heard, and obeyed (3:3). Unlike the Smyrnaean brothers and sisters who had doubled down in their efforts to remain faithful while being marginalized due to their economic status and oppressed vis-à-vis their religious commitments in that city, the Sardian Christians appear to exist in a much less tense and relatively peaceful (rather than conflict-ridden) environment, one that suggests they had accommodated to their context and begun perhaps to coexist and cooperate with the broader status quo.[1]

That the Sardians are told to awaken (3:2a) or they will be caught unawares by Jesus' coming like a thief (cf. 16:15 also) may connect to some historical background that would give this warning more peculiar significance for this congregation. The geophysical location of the city—on the edge of a cliff 1,500 feet up that formed a kind of natural fortress or citadel that gave the inhabitants the feel of having "an almost impregnable defense" against invasion[2]—may be illuminating for how this letter sounded to the Sardian ears. Because of their sense of invincibility and invulnerability to attack, there were at least two prior historical occasions in which laxity led to their being breached and conquered by foreign armies (Cyrus of Persia in the sixth century BCE and Antiochus the Great in the third century BCE). The Sardian church was seemingly reproached for the kind of nonchalance that led to the demise of their ancestors.

There was also a devastating earthquake, that also came unexpectedly, in 17 CE. To their credit, and with an influx of support from Tiberius Caesar, the Sardians rebuilt their municipality energetically and quickly, to the point that less than a decade later, the city "competed with ten other Asian cities for the honour of obtaining an imperial temple."[3] This sequence of events may lie in the background of Jesus' insistence that the congregants "wake up, and strengthen what remains and is on the point of death" (3:2a). If the city showed the capacity to recover from such a near-apocalyptic

---

1. See Richard S. Ascough, "Religious Coexistence, Co-operation, Competition, and Conflict in Sardis and Smyrna," in Richard S. Ascough, ed., *Religious Rivalries and the Struggle for Success in Sardis and Smyrna*, Studies in Christianity and Judaism/Études sur le christianisme et le judaïsme 14 (Waterloo, Canada: Wilfred Laurier University Press, 2005), 245–52.
2. Thomas, *The Apocalypse*, 159.
3. Hemer, *The Letters to the Seven Churches of Asia*, 134.

catastrophe, maybe it was possible that those on their deathbed, so to speak, might yet be revived.

If awakening and repentance were a set of first steps toward renewal and revitalization, it would seem that sure creaturely reorientation and rededication would still be in serious need of divine enablement in order for that which is "on the point of death," if not actually already expired, to have any hope of actually conquering and overcoming, especially when the wider environment bolsters such "death" (acquiescence) or punishes any countercultural resistance. Whereas the Sardians were commended, as were their Ephesian brothers and sisters, to remember—"what you have received and heard" for the Sardians (3:3a) and "from what you have fallen" for the Ephesians (2:5a)—they may also draw encouragement from the Pauline letter to the Ephesians, addressed as it was to those declared "dead in their trespasses" (Eph. 2:4), but yet also announcing Jews and Gentiles to be "made alive together with Christ," thereby having "access in one Spirit to the Father" and being "built together spiritually into a dwelling place for God" (Eph. 2:4, 18, 22). If creaturely death cannot be overcome except spiritually through divine potencies, then it is perhaps not arbitrary that Jesus comes to the Sardians as one "who has the seven spirits of God and the seven stars" (3:1b). Is it not fitting that he who has these seven spirits is therefore able to breathe upon, in, and through those "on the point of death"?

> Thus, it is said that Revelation is "resistant discourse that unthinks the logic of empire and asserts in its place an alternative vision of reality."
>
> Anathea E. Portier-Young, *Apocalypse against Empire: Theologies of Resistance in Early Judaism* (Grand Rapids: Eerdmans, 2011), 44.

Of course, we have already indicated that we should not read back into these seven spirits the notion of the holy spirit as developed over the last two millennia, especially that envisioned through the Nicene Creed. Instead, what we call the holy spirit, which does not appear in Revelation in that name, is anticipated in the seer's visions variously, including in the image of these seven spirits that are before the divine throne (1:4b, 4:5b) but yet also "sent out into all the earth" (5:6b). Further, the Sardians come to see that the Lord has both the seven spirits and the seven stars (3:1b), and we know already that the seven stars are held in Jesus' right hand and refer to the seven angels of the seven churches (1:20). Hence, the power of the divine spirit is here interwoven with the seven angels/churches so that the breath of God and of his Son below are available to the Sardians also through their interrelatedness with the other churches, the church catholic.

These churches are addressed individually and in that sense may feel that their joys and sorrows are their own. Yet without undermining the particularity of what is experienced as challenges and opportunities in each local context, participation in the universal body of Christ and people of God through fellowship of the divine spirit means that none have to confront their trials on their own and that the resources available to each are in principle offered through them to others. Thus, Jesus' promise to victorious Sardians who remember, repent, and join their fellow congregants in white robes is both that their names will be preserved in the book of life—first seen in the Torah (e.g., Exod. 32:32) and with a long pedigree in ancient Israel and then in Revelation (multiple references later to be discussed)—and confessed before the Father and the (seven) angels (3:5). Whereas in much of the rest of the Christian Testament confession is done by human creatures acknowledging their sinfulness and their allegiance to Jesus, here it is Jesus who is declaring his fidelity to those who walk with him (3:4).

FURTHER REFLECTIONS
Cultural Accommodation and Following the Spirit

When I think specifically about second and later generations of Asian Americans, those who have come from immigrant backgrounds but have worked to integrate, to the degree possible for those who appear to be "perpetual foreigners," into the dominant host culture, I think of those who acclimatize themselves to majority white evangelical and Christian cultures in the North American context. Asian Americans succeed in these "white" spaces by not rocking the boat, so to speak, or by deferring to and/or adopting the majority culture's ways, habits, and values. This involves minimizing as much of the "Asian" or alien identity as possible, even as we strive to demonstrate excellence—for promotions and all of the benefits accruing to such behaviors—in ways that are appreciated by and reinforce white cultural normativity. But what if such cultural adaptation involves also the subordination of the gospel to prevailing Eurocentric or white norms, and what if one attains the advancements one aspires to in this context at the cost of living out the gospel witness?[4] My worry is that climbing up the ladder of economic success will acclimate even those who have the appearance of difference to the dominant culture so thoroughly that they no longer see themselves as foreign and become impotent to the ongoing repentance called for by the gospel.

So, what are we known for and what kind of reputation do we have? Even if we are renowned for this or that reason, the Sardian case prompts introspection about how Jesus might see us, whether we continue in ways that enable reception of the one whose return is always imminent and whether our lives and witness are appropriate to the purity that his identity calls for. Presumptuousness about our faithfulness is hazardous to our health. Whatever our notoriety, what matters is how we measure up to Jesus' name, and how he might name us, since being asleep on this issue may lead to the removal of our names from that of the book of life, the Sardians are told (3:5a).[5] While I do not intend to argue against certain doctrines regarding the security of salvation that may be developed from other scriptural texts, this one ought to prompt not anxiety about the state of our souls but self-reflection about the condition of our hearts and lives in the present world. Such attentiveness will hear and then listen and appropriately adjust to "what the Spirit is saying to the churches" (3:6).

---

4. See my article, "Is There a Future for Evangelical Theology? API Retrospects and Prospects," *Inheritance: Heritage—Culture—Faith* 64 (2019): 42–49.

5. See the discussion in Robert M. Royalty Jr., "Etched or Sketched? Inscriptions and Erasures in the Messages to Sardis and Philadelphia (Rev. 3.1–13)," *Journal of the Study for the New Testament* 21 (2005): 447–63, which although comparing the relative contingency of Sardian names in the book of life with the more apparent permanence of Philadelphian names inscribed on temple pillars (see 3:12), nevertheless concludes by observing that the open gates of the New Jerusalem (21:25) suggests not only that outsiders might enter (22:14) but also that insiders might leave, thus extending eschatologically the dynamic possibilities of creaturely existence and historical decisions. See also our further commentary on 21:22–22:5.

3:7–13

Philadelphia: Little Power, Worldwide Witness? Enduring through the Promises

If with the Smyrnaeans, "Christ selects his most loyal followers to receive ever more extreme testing,"[1] then with the Philadelphians, who with the former are the two churches harassed by those from the synagogue of the satan and exempt from negative criticism and urgent warning, we can say that Jesus selects his exemplary devotees to receive the most expansive set of promises. Notably, the community of believers in Philadelphia may have been the smallest of the seven, as noted by their being recognized as having "little power" (3:8), particularly when the remnant and faithful few are not disaggregated from the whole of what at least outwardly constituted the Thyatiran and Sardian congregations. So how does such a relatively tiny group not just receive the accolades they do from Jesus but also educe the multiple promises made to them, and what might that have to say to many today who attend coffeeshop and house churches rather than megachurches?

Jesus' self-introduction to the Philadelphians as the one who is not only holy and true but also "who has the key of David, who opens and no one will shut, who shuts and no one opens" (3:7b), is perhaps the closest John comes to directly quoting from the Old Testament.[2] But more importantly, it is on the basis of his Davidic, and messianic, kingship that Jesus encourages this diminutive community: "Look, I have set before you an open door, which no one is

1. Paul S. Minear, *I Saw a New Earth: An Introduction to the Visions of the Apocalypse* (1968; reprint, Eugene: Wipf & Stock, 2003), 54.
2. Viz., "I will place on his shoulder the key of the house of David; he shall open, and no one shall shut; he shall shut, and no one shall open" (Isa. 22:22); see Beale, *The Book of Revelation*, 283–85, who understands John here to be quoting from the prophet.

able to shut" (3:8). Their works, keeping of his word, retaining commitments to his name, patiently enduring, and holding fast to what they have had, are all superlatively recognized.

It is from this perspective that we can begin to appreciate the seven rewards or pledges made to these faithful servants. Beyond availing to them the open door none can close (first) associated with his Davidic self-identification, Jesus also makes two promises of vindication (second and third) before the Philadelphian opponents, "those of the synagogue of Satan who say that they are Jews and are not, but are lying" (3:9a): that "I will make them come and bow down before your feet," and that "they will learn that I have loved you" (3:9b). Although the Smyrnaeans also suffered at the hands of those from the synagogue of the satan, only the Philadelphians will be exonerated and absolved publicly before these duplicitous foes. Fourth (of the rewards), the Philadelphian patient endurance has merited preservation "from the hour of trial that is coming on the whole world to test the inhabitants of the earth" (3:10); we will say more (below) about this trial relative to contemporary eschatological speculations but the point to be made is that these servants will be kept safe from wider tribulations. Fifth, Jesus pledged to return soon, also communicated to the other churches (2:5, 16; 3:3), but only in this instance does his arrival include not just the provision of relief but the finalization of their reward, symbolized in their crowns (3:11b; also promised to the Smyrnaeans, 2:10b).

Two interrelated guarantees are additionally granted to those who persevere in overcoming: (sixth) "I will make you a pillar in the temple of my God; you will never go out of it," and (seventh) "I will write on you the name of my God, and the name of the city of my God, the new Jerusalem that comes down from my God out of heaven, and my own new name" (3:11; cf. 21:2, 10).[3] The former

---

3. It has already been noted that in this letter, John is drawing (even coming close to quoting) from the prophet Isaiah, and it is hence notable that the latter part of that Old Testament prophetic book plays a central role throughout this letter to Philadelphia, including here with regard to these interrelated eschatological promises, so that the reference to the new name arguably derives from Isa. 56:5, and esp. 62:2 and 65:15; see Jan Fekkes III, *Isaiah and Prophetic Traditions in the Book of Revelation: Visionary Antecedents and Their Development*, Journal for the Study of the New Testament Supplement Series 93 (Sheffield: Sheffield Academic Press, 1994), 130–40, for discussion of these, as well as John's wider allusions to his predecessor's text.

certification of security may be related to the displacement that the Philadelphians suffered being pushed from the ruins of the city into the rural areas by the previously referred to earthquake that struck the broader region including Sardis (see p. 67)—but which aftershocks rattled those in the so-called city of brotherly love (the literal meaning of the Greek *philadelphia*, love of brothers) longer because theirs was closer to the quake's epicenter—so that they can rest confident that they "will never again be dislodged from their homes."[4] Those who persevere in faithfulness, regardless of their size, status, stature, or other constraints, will be established in the divine presence, signified by being given a new name, effectively transformed in their identity as well so that the name coincides with their being. The Philadelphians, and anyone else who hears what the divine spirit says to them and heeds similarly, will be an authentically redeemed people because their name is not disassociated from who and what they have now become: the people of God, of his city, and of his Son, Jesus Christ. Herein the nomination and the reality will be integrated, unlike the case of the Sardians whose name and condition were starkly at odds (3:1b).

Without valorizing the immigrant community, especially those who strive in English as a second language, such congregations can also be seen through the prism or lens of Philadelphian minority faithfulness. Immigrant groups take major risks in making transnational—often transcontinental and transoceanic—journeys in the hopes of achieving a better life for their children. Such is the promise-driven character of transnational migration, and this motivates strenuous efforts in order to secure a better set of possibilities for their children and their children's children. Sometimes, because of language constraints, such immigrant congregations can become quite insular, but many immigrant churches have striven to combat such siloed by attempting to renew and revitalize their sense of Christian witness in the alien environment. If their hosts have not been welcoming as is often the case in xenophobic communities, or even adversarial as in the Philadelphian case vis-à-vis the Jews of that city, immigrants avoid conflict, preferring to identify alternative

---

4. Grant R. Osborne, *Revelation*, Baker Exegetical Commentary on the New Testament (Grand Rapids: Baker Academic, 2002), 197.

routes forward. This is hardly to overlook the fact that immigrants are no less prone to the sins of the seven churches, but it is to also recognize that many are functionally disempowered as were their fellow believers in this late first-century Asian congregation. And in this case, the multiple promises to these with little clout belongs to all who persist faithfully in similar conditions.[5]

I wish to pause here for a moment to comment further on "the hour of trial that is coming on the whole world to test the inhabitants of the earth" since this plays a central role especially in Dispensationalist interpretations of this passage and of the book as a whole. Clearly, if the Sardian testing seemed to be more localized to their context and situation (2:10), the ordeal spoken of to the Philadelphians will fall upon "the whole world." More to the point, it is those who oppose God and God's Son that "the inhabitants of the earth" refer to consistently in the rest of the book (e.g., 6:10; 8:13; 11:10; 13:8; 17:2, 8), so the sense is clear that keepers of Jesus' word (mentioned twice here: 3:8b and 3:10a) will in turn be saved from the coming trial. The Dispensationalist interpretation usually connects this "hour of trial" with the "great ordeal" mentioned later (7:14) even as most scholars see an allusion here to the "time of anguish" referred to in Daniel's prophecy (Dan. 12:1). The promised preservation is understood not generally as keeping the church *amid* the affliction but as removing the church *from* the tribulation, often via a postulated rapture or rescue of the faithful by Jesus *before* the onset of such a troubling period.[6] Drawn more specifically from an early Pauline text (1 Thess. 4:16–17), what is believed to be a clear teaching about this rapture there is then understood also to be intimated in Revelation, at least symbolically, when a trumpet-sounding voice calls John, representative of the faithful as a whole, up to heaven, and he is effectively transported there in the spirit (4:1–2).[7] The rest of the visions (Rev. 4–22) are about the future, "what must take place after this" (4:1b), and it is from this that the faithful (like the Philadelphians) are spared.

5. See also my homily, "From the Jewish Diaspora to the Indian (Christian) Diaspora: An Autobiographical Look at 1 Peter's Message to West Asia" edited by John Alex, *New Life Theological Journal* 9:1 (2019): 7–18.

6. Steve Gregg, ed., *Revelation: Four Views—A Parallel Commentary* (Nashville: Thomas Nelson, 1997), 76.

7. Gregg, ed., *Revelation: Four Views*, 84–85.

FURTHER REFLECTIONS
Countercultural Assurances for "the End"

Those convinced by the Dispensationalist model will believe that version of the unfolding of events, including the so-called pretribulation rapture of the church, to be self-evident in the pages of Revelation. On the other hand, to see the promise of safeguarding parallel to how the Hebrews of old were around but secured amid, rather than removed completely (airlifted!) from, the plagues afflicting the Egyptians would be consistent with other New Testament teachings, including two of Jesus' own: "I am not asking you to take them out of the world, but I ask you to protect them from the evil one" (John 17:15), and the daily invocation he commended: "do not bring us to the time of trial, but rescue us from the evil one" (Matt. 6:13). The power of this eschatological promise is its partially realized character: that no matter what the form of the testing, the keeping of the faithful means that they will know the open doorway to safety is theirs, that their enemies will recognize that the faithful are divinely loved and cherished, that their crowns are secure, that their God and his Lord will be soon arriving, and that their new names are being forged in and through the surrounding adversity.

All these promises belong to those who are not only few in number but also severely limited in resources and capacities. Yet a wider renown is theirs, indeed one resonating among all those who inhabit the earth. This may not have been the reward that they were looking for, but it is one that is bestowed upon them. Faithfulness to God and God's Son cannot be done in secret and inevitably charts courses that are visibly contrary to the imperial and hostile regimes of this world. Eventually, our commitments will be felt as not only distinct from that of the whole world but also as effectively judging and condemning their antichristic and godless ways. We cannot be completely at home in this world in the sense that, like the perpetual foreigner condition, we find ourselves negotiating the trials and tribulations in many respects with our fellow human beings yet oriented to another hope and guided by a different light. Such witness is not achievable according to conventional wisdom and self-generated aspiration and persistence. The promises of God and the divine spirit that speaks them shape, nurture, and create the people who may otherwise falter if reliant only on their own powers.

3:14-22

Laodicea: Prosperity and the Absence of Jesus? Paying the Price of Affluence

If the first of the seven churches (in Ephesus) was one to whom another letter in the New Testament was addressed, the last of these churches, Laodicea, was also one to whom another epistle was intended to be read—that written to the neighboring city of Colossae (ten miles away); in that same breath giving these instructions, the author of the Colossian missive says to that congregation that he wants them to "read also the letter from Laodicea" (Col. 4:16), although the latter is no longer extant. There is some speculation that since it does not appear Paul ever visited Laodicea (Col. 2:1), his apostolic colleague Epaphras may have established congregations there and in the closely related sister city Hierapolis (Col. 1:7; 4:12–13).[1] In any case, the closeness of Laodicea and Colossae leads many to observe that Jesus' self-identification to the former as, in part, "the origin of God's creation" (3:14a) is not far from how he is described by Paul in his letter to the latter: as "the firstborn of all creation" (Col. 1:15b).

The triad of Colossae-Laodicea-Hierapolis has also led many interpreters to see the Lord's condemnation of Laodicea as "lukewarm, and neither cold nor hot" (3:16a), as having to do with the reputed water supply to these cities: cold springs for Colossae and hot springs for Hierapolis, but "warm water, which was not very palatable and caused nausea" for Laodicea.[2] I am inclined to agree

1. A. Kirkland, "The Beginnings of Christianity in the Lycus Valley: An Exercise in Historical Reconstruction," *Neotestamentica* 29:1 (1995): 109–24. For more on Epaphras as spirit-filled apostolic leader, see my *Mission after Pentecost*, §3.7.
2. Beale, *The Book of Revelation*, 303; see also Aune, *Revelation 1–5*, 263.

more with Craig Koester that Laodicean lukewarmness has more
to do with their severely dull spiritual self-awareness and lack of
faithful witness than with actual water supply conditions.[3] To see
why, consider the nature of the further indictments cast on the
Laodiceans and then the resolution proposed: "For you say, 'I am
rich, I have prospered, and I need nothing.' You do not realize that
you are wretched, pitiable, poor, blind, and naked. Therefore I coun-
sel you to buy from me gold refined by fire so that you may be rich;
and white robes to clothe you and to keep the shame of your nakedness from being seen; and salve to anoint your eyes so that you may
see" (3:17–18). There are three basic charges clarifying Laodicean
lukewarmness: their relative affluence, alongside being spiritually
destitute; their social self-sufficiency, alongside their being spiritually pathetic; and their spiritual overconfidence, alongside being
in reality spiritually blind. Given that the city of Laodicea was a
regional banking, finance, trade, manufacturing, textile production, and medical center, it is not inconceivable that this congregation was overly accommodated to the socioeconomic structures of
the Roman imperium and, having achieved a modicum (at least) of
success in this arena, had become assimilated at least economically
speaking to the guilds networked with the imperial cults and activities and to the economic system and social realities of Roman con-
trolled Asia Minor.[4] Gregory Beale writes,

> That some kind of boast about material welfare is in mind is
> likely from the observation that wherever [*plousios*] ("rich")
> and [*plouteō*] ("I am rich") are used negatively in Revelation,
> the reference is to unbelievers who have prospered materially
> because of their willing intercourse with the ungodly world
> system (6:15; 13:16; 18:3, 15, 19). The same idea is present
> here. Indeed, this church is on the brink of becoming identi-
> fied with such an ungodly system, as the second part of 3:17
> bears out.[5]

3. Craig R. Koester, "The Message to Laodicea and the Problem of Its Local Context: A Study of
the Imagery in Rev. 3.14–22," *New Testament Studies* 49:3 (2003): 407–24.
4. Ch. 5 of Robert M. Royalty Jr., *The Streets of Heaven: The Ideology of Wealth in the Apocalypse of
John* (Macon, GA: Mercer University Press, 1998), elaborates on the Laodicean participation
in the Roman economy.
5. Beale, *The Book of Revelation*, 304 (brackets are Beale's).

Such concession was devastating in at least two senses. First, the Laodicean Christians were indeed prosperous but in that respect too comfortably ensconced now in the affluent segments of West Asian society as evidenced by the tepidity of their public witness and their own sense of self-sufficiency.[6] Second, then, Jesus admonishes, "I am about to spit you out of my mouth" (3:16b), here resonating the warning to Israel that their disobedience to the covenant with YHWH would result in their being spewed forth from the land of promise (Lev. 18:25, 28; 20:22). Laodicean complacency would mean that they would no longer be distinguishable from the wider affluent Roman society and that their witness would be so compromised that they could no longer either represent or have fellowship with Jesus.

The first set of recommendations thus addresses the symptoms of lukewarmness (3:18): to ensure that there is spiritual and not just financial substance (the latter represented in gold); to cover up their spiritual nakedness (via white robes) rather than rely on the endowments of fine outward clothing; and to attain spiritual salve to see instead of being spiritually blind (3:18).[7] The second set of commendations more starkly insists: "Be earnest, therefore, and repent" (3:19b); only if they attend with solemnity to the gravity of their condition will they be able to get more to the root of their dis-ease. The final set of suggestions is intriguing in this context: "Listen! I am standing at the door, knocking; if you hear my voice and open the door, I will come in to you and eat with you, and you with me" (3:20). The injunctions are to listen (for a knock at the door), hear (Jesus' voice and what the divine spirit is saying to them), open (to reconnect), and eat together (have fellowship). Again, interpreters have wondered if the eating together may have overtones of the messianic banquet (depicted later: e.g., 19:9a) or even of the sacred meal

---

6. Mark R. Fairchild, "Laodicea's 'Lukewarm' Legacy: Conflicts of Prosperity in an Ancient Christian City," *Biblical Archaeology Review* 43:2 (2017): 31–39 and 67–68.

7. In each case possibly connecting to the socioeconomic background of the city, whether the banking and financial district, the textile manufacturing industry, or the medical establishment, including evidence of ophthalmological specialists as well; see Celal Şimşek, *Church of Laodikeia: Christianity in the Lykos Valley*, trans. Inci Türkoğlu (Denizli, Turkey: Denizli Metropolitan Municipality, 2015), 18–19.

and supper of the early messianists, but there is no reason why the fellowship Jesus is desiring to have with the Laodiceans (and any other of his followers in the other churches) needs to be mono-dimensional in expression.

FURTHER REFLECTIONS
The Cost of Wealth

Might the Laodicean believers have been struck by the image of Jesus standing outside of their intimate spaces? Many contemporary Christians, especially in pietist traditions and middle- to upper-middle-class Western contexts, including many second and later generation Asian Americans in their pan-Asian or multiethnic churches, would have assumed that Jesus was already in their hearts, having accepted and invited him in long before, maybe on multiple occasions. While not wishing to be unfair to second and later generations of Asian Americans in their own sojourn toward meaning in their lives, such evangelical pietism includes a heavy dose of modern Western individualism precisely of the sort that undergirds upward socioeconomic mobility in this culture. One result is that such a posture undermines the ecclesiality commended to these Asian churches. Christian faith is effectively individualized so that Christian life and witness is reduced to the personal and thoroughly subjective dimension. Christian discipleship exists, however, ecclesially, within the local congregation but also between that and the church catholic. These letters to particular communities nevertheless invite an interdependent and inter- and trans-personal Christian witness, one empowering the many individuals across various localities listening to and responding collaboratively in the power of the divine spirit.

Another result of such embrace of Western individualism is the consumerism that comes with it. Yet Jesus is found not in the comforts of our upper-middle-class lifestyles but, as was told in another parable elsewhere (Matt. 25:31–46), among the hungry (those making it from paycheck to paycheck), the stranger (the immigrant), the unclothed (impoverished), the sick (oppressed), and those in prison (rightly or wrongly: the so-called dregs of society). Laodicean prosperity had led them away from fellowshipping with and engaging Jesus, as represented on these social margins. No wonder Jesus begins by calling attention to their works, either the lack thereof (works of witness) or of the wrong type (of climbing the ladder of upward socioeconomic mobility). Not surprisingly, Jesus insists he knows the works of five of the seven congregations (Smyrna and Pergamum excepted), and we are later told that the final judgment will also be according to works (20:12). The cumulative message to the churches therefore is to encourage both their attentiveness to and realization of what Jesus considers important. Laodicean energies were at work but if not in demonstrating love for Jesus and those he loves, then their Lord is increasingly distanced, to the point where the chasm opened up is unbridgeable (after the final vomiting forth).

Are any of us readers of this and the other letters beneficiaries of social and other forms of privilege?[8] If so, this Laodicean letter is unlikely to be one of our favorites. The Laodiceans are counseled "to buy from me gold refined by fire" (3:18a). This may not be the fire announced to the Philadelphians as the coming great ordeal but instead may be the fire experienced by Smyrnaeans from civil, governmental, and political agents who sought to thrown them in jail, precisely because of their faithful witness. Such fire is fed not by divine wrath but by countercultural messianic discipleship. In the case of the Pentecost community, it cost those with means their land and property so they could be in solidarity with those without (Acts 2:42–47; 4:32–37).[9] Obtaining, retaining, and expanding wealth is costly in that sense, and so is following the Jesus path.

Yet we are not alone. Jesus warns and reproves those he loves (3:19a). Those who heed the words of the divine spirit spoken through these visionary messages, then, will both enjoy eternal— here and now and evermore after—fellowship with Jesus, and will

8. Harry O. Maier, *Apocalypse Recalled: The Book of Revelation after Christendom* (Minneapolis: Fortress, 2002), 30–39, confesses that if he were to be honest about his "reading as a Laodicean," that would entail recognizing his white male, educated, and privileged social location.

9. See my book on Acts and Luke, *Who Is the Holy Spirit? A Walk with the Apostles* (Brewster, MA: Paraclete Press, 2011), part III.

also take up a seat along his side at his throne, that also alongside
the Father (3:21; cf. 20:4). The promise is not mere health, wealth,
and prosperity in this life, particularly not if that compromises discipleship in the way of the slain Lamb, but rather, of his presence, by
his spirit, in our efforts to bear faithful witness to the world.

4:1–11
Around the Heavenly Throne: Invitation to Worship

If we followed the internal divisions of the Apocalypse marked by when John is "in the spirit" (4:2a), then this vision sets up a cosmic platform from which readers and listeners can see and hear the judgments related to the opening of the seals, the blowing of the trumpets, and the outpouring of the bowls—effectively chapters 4–16 in the book—all until the seer is "carried . . . away in the spirit into a wilderness" (17:3a). It is this elevated position that is important. This vision tells us about who and what is in heaven and what is being done there; we, in turn, can explore its implications for who we are today and what we ought to be doing.

These four strategic references to the work of the divine wind suggest that "the Divine Spirit can be called to play a role as a ubiquitous networking coordinator in the whole cosmos in terms of fundamental-semantic structure."

Hee Youl Lee, *A Dynamic Reading of the Holy Spirit in Revelation* (Eugene, OR: Wipf & Stock, 2014), 214.

Most important, upon entering into the heavenly portal (4:1), John envisions the throne and "the one seated there" in all its rainbowlike brilliance when refracted through the colors of precious stones such as jasper, carnelian, and emerald (4:2b–3).[1] We need to keep in mind that here, and wherever it follows in the Apocalypse that the heavenly throne is mentioned, Jesus is already said to be seated there, either on or more probably with the Father (3:21;

---

1. On Revelation being a very colorful book, see Lourdes García, "The Book of Revelation: A Chromatic Story," in Collins, *New Perspectives on the Book of Revelation*, 393–419.

also 22:1, 3),[2] so that the dazzling one is always with his Son, also the Lamb (see 5:6). Yet the focus here is on the magnificence of the throne's appearance. The vividness of this lightning- and torch-filled scene—notice here the illumination "in front of the throne [of the] seven flaming torches, which are the seven spirits of God"—is audibly reverberated through the "rumblings and peals of thunder" that are "coming from the throne" (4:5) on the one hand and yet calmed through what manifests "like a sea of glass, like crystal" (4:6a) on the other. If in ancient Israel the sea symbolized the chaos that needed constant ordering by the deity and in Revelation the beast arises out of the sea (13:1) and the waters of the seas harbors the dead (16:3b; 20:13a), then the apparent bed of glass—fully transparent as crystallite rather than hiding or obscuring what may be under the surface—in this initial heavenly vision portends both that the chaotic forces of the deep have been subjugated for divine purposes (see 15:2), and all of the darkness and deception that it represents are eventually vanquished (21:1).

Surrounding each side of the throne are four living creatures, looking, respectively, like a lion, an ox, a human (facially at least), and a flying eagle (4:6b–7). These living creatures represent the full expanse of the creaturely cosmos, the human animal along with its domestic (ox) and wild (lion) associates, as well as that in the skies above (none in the sea, of course, as that is already transformed and stilled in this heavenly vision).[3] Their characterization is re-visioned from the prophet Ezekiel where they also were "full of eyes in front and behind" and "all around and inside," albeit with six rather than four wings each (4:6b, 8; cf Isa. 6:2 and Ezek. 1:18; 10:12). With wings representing mobility, life, and dynamicity and eyes symbolizing omniscience, these four living creatures are relentlessly, "[d]ay and night without ceasing," singing and declaring, "Holy, holy, holy, the Lord God the Almighty, who was and is and is to come" (4:8b). Befitting this everlastingly living deity, they "give glory and honor and thanks to the one who is seated on the throne" (4:9).

But if all creation, as represented by these four living creatures,

---

2. Helpful here is Murphy, *Fallen Is Babylon*, 404.
3. For a thorough theological overview of Revelation's animals, see Richard Bauckham, *Living with Other Creatures: Green Exegesis and Theology* (Waco, TX: Baylor University Press, 2011).

unremittingly worship the one who was, is, and is to come, that includes human creatures, surely symbolized by the one with such a face. These human beings are also clearly envisioned as twenty-four elders, often believed to stand for the twelve tribes of Israel and the twelve apostles, but representative of the peoples of God considered all together (including Old and New Covenants).[4] These were seated on twenty-four thrones that encircle the throne of the Lord God Almighty, and they are "dressed in white robes, with golden crowns on their heads" (4:4). Surely readers and hearers of the book remember the victorious Sardians were promised white robes even as the lackadaisical Laodiceans were invited to put such on, even as the Philadelphians were reminded to guard the crowns on their heads through faithfulness. As the entirety of creation itself worshiped the one on the throne, through the four living creatures, so did the twenty-four elders, and the latter do so by prostrating themselves before the throne and laying down their crowns there (4:10). The twenty-four elders also add to the singing of the four living creatures, both glorifying and honoring the Lord their God but including alongside the thanksgiving of the four living creatures their own elderly acknowledgment of the deity's power: "for you created all things, and by your will they existed and were created" (4:11b). Echoing from the (earthly) background where/when the unrepentant Jezebel is thrown or cast down on her sickbed (*ballō*, 2:22a), the twenty-four elders instead cast (*balloūsin*) their crowns (4:10b) before the one who is worthy.

The hymn or song chanted by the four living creatures and twenty-four elders is the first of eight found in the book of Revelation (see also 5:12–14; 7:10–12; 11:15–18; 12:10–12; 15:3–4; 16:5–7; and 19:1–8). Whether or not the visions as a whole can be correlated with the liturgical practices of the early Christians, there is surely an implicit theology of worship and even an explicit commendation of and invitation to worship spread out across these pages.[5] The worship around the throne, though, is remarkable in its cosmic phenomenology. The ambiance of this worship around the throne

---

4. See Beale, *The Book of Revelation*, 322; Keener, *Revelation*, 172–73.
5. See Thomas Allen Seel, *A Theology of Music for Worship Derived from the Book of Revelation*, Studies in Liturgical Musicology 3 (Lanham, MD: Scarecrow Press, 1995).

insists that worship of the Lord Almighty cannot but be full-orbed, being caught up in the glory of the divine presence, enraptured by the sights, sounds, and perceptions, fully and wholly engaged with all that we are, and all that creation is, in extolling the one who lives forever and ever. Worship before the throne, heaven, is no mere conceptual, abstract, or speculative affair, but wholly affective (with hearts devoted), embodied (via prostration of our lives and achievements), and cosmic (alongside one another and the living creatures of God).[6]

FURTHER REFLECTIONS
Let Us Worship God

Yet there is a sense in which the heavenly worship is not for its own sake or only for the sake of the one who is on the throne but perhaps mirrors, or seeks to arouse and enact, what ought to transpire on earth. Revelation portrays not just that there is one worthy of worship on the heavenly throne but that there are other thrones—for instance of the satan, of the dragon, and of the sea beast (2:13a, 13:2b, 16:10a)—that also attempt to secure creaturely adulation. This is not then merely about worshiping God rather than the devil and all of the self- and creaturely-absorption that this symbol represents, although at one level, it is about as simple as that. On the contrary, it is precisely because the satan's throne is historically located and tied in with the social, civil, economic, and political powers of its time and space, not just at Pergamum but all along the seven mountains (17:9), that the demonic throne and its devious extensions invite our allegiance: our service, time, energy, and efforts. From that perspective, then, one might even be able to enter into congregational worship on Sunday mornings and give glory, honor, thanks, and power to the living God, but then devote the other six days to working for the "deities" of this world, enslaving ourselves to the altars of work and thrones of consumption. The heavenly worship, then, demands incessant participation since anything less

6. See also Melissa L. Archer, 'I Was in the Spirit on the Lord's Day': A Pentecostal Engagement with Worship in the Apocalypse (Cleveland, TN: CPT Press, 2015).

than that offers occasion for other earthly (social, economic, political) idols and divinities to receive our veneration.[7]

Last but not least, then, these hymns are not only directed toward the divine but also turned away from and in that sense defiant against what opposes the rule and reign of God. Brian Blount hence calls these "songs of resistance"—the modes through which we fight the good fight of faith, rendering our fidelity to God on the one side and renouncing and repelling the powers of darkness on the other side.[8] *Holy, holy, holy*—what in Greek is called the *Trisagion,* or the thrice-said-holy—orients us toward the divine purity and away from the ungodly and unholy. Glorifying and honoring God means recognizing our creatureliness and the deceitful nonbeing of the unholy triad. Thanking God means gratefully receiving divine grace, even creatureliness and life itself, rather than arrogantly being presumptive about our own capacities and potencies. In short, singing is a wholesome activity of fully prostrating ourselves toward the one who alone deserves worship, and this activity in turn refuses to recognize any other claims on our lives, loves, hopes, and dedication. Can we participate, however momentarily in our times and places, in realizing the eternal heavenly worship of the four living creatures and the twenty-four elders?

7. E.g., J. Nelson Kraybill, *Apocalypse and Allegiance: Worship, Politics and Devotion in the Book of Revelation* (Grand Rapids: Brazos, 2010).
8. Brian K. Blount, *Revelation: A Commentary*, New Testament Library (Louisville, KY: Westminster John Knox Press, 2009), 75.

5:1–14

The Lamb and the Scroll: Preparing for/amid the Storm

Whereas Revelation 4 focuses on the one on the throne, the next chapter turns to the Lamb between the throne, the creatures, and the elders (5:6a). The central throne-room scene in chapters 4–5 portrays powerfully the central biblical dramas of creation (the Lord Almighty on the throne) and redemption (the Lamb slain before the throne).[1] Yet the Lamb-throne scene not only connects backward but also looks ahead since the Lamb is the response to the seven-sealed scroll in the right hand of the one on the throne, and the Lamb's worthiness and ability to open the seven seals is what unleashes the judgments of the scroll in chapters 6–8. What can observation of the Lamb in the throne room tell us about anticipating the judgments of the unsealed scroll? As the Apocalypse is about the uncovering of Jesus Christ, we shall see in this chapter how the slain Lamb is central both to the divine presence and to the activity of the saints in its faithful witness.

The worshipful scene of the Lord God Almighty on the throne is interrupted when an angel asks with a loud voice, "Who is worthy to open the scroll and break its seals?" (5:2b), and the seer begins to "weep bitterly" because "no one in heaven or on earth or under the earth" was found worthy or able to open the scroll or to look into it (5:3–4). It is here that the one worthy and able is identified by one of the elders: "Do not weep. See, the Lion of the tribe of Judah, the

---

1. Loren L. Johns, "Facing Revelation's Beasts: The Opportunities and Challenges of Pastoral Ministry at the Edge of History," in Loren L. Johns, ed., *Apocalypticism and Millennialism: Shaping a Believer's Church Eschatology for the Twenty-first Century* (Kitchener, ON: Pandora Press; Scottdale, PN: Herald Press, 2000), 364–79.

Root of David, has conquered, so that he can open the scroll and its seven seals" (5:5). Yet when John looks for this lion—"Judah is a lion's whelp" (Gen. 49:9 says)—he sees "a Lamb standing as if it had been slaughtered, having seven horns and seven eyes, which are the seven spirits of God sent out into all the earth" (5:6b). This is not just a vulnerable and tender lamb but a military-like and warring ram, fully loaded with seven horns (so to speak) to be the "messianic conqueror who leads the people of God to victory" (cf. 6:16–17; 17:14).[2]

Jesus is hence revealed as both lion and lamb, conqueror and butchered one, four-footed yet standing as if on two.[3] Intriguingly, Revelation's high Christology is at its apex when viewed animalistically and quadrupedally through images of lion and lamb (and later when riding a white horse).[4] Besides being killed and bloodied (cf. 7:14b; 12:11; 13:8), elsewhere in Revelation, John's visions of the Lamb unveil other christological truths: that the Lamb is also at the "center of the throne" (7:17a); that there is wrath associated with the Lamb and the Lamb's presence (6:16; 14:10); that the Lamb is a guide to and conduit of springs of living water (17:7b; 22:1); and that the Lamb has the book of life and will light up the New Jerusalem (21:23, 27). Precisely because he is able to take the scroll "from the right hand of the one who was seated on the throne" (5:7b), he is worshiped by the four living creatures and the twenty-four elders (5:8a). The Lamb's co-equivalent divinity with the one on the throne is confirmed by the worship given to the Lamb.

Yet the Lamb's taking of the scroll at the throne has earthly connections and implications. The first inkling of this is that the crushed Lamb has "seven horns and seven eyes, which are the seven spirits of God sent out into all the earth" (5:6). With allusions to the prophecy of Zechariah again (Zech. 4:10b)—note this is from the same passage in Zechariah 4 related to the initial vision of the lampstands (see also discussion of 1:10–20 above)—this is less about John

---

2. Osborne, *Revelation*, 256.
3. See Graeme Goldsworthy, *The Lion and the Lamb: The Gospel in Revelation* (Nashville: Thomas Nelson, 1985).
4. See Stephen D. Moore, *Untold Tales from the Book of Revelation: Sex and Gender, Empire and Ecology* (Atlanta: SBL Press, 2014), ch. 9; cf. Christopher A. Frilingos, *Spectacles of Empire: Monsters, Martyrs, and the Book of Revelation*, Divinations: Rereading Late Ancient Religion (Philadelphia: University of Pennsylvania Press, 2004), chs. 4–5.

attempting to parse intra-trinitarian relations (e.g., how the seven spirits of holy spirit can be reduced to being the Lamb's or Son's eyes) than it is about the divine omniscience and how the Lamb and the one who sits on the throne's relatedness to the creaturely and cosmic realm is pneumatologically illumined. Herein, then, are the interlinkages between transcendent knowing (the all-seeing eyes) and cosmic reality (all the earth) indicated by the elders' "golden bowls full of incense, which are the prayers of the saints" (5:8b). Because nothing that happens at the ends of the earth escapes the surveying knowledge of the God of Jesus Christ, the prayers of the saints from around the earth arise before the throne as if through the Lamb's eyes—the seven spirits—going forth into the world and then harvesting what is seen and conveying them back to the throne room in the form of incense.[5] Thus, the elders "sing a new song: 'You are worthy to take the scroll and to open its seals, for you were slaughtered and by your blood you ransomed for God saints from every tribe and language and people and nation;[6] you have made them to be a kingdom and priests serving our God, and they will reign on earth'" (5:9–10). If the demonic triad later is exposed in their attempts to deceive all the earth's inhabitants and delude the kings of the entire world (13:3–4, 7–8; 16:13–14), here the divine spirit connects the eyes of the Lamb at the center of the heavenly throne room to all the earth.[7]

Whereas the initial throne room scene heralded the worship of the four living creatures and the twenty-four elders, here, the spotlight on the slain Lamb prompts them to sing a new song, one that is not only

5. I thus am sympathetic with a section, "Spirit of Pentecost (Acts 2) as the Seven Spirits of Rev: A Synthesis," in the concluding section of Ingo Willy Sorke, "The Identity and Function of the Seven Spirits in the Book of Revelation" (PhD diss., Southwestern Baptist Theological Seminary, 2009), 279–89, where he urges that the Lukan text provides an earthly viewpoint while the apocalyptic one offers a heavenly perspective.

6. Likely riffing off Daniel's prophecy where the triad of "peoples, nations, and languages" appears a half dozen times (Dan. 3:4, 7; 4:1; 5:19; 6:25; 7:14), perhaps especially "the LXX [Septuagint] version of Dan. 3.4 [that] mentions *four* such units ('nations and lands, peoples and tongues')"; Smalley, *The Revelation of John*, 137 (his italics and brackets). See also Justo L. González, *For the Healing of the Nations: The Book of Revelation in an Age of Cultural Conflict* (Maryknoll, NY: Orbis Books, 1999), 70–71.

7. Thanks to Frank D. Macchia (personal correspondence) for this connection; see also Macchia, "The Spirit of the Lamb: A Reflection on the Pneumatology of Revelation," in Craig S. Keener, Jeremy S. Crenshaw, and Jordan Daniel May, eds., *But These Are Written . . . : Essays on Johannine Literature in Honor of Professor Benny C. Aker* (Eugene, OR: Pickwick, 2014), 214–20.

flavored by incense of the prayers of the saints but also extols their ransom by the Lamb for priestly service and participation in divine rule on earth. With this choral, that which is implicit about the cosmic worship of the one on the throne is made explicit as including "myriads of myriads and thousands of thousands" of angels and "every creature in heaven and on earth and under the earth and in the sea, and all that is in them" (5:11b, 13a). Along with the four living creatures and twenty-four elders, now arises a truly comprehensive heavenly and earthly choir, with the seer envisioning almost literally every creature and the entirety of creation itself singing: "Worthy is the Lamb that was slaughtered to receive power and wealth and wisdom and might and honor and glory and blessing!" and "To the one seated on the throne and to the Lamb be blessing and honor and glory and might forever and ever!" (5:12, 13b). Whereas the one on the throne extracted a combined (from the four living creatures and the twenty-four elders) fourfold veneration of the divine glory, honor, power, and thanks, the Lamb receives an even more complete—imagine that!—adoration: fourfold from the creaturely realm (5:13b) and sevenfold from the heavenly band (5:12). With this, the worship climaxes before the Lamb: "the four living creatures said, 'Amen!' And the elders fell down and worshiped" (5:14).

Richard Bauckham puts it succinctly: whereas "Rev 4:6b–8 portrays the four living creatures as the central worshippers in creation, who, as heavenly representatives of the animate creatures of earth, unceasingly give to God the praise that all creation owes him," the enthronement of the Lamb in Revelation 5 moves us "from the worship of the living creatures to the worship of the whole creation."

Richard Bauckham, *Living with Other Creatures: Green Exegesis and Theology* (Waco, TX: Baylor University Press, 2011), 179 and 181–82.

FURTHER REFLECTIONS
Pathways through the Tempest

It is important here for an admonition that can also serve as a hermeneutical plumb line guiding our theological interpretation of the

rest of the book of Revelation. While this heavenly worship is unfolding with all its perceived pomp and circumstance, such is only partially—minimally in most cases—realized on earth where there is a
lot more going on besides orientation to the throne and the Lamb
in its midst. The difference between heavenly and earthly realities
are thus stark: the worship of the Lamb anticipates the opening of
the seven seals, and the destructions and judgments thereby catalyzed. Postcolonial readings of the throne room worship scenes
are thus correct to put before us at least two trajectories of considerations. On the one hand, that its imperial setting, the signs and
wonders characteristic of imperial majesty, the council of regent
(the twenty-four elders), the ritual performances of obeisance, the
liturgical hymn singing of the entire imperial domain, and the liturgical performance as a prelude to engaging with the oppositional
powers of evil—all these could be viewed as part of the colonized
mimicking the colonizer so that the imperial symbols are reappro-
priated for religious and even liturgical purposes.[8]

On the other hand, there is also a kind of dual consciousness
whereby the exile on Patmos also sees the divine victory as achieved
first and foremost through a slaughtered Lamb. It's the symbol of
a vulnerable and slain Lamb, intersecting here in important ways
with what the Lutheran theological tradition has called a *theology of
the cross*, that could become the hermeneutical pivot around which
the understanding of Revelation turns, and in that sense also provide an interpretive key for the full scope of the biblical drama of
creation and redemption.[9] God is disclosed in Jesus Christ who is
imaged in this starkest of revelations as a sacrificial and exposed
Lamb. Lambs are defenseless and helpless, in need of shepherds;
in this case, the guardians were not able to prevent the sacrifice
of the lamb, so it became a victim at the hands of its slaughterers.
Perhaps John and his original readers and hearers felt they were at
the mercy of the powers that be or had even (at least in the case of
Antipas of Pergamum) experienced first-hand the devastating grip

8. See Stephen D. Moore, *Empire and Apocalypse: Postcolonialism and the New Testament*
   (Sheffield: Sheffield Phoenix Press, 2006), esp. ch. 5.
9. Loren L. Johns, *The Lamb Christology of the Apocalypse of John*, Wissenschaftliche
   Untersuchungen zum Neuen Testament 2.167 (Tübingen: Mohr Siebeck, 2003).

of those powers as Jesus did through his death on the cross; and if that is the case, they may have seen their own situation as being aligned with the fortunes of the slain Lamb or believed that in the Lamb, once crushed but raised to life and the throne, God saw their plight and promised final resurrection.

The challenge, of course, is where readers or hearers are located vis-à-vis the original audience. Those on the underside of history would be less able to reproduce the trappings of power and embrace instead the symbolic solidarity of the slain Lamb. Those on the upper side of history, and even more worrisome, those at the centers of society or inhabiting the halls of economic and political power will be tempted by the authoritativeness of the Apocalypse to erect, extend, and deploy new discourses and practices of domination.[10]

In democratic societies, in principle nothing inhibits any person or group of persons from upward socioeconomic and even political mobility, and in that sense Revelation both encourages the underprivileged and can be mesmerizing for those either born into or have worked up toward such privileges. An Asian (American) perpetual foreigner hermeneutical stance, then, provides an angle on cultivating vigilance so that we are not ensnared by imperial allurement. The key here is to prioritize the potency of the slaughtered Lamb (mentioned twenty more times in the rest of the book) over that of the Lion figure (which appears four other times, although never again in relationship to Jesus and only in one of those instances not referring to anti-christic forces and realities). Doing so enables recognition that our pathways through the storms of life and history, about to unfold with full force (in Revelation 6 and following), are steadied through camaraderie with the worthy Lamb.

10. Greg Carey, *Elusive Apocalypse: Reading Authority in the Revelation to John* (Macon, GA: Mercer University Press, 1999), 175.

Excursus B
Seven Seals-Trumpets-Bowls (Chapters 6–16)

Before diving into the seven seals in Revelation 6, we need to step back to situate that heptad amid the bigger picture of the book. The Apocalypse is structured heptadically, and we have just completed discussion of the seven churches. The throne room scenes introduce the seven seals, and their unfolding (6:1–8:1) is related in turn to the seven trumpets (8:2–11:19) and seven bowls (15:5–16:21). Now there is some question about the degree the judgments of the seventh bowl extend to include Revelation 17–18, and we will comment further on that question in the final excursus (D). For the moment, we consider the togetherness of the seals, trumpets, and bowls since they are divulged out of the throne room scenes unveiled to John when he was lifted up in the spirit to heaven (4:2) and before he is next carried by an angel "in the spirit into a wilderness" (17:3a).

As by now we have already seen that the seer has led his hearers and readers to understand that the Apocalypse concerns "what must take place after this" (4:1a; cf. 1:1a, 19b), for much of Revelation's reception and interpretive history the assumption was that starting with the vision of the seals in chapter 6, we were being given a glimpse into what would happen next after John's heavenly exaltation. Hence, during the medieval period, expositors of the book interpreted these middle chapters of the Apocalypse historically and ecclesially, as mapping the development of the church, and these correlational endeavors not only grew more and more sophisticated over the centuries but also gained in intensity and fervor the closer it was that the church of that time felt they were running up against or toward the final conflagration.[1] Of course, there were debates about precisely how to construe these visions. Were the seals, trumpets, and bowls to be unraveled sequentially (or chronologically) or deciphered as unfolding simultaneously, for instance? Indications of a progressive development across the Revelation narrative with each series of the three heptads affecting first one-fourth (6:8), then one-third (8:7–12), and then all (16:17), suggests a linear perspective.[2] On the flip side, the final announcements at the end of the book, concluding with, "It is done!" (21:6), suggests perhaps a parallelist depiction.[3]

---

1. For instance, was Francis of Assisi (1181/1182–1226) the angel of the sixth seal (Rev. 7:2) or did the Franciscans believe they were Joachim of Fiore's (1135–1202) "spiritual men" of the last days? See Francis X. Gumerlock, trans., *The Seven Seals of the Apocalypse: Medieval Texts in Translation* (Kalamazoo, MI: Medieval Institute Publications, 2009), 21.
2. James L. Resseguie, *Revelation Unsealed: A Narrative Critical Approach to John's Apocalypse*, Biblical Interpretation 32 (Leiden and Boston: Brill, 1998), 162.
3. Ryan Leif Hansen, *Silence and Praise: Rhetorical Cosmology and Political Theology in the Book of Revelation* (Minneapolis: Fortress, 2014), 73.

It is in part for these reasons that fairly early on, by the fourth century in most accounts,[4] a mediating view emerged, one that observed how each successive heptad is included in some sense in the preceding one. There are certainly variations to what must be seen hence as a spectrum of views—from contested interpretations about how much of a preceding heptad overlaps with a succeeding one to that which insists that the final seal opens up to the trumpets and the final trumpet to the bowls[5]—but the point is that this *recapitulative* perspective, as it has come to be known, emphasizes logical and theological intensification rather than chronological succession following the cues internal to the Revelation narrative. One such hint is the literary structure that organizes each heptad, arguably, in a four-two-interval-one movement, with the first four separated out from the next two, and the latter pair elongated in ways that exceed the length of their combined four predecessors. Another is the interruption that happens at the end of the sixth seal and the sixth trumpet—interludes, as these have come to be known[6]—that structure the narrative, with a parenthetical aside inserted between the sixth and seventh bowl. A third signal is that the end of each heptad prompts peals of thunder, rumblings, flashes of lightning, and an earthquake, not always in that order, with the final trumpet and bowl unshackling "heavy hail" and "huge hailstones" (8:5; 11:19; 16:18, 21).[7] The point is that seeing the trumpets as recapitulating the seals in some way and the bowls as recapitulating the trumpets (and seals) further is faithful to John's visionary narrative and serves the purposes of those interested in theological commentary rather than in matching historical events with biblical prophecy understood in predictive terms.[8]

4. Dating back to Victorinus of Poetovio (d. *c.* 304), perhaps in part because he expected the end to occur imminently, although he stopped short of predicting the end of the world; see Douglas W. Lumsden, *And Then the End Will Come: Early Latin Christian Interpretations of the Opening of the Seven Seals* (New York and London: Garland Publishing, 2001), ch. 2.

5. See Mark Wilson, *Charts on the Book of Revelation: Literary, Historical, and Theological Perspectives* (Grand Rapids: Kregel Academic & Professional, 2007), 78.

6. Which function like parentheses in the narrative, to be used and acknowledged as such "only on the condition that they are understood to describe the form only and not the contents of the text," the latter about which nothing is marginal; see Resseguie, *Revelation Unsealed*, 324.

7. Dale Ralph Davis, "The Relationship between the Seals, Trumpets, and Bowls in the Book of Revelation," *Journal of the Evangelical Theological Society* 16:3 (1973): 149–58. Other parallels not directly impinging on the parallel-versus-progression question have been identified, such as that explored by Andrew E. Steinmann, "The Tripartite Structure of the Sixth Seal, the Sixth Trumpet, and the Sixth Bowl of John's Apocalypse (Rev. 6:12–7:17; 9:13–11:14; 16:12–16)," *Journal of the Evangelical Theological Society* 35:1 (1992): 68–79.

8. Such a recapitulative hypothesis makes even more sense when we see how later cycles reintegrate earlier ones, which reincorporation is especially crucial given that the septets of judgments are themselves on the way toward the ultimate re-creative task that happens with the new Jerusalem. I owe this important insight about Revelation redemptively encompassing everything going back to the primordial creation to T. Craig Isaacs, *John's Apocalypse: A Study in Dream Interpretation* (Eugene, OR: Cascade Books, 2016).

Asian Australian pentecostal biblical scholar U-Wen Low notes (personal communication, October 2019): "I actually fully agree with the recapitulation idea here, and think that there are many advantages to it—I wonder if there is some sort of Asian influence/worldview here which allows us to grasp this [recapitulative] concept more readily (a non-linear reading)."

I'd like to make one more observation about the extended moments between what is penultimate within and what concludes each heptad. In the seal sequence, there is a lengthy interlude before the opening of the seventh seal that features two large groups: the 144,000 (7:3–8) and great multitude (7:9–17); and in the trumpet series, there is another interval before the sounding of the final trumpet that focuses first on one witness, that of John the seer himself (10:1–11), and second on two witnesses (11:3–13). There is not much of a discernible intermezzo between the sixth and seventh bowl, but there is a subtle pause that in English translations is rightly characterized as a bracketed moment, one in which Jesus' voice interrupts the narrative with a warning about his soon return and an invitation to the reader or hearer to be ready (16:15). These pauses allow for a building up of intensity within each heptad, anticipating the final seal, trumpet, and bowl, encouraging the people of God—the addressees of this Apocalypse—to be faithful in worshipful obedience even amid trials, persecution, and tragedy.[9]

And it is this big picture of covenant renewal, purification, and expanded (from Jews to the rest of the world) restoration that ought not to be lost amid foci on the particularities of the heptads and their constitutive elements. The seals are unbounded by the slain but standing Lamb, and this reminds us that the unveiling is less about the apocalyptic destruction of the world (without minimizing the horrific nature of what is portrayed as coming to pass) than it is about the reordering of the cosmos toward the throne of the Lord God Almighty.[10] The trumpets then bring us right up to the cusp of rewards (for God's servants and saints) and judgments for rebellious nations and those who destroy the earth (11:18), even as the bowls reveal and finalize the divine judgments (15:4b).[11] As we embarked on what some might anticipate to be a

---

9. See Peter S. Perry, *The Rhetoric of Digressions: Revelation 7:1–17 and 10:1–11:13 and Ancient Communication*, Wissenschaftliche Untersuchungen zum Neuen Testament 2:268 (Tübingen: Mohr Siebeck, 2009).

10. Gordon Campbell, "Findings, Seals, Trumpets, and Bowls: Variations upon the Theme of Covenant Rupture and Restoration in the Book of Revelation," *Westminster Theological Journal* 66 (2004): 71–96, at 84.

11. Josephine Ford suggests (*Revelation*, 266–68, 282–83) that the four promises of judgments (wild animals, sword, pestilence, and scarcity of bread symbolized in its selling by weight)

decoding of the dense symbolism of the seals, and the trumpets and bowls to follow, let us not forget that all this ought to occur in a doxological posture, one that is rightly attending to the slain Lamb that saves amid judgments and that judges as part of saving, even as it is appropriately responding, in this worshipful stance, toward the personal, relational, and political dynamics of earthly and creaturely existence.

---

in Lev. 26:18, 21, 24, 28—that so long as Israel remains unrepentant of its sins, it would be punished sevenfold—are here quadratically fulfilled in the seals-trumpets-bowls heptads plus in the losses suffered by seven groups or figures in Rev. 17–19: the harlot, the kings of the earth, the merchants, the sailors, the classes of human beings, the sea and earth beasts, and the satan. If we stayed within the main frame of Rev. 6–16, the seven angelic sign-messages of judgments in 14:6–20 (see commentary on this passage below) would be the third (after seals and trumpets) of four (followed by bowls) heptads pronounced or performed, again mapping onto the Levitical warnings.

6:1–8

The First Four Seals and the Four Horsemen: Unveiling a Broken Creation

This sixth chapter plunges us into the heart of the coming apocalypse, the details of which John has been promising would be unfolded to his readers and hearers. We will make some general comments about the first four seals and their accompanying four horsemen before going into some specifics about what each of these horsemen represent. We will conclude with some reflections on the nature of the world that feature these horsemen and how the church today is to understand its engagement with that world. We must keep in mind, however, that with the following we are merely entering into the apocalyptic domain; more seals await opening, and all that comes with them.

The popular imagination has long been gripped by these four horsemen.[1] Let us attempt to situate these horsemen both intra-textually within the Apocalypse and inter-textually with other portions of the scriptural canon. With regard to the former, the 4+2+1 structure of the seals, trumpets, and bowls invites at least some comparative perspective. In this case, the trumpets and bowls speak with much more unanimity in that both generally parallel the Egyptian plagues (Exod. 7:14–11:10), although the apocalyptic arrangements follows their own ordering: the first trumpet and bowl consume the earth and assault its human inhabitants (8:7; 16:2); the second pair turn the sea into blood and kill its creatures (8:8–9; 16:3); the third duo strike the fresh springs and rivers of the world (8:11; 16:4), and the fourth couple darken the world and scorch the sun, impacting the

---

1. E.g., Billy Graham, *Approaching Hoofbeats: The Four Horsemen of the Apocalypse* (New York: Avon, 1985).

heavenly and cosmic realms (8:12; 16:8–9). More may be said, but this provides a backdrop to comprehend the four horsemen as unloosing war, killing, famine, and death.[2] The parallels are rough but present.

Further, read inter-textually, it is unimaginable that John was neither alluding to nor riffing off the initial and concluding of Zechariah's eight visions, which feature four horses of almost equivalent colors (two reds but no black) and four chariots of exactly matching colors (Zech. 1:8; 6:2–3). As important, the parallels between the six seals and the apocalypses in the Synoptic Gospels are striking. A grid depicts more starkly the convergences across the New Testament:[3]

Comparing Revelation and the Apocalyptic Passages of the Synoptic Gospels			
Revelation *ch. 6*	*Matthew* *ch. 24*	*Mark* *ch. 13*	*Luke* *ch. 21*
conquering and to conquer	wars and rumors of wars (v. 6)	wars and rumors of wars (v. 7a)	wars and insurrections (v. 9)
war and killing	international strife (v. 7a)	international strife (v. 8a)	international strife (v. 10)
famine	famines (v. 7b)	earthquakes (v. 8b)	famines (v. 11a)
death	earthquakes (v. 7c)	famines (v. 8c)	earthquakes (v. 11b)
persecution	persecution (v. 9)	persecution (v. 9)	persecution (v. 12)
cosmic perturbations	cosmic perturbations (v. 29)	cosmic perturbations (v. 24)	cosmic perturbations (vv. 25–26)

2. Laurenţiu Florentin Moţ, *Angels and Beasts: The Relationship between the Four Living Creatures and the Four Riders in Revelation 6:1–8* (Eugene, OR: Wipf & Stock, 2017), 48–54, suggests that the sequence of the four horsemen is the inverse of the humanization in Jesus Christ, which is manifest in and through the four living creatures at the throne room in the previous vision and thus meant to encourage faithfulness among the saints and repentance and the experience of redemption among others.

3. The following is found variously in other sources, e.g., Ford, *Revelation*, 104; Murphy, *Fallen Is Babylon*, 202; Wilson, *Charts on the Book of Revelation*, 77.

The big questions coming from this insight is how to comprehend and enact messianic discipleship against apocalyptically understood historical realities. These four horsemen and the six seals taken together approximate the message of Jesus' own teachings about how to orient our lives faithfully amid challenging circumstances, at least as recorded in these sections of the synoptic evangelists.

From this perspective, then, we can explore the opening of each seal in order. The first discharges "a white horse! Its rider had a bow; a crown was given to him, and he came out conquering and to conquer" (6:2). At first blush, this is rather confusing since we have come to expect whiteness to be associated with Jesus and goodness, as it has been on multiple occasions in the first five chapters of the Apocalypse; but here, Jesus is the one, in the form of the Lamb, opening the seal (6:1), and he has already been presented as a giver, not receiver, of crowns (2:10). Things get even more puzzling if we fast-forward to the end of the Apocalypse where Jesus also comes riding a white horse (19:11). The obfuscation may be alleviated a bit once we realize that the beast that emerges from out of the bottomless pit and the sea also makes war against and conquers the two witnesses and the saints (11:7; 13:7). At best, this rider on a white horse is a lesser angel paving the way for destructive judgment;[4] at worse, it is a "demonic parody of Christ."[5] The symbolism is most important: that the work of the slaughtered Lamb, now having ascended to heaven, is intended to accomplish thoroughly the redemption of all creation to the one who sits on the throne, and that this task will involve a final conflict so that both judgment and salvation can be achieved.

As with any conflict, what ensues is war, famine, and death.[6] The unlocking of the second seal released a rider on a bright red horse given a "great sword" that "was permitted to take peace from the earth, so that people would slaughter one another" (6:4), and that of the third seal divulges a "black horse! Its rider held a pair of scales in his hand" (6:5b). The symbolism here is clarified by "what seemed

---

4. Ford, *Revelation*, 106.
5. Gordon D. Fee, *Revelation*, New Covenant Commentary Series (Eugene, OR: Cascade Books, 2011), 43.
6. This logical progression is observed by Osborne, *Revelation*, 272.

to be a voice in the midst of the four living creatures saying, 'A quart of wheat for a day's pay, and three quarts of barley for a day's pay...'" (6:6). Conditions of famine striking these subsistence products mean that workers will not be able to provide for their families and that everyone other than the wealthy and affluent will struggle, be affected, and suffer.[7] Last but not least, the unlatching of the fourth seal bares a "pale green horse! Its rider's name was Death, and Hades followed with him; they were given authority over a fourth of the earth, to kill with sword, famine, and pestilence, and by the wild animals of the earth" (6:8). This is in some respects an intensification of what the bright red and black horses inflict, but now much more expansively and extensively strewn.

Overindulgence in or excessive speculation about the details of these four horsemen can occlude what is really happening here: that these are judgments of divine provenance and under divine providence. First, the Lamb is the one who opens each of the seals. Second, as each of these first four seals is unfastened, one of the four living creatures, each also in turn, calls out in a thunderous voice (this is clearly said of the first living creature's announcement), "Come!" (6:1b, 3b, 5a, 7), and it is this which brings forth the horsemen. Third, while the havoc wreaked on earth by these horsemen ought not to be underestimated, God remains in control. The rider on the white horse is given the powers to conquer, while that on the bright red horse is clearly said to be "*permitted* to take peace from the earth" (6:4, italics added). Further, the famines strike a fourth of the earth, but a voice from the center of the throne room, from amid precisely the four living creatures that are calling forth these horsemen, also draws a line over which the scourge of famine cannot cross: "but do not damage the olive oil and the wine!" (6:6b). With oil and wine being used for festivities, yes, this might be an ironically sarcastic expression of how the final judgments will sweep over an evil world bent on continuing their God-ignoring ways in their partying amid the felt cataclysms;[8] but I also see this as a further indicator that the divine judgments are measured, not indiscriminate. Last but not least along these lines, do not overlook that Death, the pale green

7. Murphy, *Fallen Is Babylon*, 366.
8. Blount, *Revelation*, 129–30.

horse rider, and Hades in its stead (pun intended), is "given authority," and this authority is also demarcated to affect and destroy no
more than "a fourth of the earth" (6:8). As such, bad things are happening all around, and even to the saints (as will be clear momentarily in the next section), but whatever is occurring transpires only
under the aegis of the Lamb and the one on the throne.

FURTHER REFLECTIONS
Laying Bare the Human Condition

If Dispensationalist schemes often put off these developments to
the end of the age, precipitating events like the rapture of believers
and of the great tribulation, our own theological approach prefers to
view these calamitous horsemen as symbolic of the kinds of upheavals normative for a fallen, sinful, and evil world. In other words, the
four horsemen describe at least the age of the church as that which
has been unfolding since the apostolic times.[9] Wars, strife, famines,
death: these wax and wane on the one hand but also persist perva-
sively through the human condition on the other hand. But these
human atrocities are precisely the forms of destruction and tragedy
through and for which the Lamb was slain in order to redeem the
world. Indeed, apart from such imperial destructiveness, the Lamb
would never have been threatened to begin with, and this invites
our own consideration that the present age of testing is constituted
precisely by a terrestrial environment groaning for renewal and the
flux of historical circumstances that cry out for redemption. Seen
from such a wider cosmic lens, then, the horsemen of the apocalypse are characteristic of the fallen creaturely order unleashed
since the primordial sin of creaturely self-preoccupation.

   Hence, the opening of the seven seals can be understood as part
of what brings to fulfillment the salvation accomplished through
the Lamb's slaughter. Yes, creation is broken, but we already knew
that, even if the portrayal of the four horsemen is a vivid reminder
that we travail in a damaged and malfunctioning world. Yet the

---

9. Thus does Gregory Beale categorize the opening of the seals as what occurs "throughout the
church age for either purification or punishment" (*The Book of Revelation*, 370).

opening of these seals also keeps before us that the deliverance wrought through the slain Lamb will not remain incomplete and that the one who sits on the throne intends to salvage fully the world that the divine power brought into being, and seeks to do so in part through empowering Christian witness and discipleship in the present time through these apocalyptic visions.

6:9–17

Under the Heavenly Altar and among the Caves and Mountains: Can I Get a Witness?

In the previous section we noted the congruence between the six seals and the Gospel apocalypses,[1] so now we turn to addressing specifically how the issues of persecution and cosmic reverberations that are undraped by the loosening of the fifth and sixth seals can be part of the evangel or good news of Jesus Christ. This is part of furthering the query initiated in the preceding: if the seals describe not just what will happen at the end of time/history but also depict the character of the age of the church, then how do the images related to these two seals specifically form viable Christian witness for the present (and any ecclesial) time? Our discussion will foreground both the missional opportunity and challenge and suggest an Asian (American) perpetual foreigner via media through the thickets.

The opening of the fifth seal leads John to see "under the altar the souls of those who had been slaughtered for the word of God and for the testimony they had given" (6:9). These martyrs are clothed in white robes (6:11a), fulfilling the promises made to the churches (3:5, 18), and replicative of what was worn by the twenty-four elders (4:4). Although this is the first time that the altar in heaven is mentioned, we are told later that it is a golden altar and that it plays a prominent role in the rest of the visions, mostly related to being the source of or channels for judgments on the earth (8:3–5; 9:13; 14:18; 16:7). This is because these are those who have been, as if in the footsteps (or hoof-steps, as the case may be) of the Lamb found worthy to break open the seals of the scroll, slaughtered for their

---

1. As we turn now to Rev. 6, see also C. Marvin Pate, "Revelation 6: An Early Interpretation of the Olivet Discourse," *Criswell Theological Review* 8:2 (2011): 45–55, esp. 46–51.

witness, and it is as such souls that their prayers are loudly voiced, "Sovereign Lord, holy and true, how long will it be before you judge and avenge our blood on the inhabitants of the earth?" (6:10). In some respects, the rest of the judgments that are unfolded in the Apocalypse can be understood as God's response to this cry. From this perspective, "the altar does not represent killing; it personifies the divine response to it."[2]

The seer then envisages that the souls under the altar "were each given a white robe and told to rest a little longer, until the number would be complete both of their fellow servants and of their brothers and sisters, who were soon to be killed as they themselves had been killed" (6:11). The English translation is a bit misleading, as if there were a predetermined sum of martyrs expected before divine intervention would accomplish their exculpation. The original Greek, however, does not mention any actual quantity, and a more literal translation is perhaps more accurate: "until their fellow servants and also their brethren, who were to be killed as they were, should be fulfilled" (twenty-first-century KJV). This suggests that what is being awaited is not for x-number of sacrificial victims but the completion of their work and witness.[3] There therefore appear to be two forms of witness that the altar resounds: that of the dead longing for vengeance—a form of petitionary prayer pervasive across the Old Testament canon—and exoneration, and those who are still alive but whose witness puts them on a course toward martyrdom.

The opening of the sixth seal booms forth two other forms of "witness": that of the cosmos as a whole and that of the "inhabitants of the earth" that the souls under the altar sought retribution on. John now sees a thoroughly apocalyptic set of images: "there came a great earthquake; the sun became black as sackcloth, the full moon became like blood, and the stars of the sky fell to the earth as the fig tree drops its winter fruit when shaken by a gale. The sky vanished like a scroll rolling itself up, and every mountain and island was removed from its place" (6:12–14). If justice is called for by those given voice through the breaking of the fifth seal, then justice is initiated with the cracking of the sixth seal, and this flowing forth

---

2. Blount, *Revelation*, 133.
3. Blount, *Revelation*, 137.

of divine judgment brings with it, according to the apocalyptic scenarios foreseen by the prophets of ancient Israel, cosmic shocks and effects. Intriguingly, our seer here alludes especially (if not only) to the prophet Joel,[4] not coincidentally for our purposes from the same passage that Luke also draws on in explaining the Pentecost event as the outpouring of the divine spirit heralding the Day of the Lord (see Acts 2:17–21; cf. Joel 2:28–32). So, if for Luke the outpouring of the spirit on all flesh inaugurates the great Day of the Lord, then in Revelation, the going forth of the seven spirits to the edges of the earth (5:6) initiates what the powerful of the world recognize as the "great day" of the wrath of the Lamb and of him who sits on the throne (6:15–17). But whereas Luke emphasizes this as the day of salvation, John views it as the day of judgment.

Ironically, then, the creation itself bears witness, in these ways, to the purifying verdicts of God. Yet the shaking of the heavens and the earth not only destroy but also, somehow, provide cover for its inhabitants. John sees in the wake of these apocalyptic developments that "the kings of the earth and the magnates and the generals and the rich and the powerful, and everyone, slave and free, hid in the caves and among the rocks of the mountains, calling to the mountains and rocks, 'Fall on us and hide us from the face of the one seated on the throne and from the wrath of the Lamb'" (6:15–16). Seeking refuge from creational resources rather than pleading for divine mercy,[5] the "witness" of these earthly inhabitants is thus one of fear, specifically anxiousness and dread regarding the Lamb's wrath. This paradoxical image is rooted in the vision's insistence that only the Lamb was found worthy and capable of breaking the seals and opening the scroll. Hence even those deemed most dominant on earth lament, "for the great day of their wrath has come, and who is able to stand?" (6:17). Certainly not the earth's inhabitants who have usually had dominion over and exploited the earth and its properties, but now seek refuge, cowering amid its caves and mountains. Those who are exposed here are precisely those deemed to utterly contrast with the

4. See Susan F. Mathews, "The Power to Endure and Be Transformed: Sun and Moon Imagery in Joel and Revelation 6," in Lawrence Boadt and Mark S. Smith, eds., *Imagery and Imagination in Biblical Literature: Essays in Honor of Aloysius Fitzgerald, F.S.C.* (Washington, DC: Catholic Biblical Association of America, 2001), 35–49.
5. See Skaggs and Benham, *Revelation*, 83.

helplessness and defenselessness of animals such as lambs. Yet the symbols here are moving in completely unexpected directions: it is the slain Lamb who is fearsome and it is the earth's powers-that-be that are the most susceptible and exposed. This theme of the Lamb's power over the earth's regents' weakness is one that we shall see again, even more intensely depicted, as we move forward in the seer's visions. Even those who are the exact opposite of the Lamb, surely not that Lamb's followers, are now testifying to the Lamb's judgments, which are emanating from the heavenly throne room.

FURTHER REFLECTIONS
Multivocal and Messianic Testifyn[^1]

The subtitle of this section, "Can I Get a Witness?," was popularized first as a song in the dancehalls of the emerging counterculture of the 1960s.[6] Although the lyrics went in directions quite different from what John would have considered as relevant for messianic witness, nevertheless the counterculturality of the artists and bands that propagated the hit single connects with our current consideration. In this case, one might say that there are multiple dimensions of counterconventional witnesses disclosed by the fifth and sixth seals: (1) that of the martyred souls and those who will be following closely in their steps calling for retaliation; (2) that of the creational elements, in their own (apocalyptic) way, manifesting the sovereignty, holiness, and truthfulness of God (recall that the souls under the altar addressed their prayers to the "sovereign Lord, holy and true"); and (3) the presumed rulers of the earth, including the kings, generals, magnates, rich, and powerful, who truthfully testify to the

---

6. Led by crossover gospel artist Marvin Gaye in 1963; on Gaye's pentecostal-holiness background and its impact on his music, see Louis B. Gallien Jr., "Crossing Over Jordan: Navigating the Music of Heavenly Bliss and Earthly Desire in the Lives and Careers of Three 20th Century African American Holiness-Pentecostal 'Cross-over' Artists," in Estrelda Y. Alexander and Amos Yong, eds., *Afro-Pentecostalism: Black Pentecostal and Charismatic Christianity in History and Culture*, Religion, Race, and Ethnicity series (New York: New York University Press, 2011), 117–37, esp. 127–32. See also Brian K. Blount, *Can I Get a Witness? Reading Revelation through African American Culture* (Louisville, KY: Westminster John Knox Press, 2005), ch. 4, on the gospel/spirituals-blues perspective on Revelation, although Blount does not discuss Gaye specifically.

horrifying wrath of the Lamb. Both who is doing the testifying and what they are witnessing to in at least two of the cases are counter-intuitive for many Christians. We usually do not expect the natural world to attest as loudly as it does in this case, although theirs is the most expected testimony: that the divine judgments will indeed quake the world. Otherwise, Christians will generally not desire, nor volunteer for, a martyrological witness, much less one that seeks their deaths to be avenged—since Jesus sought forgiveness for his murderers, and they would not normally also expect that the earthly powers will give such truthful witness, particularly one so unimagi-nable as that of a wrathful Lamb. The Day of Pentecost outpouring of the divine spirit, however, inspired many different tongues to tes-tify, each in their own idiom and accent, to the bewilderment and perplexity of those listening, of the wondrous works of God. What kind of multiplicity of witness have ensued from the breaking of these seals, and what further testimonies might resound regarding Christian faithfulness two thousand years removed from their initial disclosures?

Perhaps the perpetual foreigner perspective of the Asian Ameri-can experience can chart a path forward. This may not be one that seeks persecution for the sake of martyrdom, and it certainly would not be one that embraces earthly power for the purpose of coming under the wrath of the Lamb. Rather, being both insiders in some respects but outsiders in other aspects means that we can identify with both sides in important capacities and then bear appropriate witness in either direction as the circumstances may avail. This is hence to be able to adopt the perspective of the souls under the altar if and when we may have access to earthly authority or to be able to remember that our witness is first and foremost, if not also always, to the word of God (6:1b), and that is what we want to be renowned for, rather than as purveyors of the Lamb's wrath (which then even the inhabitants of the world will bear witness to). Can we hereby get authentic but yet unforeseen witnesses, not strictly following the scripts of the fifth and sixth seals but nevertheless informed by their images? If so, we may yet contribute to the fulfill-ment and completion of the witness of the souls under the altar even if we might not be literally numbered among the martyrs gathered there. I would imagine that most of my readers might think avoiding such an end would be a good thing, although the flip side then is not to find ourselves so assimilated to the powers of this world that we are unable to extricate ourselves from those cavernous and mountainous testimonies bemoaned with the breaking of the sixth seal.

7:1–17

144,000 and the Great Multitude: Standing (Out) in the Crowd?

If the breaking of the sixth seal ends with the question of the kings and the powerful, "who is able to stand" on the great day of the wrath of the Lamb and the one who sits on the throne, the next two visions are a part of an interlude anticipating the seventh seal that in effect provides a twofold answer: John sees first "four angels standing at the four corners of the earth" (7:1a), and this opens up to his hearing of 144,000 servants of God, and second, "a great multitude that no one could count, from every nation, from all tribes and peoples and languages, standing before the throne and before the Lamb" (7:9). The two visions of Revelation 7, including the introduction of the huge groups of persons in the second set of images, invite consideration of how they might speak theologically to the church today.

Note first that the four angels are those "who had been given power to damage earth and sea" (7:2b), and their task was to hold back the destructive winds of the earth and sea (7:1b) until "another angel ascending from the rising of the sun [from the East], having the seal of the living God" was able to "have marked the servants of our God with a seal on their foreheads" (7:2a, 3b). We know that the sixth seal has already shaken the very foundations of the heavens and the earth (6:12–14), which is why the restraining of the winds of the earth here from wreaking destruction is not to be understood in a strictly chronological sense. Hence, as part of the heightening of the tension during this intercalation while we await the breaking of the seventh seal, John tells us he "heard the number of those who were sealed, one hundred forty-four thousand, sealed out of every tribe of the people of Israel" (7:4). Then 12,000 are specified from each of the twelve tribes, Dan excepted and Manasseh son of Joseph in its place.[1]

How do we understand these 144,000 sealed servants of God? There are at least eighteen different listings of the twelve tribes throughout the Old Testament and so John's unique rendering is not out of the ordinary.[2] Perhaps he begins with Judah since Jesus comes from that line, indeed already named as the Lion of that tribe (5:8), but other than this, there is a lot of conjecture but little definitive rationale for this enumeration since it had already grown very difficult by the time of the first century for Jews to trace their tribal lineages. Revelation 14 tells us that these 144,000 were "standing on Mount Zion" (14:1a)—there definitively answering the question of who can stand on the day of wrath—and also that they are "redeemed from the earth" (14:3b), precisely what the angel from the East suggests would happen. Further, the later vision tells us that the 144,000 are virgins, effectively pure, holy, truthful, and blameless (14:4–5). Last but not least, the seal the East angel marks on their foreheads is more explicitly disclosed as the name of the Lamb and of his Father (14:1), which is consistent with what was promised to victorious Philadelphians preserved in and through the time of testing promised to afflict the earth (3:10, 12b).

After telling that he hears the 144,000 sealed, John looks and sees the great multitude and hears them crying out loudly: "Salvation belongs to our God who is seated on the throne, and to the Lamb!" (7:10). At this, again, the angelic hosts, four living creatures and elders come back into focus: "they fell on their faces before the throne and worshiped God, singing, 'Amen! Blessing and glory and wisdom and thanksgiving and honor and power and might be to our God forever and ever! Amen'" (7:11b–12). This is almost exactly what we had seen and heard earlier around the heavenly throne (5:11–12), except differing on two points: that there they sang with a full voice

---

1. Maybe because members of the tribe of Dan were involved historically in idolatrous practice (Judg. 18, 1 Kgs. 12:29), and perhaps because Ephraim—which in some lists was included with Manasseh his brother, both as replacements for their father Joseph and Dan—was also implicated in idolatry (Hos. 4:17–18; 5:9); although in neither case was such the basis for preclusion from Israel's eschatological renewal (Ezek. 48:1a, 6b); see Beale, *The Book of Revelation*, 429–30.

2. Fee, *Revelation*, 107; see also Gert J. Steyn, "The Order of the Twelve Tribes of Israel and Its Reception in Revelation 7," in Collins, *New Perspectives on the Book of Revelation*, 523–43.

whereas here they prostrated themselves, and that among the seven almost identical accolades in both songs, the earlier emphasized *wealth* (appropriate to the creational worship milieu there, perhaps) while the present one lifts up *thanksgiving* (befitting the redemption of human creatures from the four corners of the earth here, feasibly).

What else do we know about this enormous multitude? One of the elders engages John in conversation and offers this explanation: "These are they who have come out of the great ordeal; they have washed their robes and made them white in the blood of the Lamb. For this reason they are before the throne of God, and worship him day and night within his temple, and the one who is seated on the throne will shelter them. They will hunger no more, and thirst no more; the sun will not strike them, nor any scorching heat; for the Lamb at the center of the throne will be their shepherd, and he will guide them to springs of the water of life, and God will wipe away every tear from their eyes" (7:14b–17). This elaboration locates the inordinate multitude in heaven and within an environment that not only echoes the ancient prophets about the restoration of Israel (e.g., Isa. 49:10) but also anticipates the conditions of the new heavens, new earth, and heavenly Jerusalem (see Rev. 21:2-4, 23–24; 22:1–5). More poignantly, the elder suggests that these are martyrs, perhaps constitutive of the souls under the heavenly altar unveiled by the fifth seal.

Those who believe that the marking of the 144,000 was to preserve them from the earthly destruction like the Hebrews were kept by the Passover blood from the plagues visited upon the Egyptians (e.g., Exod. 8:22–23; 9:4–7, 26; 10:23; 11:5–7; 12:12–13) have tended to view the contrast with the martyred multitude as, among other reasons, indicative of two distinct groups in these two visions. Yet neither in this nor the fourteenth chapter of Revelation is it clearly stated that the 144,000 were marked to be preserved from martyrdom. Instead, the two visions could be of the one group of all the redeemed people of God across both covenants, with the former 144,000 heard as providing an Israelite and earthly perspective and the latter vast multitude providing a more ecclesial and heavenly orientation.[3] Such a view is eminently more plausible if the "great

---

3. E.g., Keener, *Revelation*, 232; and Smalley, *The Revelation to John*, 187.

ordeal" were not limited to a specific future tribulational period (cal-culated in Dispensationalist terms) but was inclusive of the entire history of the church past as well as extending to its final periods of testing later.[4] If 144,000 is recognized as clothed in the Lamb's robes and having his name also, it is then compounded from twelve tribes multiplied by twelve apostles (twenty-four elders total) multiplied by 1,000 and becomes a maximal symbol "for the fulness of the new people of God, composed of both Jews and Gentiles."[5]

FURTHER REFLECTIONS
The Multitude on the Way to God's Reign

Recall that the New Testament expects that the restoration and renewal of Israel is being accomplished in the redemptive work of Jesus Christ but that this involves, however incomprehensibly, the grafting in of Gentiles into the new people of God, not in a way that supersedes the first covenant but as enriching its ethnic and religio-cultural homogeneity and multiplying its (Hebrew-centric) mono-linguality. This is the promise of the Pentecost outpouring of the divine spirit, here confirmed by the inclusion in this eschatological multitude of those from "every nation, from all tribes and peoples and languages." The Pauline letter to the Ephesians also clearly states that believers who "had heard the word of truth, the gospel of your salvation, and had believed in him, were marked with the seal of the promised Holy Spirit" (Eph. 1:13; cf. 2 Cor. 1:22). If the winds of the four angels do indeed rage destructively from the four corners of the globe, the breezing of the seven spirits across the earth both seal and save, preserving the remnant in and through tribulation on the one hand but also redeeming the masses in and through death on the other hand.

On the other hand, we oftentimes think that it is better to be

---

4. See Smalley, *The Revelation to John*, 196.
5. David E. Aune, *Revelation 6–16*, Word Biblical Commentary 52B (Nashville: Nelson Reference, 1998), 444; contrasting with my view (urged with the support of other previously cited scholars), Aune believes that this 144,000 constitutes "the remnant of Christians who survive the eschatological woes," as distinct from the great multitude that is martyred across history.

part of the larger group or crowd because there is safety in numbers, but the hugeness of the multitude is forged through rather than escapes (as if raptured) from the ordeal. The multitude's final vindication presumes their prior suffering, persecution, and even martyrdom;[6] there is therefore no shortcut to exculpation except through anguish, harassment, and execution. Most perpetual foreigners, understandably, wish to avoid the fate of the latter set, but that risks minimizing the foreignness and accommodating to the status quo of the majority.

The theological and missiological question for contemporary readers and hearers of what the divine spirit is saying to the churches is whether, on the one hand, we will be found to be among those finally standing in and with the prodigious multitude, and on the other hand, whether we will be welcoming of others different from us who may not be of our people, or speak our language, or derive from our tribe or ethnicity.[7] Perhaps none of us might wish to stand *out* from among this throng since doing so might result in our being at the head of the procession toward martyrdom. Yet might it also not be that to be so devoted to the Lamb is to rise above the hunger pangs of this world, to overcome creational thirst, and to no longer be threatened by the blistering heat of the sun, not because we are no longer material creatures but because we realize that the Lamb will provide springs of living water from within by the divine breath (cf. John 7:37–39), his Father will comfort the sorrowful, and that even the creational elements like the sun, moon, stars, and caves and mountains only do the Father's bidding? So, in effect, the question about who will stand in that eschatological day is preceded by the many other times that this question will be posed to us each and every day: Will we be willing to stand out now among the crowds of this world in our witness to the Lamb's way of salvation? Failure

6. These are the features of the people of God not only here in Rev. 7 (thus uniting the two groups) but throughout the book, so argues Rob Dalrymple, *Revelation and the Two Witnesses: The Implications for Understanding John's Depiction of the People of God and His Hortatory Intent* (Eugene, OR: Resource Publications, 2011), esp. ch. 6.

7. The missiological question from this text is posed helpfully by Eckhard J. Schnabel, "Early Christian Mission and Christian Identity in the Context of the Ethnic, Social, and Political Affiliations in Revelation," in Jon C. Laansma, Grant R. Osborne, and Ray F. Van Neste, eds., *New Testament Theology in Light of the Church's Mission: Essays in Honor of I. Howard Marshall* (Eugene, OR: Cascade Books, 2011), 369–86.

to stand affirmatively in response to this question today may lead to our not being found among the eschatological multitude tomorrow. To blend into the conventions of this world now may mean that we will find ourselves with the kings and the powerful in the caves and mountains along the way, and that would mean exclusion from the great assembly before the throne later. Will the perpetual foreigner ultimately stand with the salvation of the Lord or attempt, however vainly, to assimilate with the worldly crowd today?

8:1–5

Silence in Heaven, Trumpets for Earth: How Then Should We Pray?

The first verse of Revelation 8 concludes the seal heptad, but the seer immediately leaps forward to the trumpet heptad. While we will not be encountering many new elements in this passage, we will take advantage of the silence invoked by the opening of the seventh seal to probe deeper into the nature of prayer that has already been introduced above and that reappears in the seer's vision. In particular, we will explore in greater depth if and how Revelation teaches us to pray, especially in what might be perceived as apocalyptic times. To set the stage, however, observe what John describes.

First, the seventh seal's unfastening leads to "silence in heaven for about half an hour" (8:1). John hears mostly about the *hours* of trial (3:10) and especially of judgment (14:7, 15; 18:10, 17, 19), about the *hour* of the beast's rule with the ten kings (17:12), and also about an enigmatic "half a time" (12:14), but nowhere else about any *half hour* specifically. The symbol here is to slightly extend the tension already stretched between the undoing of the sixth and seventh seals (across the interlude of two visions in Revelation 7) before moving into the trumpet judgments. More important, the silence in heaven is symbolically dense in terms of its Old Testament antecedents, being a deportment of reverence before the Almighty one (Hab. 2:20) and being a posture of waiting for divine manifestation and action (Ps. 62:1, 5; Zech. 2:13).

Second, then, the opening of the seventh seal segues into the announcement of the next heptad: "And I saw the seven angels who stand before God, and seven trumpets were given to them" (8:2). These are not the seven angels that are also the seven stars of the seven churches as those were in the right hand of the Son of Man in the opening vision (1:13, 16, 20). Trumpets were given to them in their standing position, indicating (again) the sovereignty of the one on the throne over the judgments of history on the one hand, and the readiness of the angels to blow these trumpets—consistent with the time being near and short we have observed repeatedly communicated since the beginning of the book, most recently in the opening of the fifth seal when those under the altar were told the divine response would be arriving shortly, after only "a little longer (6:11b)—on the other hand. As expected, trumpets in the Old Testament announced the imminence of and embarking upon battle (e.g., Num. 10:9; Judg. 3:27; 1 Sam.13:3), including when under the inspiration and enablement of the divine breath (Judg. 6:34).

Third, John sees, "Another angel"—thus taking him (and us) away from the seven angels with the seven trumpets for a moment[1]—one with "a golden censer [that] came and stood at the altar; he was given a great quantity of incense to offer with the prayers of all the saints on the golden altar that is before the throne" (8:3). There is some scholarly discussion about whether "the altar" and "the golden altar" are one and the same, but it is possible that at least the former is the same altar unveiled by the fifth seal even as it is more assuredly the case that the golden altar is before God in the heavenlies (8:1–2). What we are told now is that the cries of vengeance from the souls of those "slaughtered for the word of God and for the testimony they had given" (6:9–10) are offered by the angel with more than sufficient incense to ensure their ascending. Hence, "the smoke of the incense, with the prayers of the saints, rose before God from the hand of the angel" (8:4).

Fourth, as the angel offers up the incense with the prayers of the saints, "the angel took the censer and filled it with fire from the altar and threw it on the earth; and there were peals of thunder, rumblings, flashes of lightning, and an earthquake" (8:5). On the one side, the incense of/with the prayers arise from the golden altar before the throne; on the other side, the

---

1. See Zdravko Stefanovic, "The Angel at the Altar (Revelation 8:3–5): A Case Study on Intercalations in Revelation," *Andrews University Seminary Studies* 44:1 (2006): 79–94.

fire of judgments descends from the altar (maybe the same as the golden altar since it is now suggested to be at an elevated site) to the earth. The worshipful silence of the heavens is broken by the apocalyptic response of the creation—in ways that are heard (thunders), seen (flashes of lightnings), and felt (an earthquake)—to the divine judgments.[2]

Intriguingly the other occasion (so far) we have seen and heard lightnings, thunderings, and rumblings was when they were "coming from the throne" room in the initial heavenly scene (4:5a), and this was connected directly to "seven flaming torches, which are the seven spirits of God," that were burning "in front of the throne" (4:5b). These seven divine spirits, we also know, are also the eyes of the slain Lamb "sent out into all the earth" (5:6b), and they have seen, heard, and effectively gathered the inestimable "great multitude . . . , from every nation, from all tribes and peoples and languages," and situated them "before the throne and before the Lamb" (7:9). The interlude showed that it was these who had "come out of the great ordeal; they have washed their robes and made them white in the blood of the Lamb"; hence, "they are before the throne of God," on the one hand "worship[ing] him day and night within his temple" (7:14b–15a), and on the other hand crying out to God for justice and vindication (6:10). In this vision following the opening of the seventh seal, it is particularly the latter appeals that are expounded upon: these supplications arising from the golden altar are what activates the response of the one on the throne so that the angel uses the same golden censor, it is implied, to now cast—recall: the same word, *ballo*, is used to threaten Jezebel's being thrown into distress (2:22)—fire from the same altar, mixed with the same incense, down onto the earth. These are hence both worshipful prayers and petitionary worship that initiate the divine judgments, mediated by the golden censor but ultimately by the seven divine spirits going out across and returning from throughout the entire earth.

2. The irony is that the silence announced here opens up to a description of a grand liturgical scene full of sights, sounds, actions, prayers, incense, etc., which also then mirrors the saints' abandonment of the imperial cult—now reduced to hushness!—in the Western Asian context; for this argument, see Ryan Leif Hansen, *Silence and Praise: Rhetorical Cosmology and Political Theology in the Book of Revelation* (Minneapolis: Fortress, 2014).

FURTHER REFLECTIONS
Contemplative Prayer

As an Asian American, pentecostal Christian who is usually deferential, both because that is inculcated in the East Asian culture
that respects tradition and because survival of the perpetual foreigner often is predicated upon not rocking the boat, my ecclesial
community might enjoin the worship before the throne but not
because such emerges from out of the fire of persecution and martyrdom. Given the pietism that characterizes much of the evangelical and pentecostal world of Asian American Christians, we would
also surely not resort to the kinds of imprecatory prayers seen in
the Psalms and predominant here in the Apocalypse. What about
turning the other cheek, forgiving our adversaries, and loving our
enemies instead, we'd ask?

Perhaps it is only those who are on the receiving end of injustice occasioned chiefly if not only because of faithfulness to Jesus
who might be able to empathize with John of Patmos and perhaps
even resoundingly emulate the entreaties of those under the altar.
More problematically, if our repetition of these prayers persists so
that they become part of who we are but our sociopolitical location
changes so that we begin to accumulate some earthly power, we
might be able to act out the judgments aspired to in these prayers
rather than having to wait upon the slain Lamb to bring about justice. Those in power rush to conclusions justifying their deployment
of that power and (conveniently) forget that such putative mimicking of the powers in texts like Revelation were developed by those
attempting to survive under imperial pressure.

Counterintuitively for many pentecostals who tend to emphasize that the divine spirit's empowerment to bear witness is manifest primarily in inspired speech (and verbal witness),[3] the caution
invited in this text is to temper our loud cries and prayers with the
posture of silence that attends to the one who sits on the throne
and to his Lamb. Silence requires a contemplative posture that

---

3. E.g., Roger Stronstad, *The Prophethood of Believers: A Study in Luke's Charismatic Theology*,
Journal of Pentecostal Theology Supplement Series 16 (Sheffield: Sheffield Academic Press,
1999).

hearkens to the depths of our embodied being but is now situated amid a cosmic throne room surrounded by many others from different tribes, cultures, and languages, including many creaturely and angelic others. The contemplative gaze may actually increase compassion even for those we perceive, rightly or not, to be our victimizers. Will adopting such a stance run counter to precisely those perlocutionary attitudes that John is attempting to foment? Will having compassion on our adversaries seduce us into being overly tolerant of their evil deeds? Or will the contemplative mood enable even deeper solidarity with the slaughtered Lamb, so that we might pray even more radically as he taught us? We shall return periodically to take up these questions as we navigate the rest of the visions of the seer from Patmos.[4]

4. The kind of contemplative prayer called for here is that which allows human hearts to connect with their Creator and, thereby, also with one another and with the world that has been given to them as their habitation. This is consistent with how the cosmic silence both allows the prayers of the saints to ascend to the divine dwelling place and also prompts terrestrial rumblings, as if the material creation itself is participating in the final judgment and redemption. Personal piety and activity, even that of prayer, and cosmic redemption are thus intertwined. I have learned a great deal from my son about how the contemplative posture allows for the compassionate enlargement of the human heart so that its capacity for solidarity with others and the world itself is expanded; see Aizaiah G. Yong, "All Mixed Up: Multi/Racial Liberation and Compassion-Based Activism," *Religions* 11:8 (2020), https://www.mdpi.com/2077-1444/11/8/402/htm. See also Richard Rohr, *Silent Compassion: Finding God in Contemplation* (Cincinnati: Franciscan Media, 2014).

8:6–13

The First Four Trumpets Blowing: What Can/Should Be Done about Global Warming?

The blowing of the seven trumpets next proceeds in swift fashion at least following the expeditiousness of the first four seals. These four trumpets wreaked havoc over a third of the earth, thus ratcheting up the intensity of the destruction that touched a fourth of the earth carried out by the pale green horseman (6:8). We will briefly comment on each before asking the bigger question about what specifically this passage, and Revelation more fully considered, might have to say about a theology of the created environment.

First, note the violence enacted by the gusting of the four trumpets (emphases added in each case): hail and fire "were *hurled* to the earth" (8:7a); a fiery mountain "was *thrown* into the sea" (8:8); a blazing star "fell from heaven" on a third of the rivers and springs of water (8:10); and "a third of the sun was *struck*" (8:12a). The result is catastrophic devastation: a third of the earth and the trees, and all the green grass, was devoured (8:7b); a third of the sea is bloodied, killing a third of marine life and destroying a third of the ships of the seas (8:9); the waters of these rivers and springs became "wormwood,"[1] murdering many with their bitterness; finally, if a third of the sun is struck, the ramifications touch on a third of the moon and a third of the stars so that "a third of their light was darkened; a third of the day was kept from shining, and likewise the night" (8:12b). The reality is that the four

---

1. One interpreter notes that "wormwood" in the Old Testament is punishment for apostasy, so this is judgment of the counterfeit to messianic truth especially since the apostates in turn persecute those who do not fall away; see Jon Paulien, *Decoding Revelation's Trumpets: Literary Allusions and the Interpretation of Revelation 8:7–12*, Andrews University Seminary Doctoral Dissertation Series 11 (Berrien Springs, MI: Andrews University Press, 1987), 403–4.

trumpet blasts ravage the known human world: the earth, the seas, the sources of life-nourishing water, and the heavens that regulate creaturely temporality and rhythms. When combined with the phenomena associated with the sixth seal and against the backdrop of restraints of the four winds that were removed after the marking of the 144,000, the mass desolation cannot be understated.

Passages in the Apocalypse such as this one, read in conjunction with other apocalyptic texts including those in the Gospels and other parts of the New Testament, contribute to the popularity of the Left Behind series, which elaborates on the destruction of the earth during the last days of tribulation after the rapture of the church and its aftermath preceding the second coming of Christ.[2] Texts like the second Petrine letter, which talk about "the coming of the day of God," when "the heavens will be set ablaze and dissolved, and the elements will melt with fire" (2 Pet. 2:12), add to the sense that the new heavens and new earth will have to emerge *de novo*, as did the first creation, rather than being regenerated from out of this floundering one. Our current world, in this scenario, will only get worse, to the point that evil's pervasiveness will be so extensive that the only recourse is a fiery judgment and a miraculous new creation from out of the annihilation of the first world.

Even if one were to reject a Dispensationalist hermeneutic, it is difficult to argue that the apocalyptic imagery in the New Testament does not prefigure some sort of cosmic calamity. In this perspective anticipating catastrophic convulsions, John's description of what unfolds with the blowing of the first four trumpets and other related visions "either prefigure or initiate the passing away of the present heaven and earth."[3] This may not lead to the Dispensational devaluation of the material creation nor must one insist on a literal cosmic obliteration, but it is difficult to otherwise not recognize a real destabilization of the current world order.

2. This is one of my very few references to Left Behind; Jon K. Newton, *Revelation Reclaimed: The Use and Misuse of the Apocalypse* (Milton Keynes, UK: Paternoster, 2009), ch. 2, rightly helps us see that it is a misuse of Revelation to identify fulfilments of prophecy in current events for our (or any other) time.

3. Edward Adams, *The Stars Will Fall from Heaven: Cosmic Catastrophe in the New Testament and Its World*, Library of New Testament Studies 347 (London and New York: T&T Clark, 2007), 17.

FURTHER REFLECTIONS
Stewards of Creation

To be sure, the question of the renewal of creation is not one that rests on human beings either doing something or not: either we care for and preserve the world or we destroy it might be how some liberals conceive of creation care, but such an either-or framing is not necessary. Of course, the starting point for any theology of creation or environmental/ecological theology is important, and from that perspective, beginning to think about the world with the first four trumpets is surely a gloomy prognosis. But if we began instead with the New Jerusalem and then read or listened to the book of Revelation from that horizon, then our participation in the missional witness of the risen Word depends less on our efforts than on our dependence on his (seven) spirit(s) and on the testimony of the slain Lamb.[4] The point is that the goodness of creation suffers under the weight of sinful creatures and that it is creaturely disobedience against and unwillingness to abide in accordance with the divine holiness that induces the groanings of the material world and its upheavals. The Bible's apocalyptic imagery, including those found in Revelation, witness to the cosmic suffering inflicted by sin even as the blowing of the trumpets initiate creational cleansing from which renewal, restoration, and re-creation—indeed, new creation!—can emerge.

So, the point is that we don't have to deny that global warming is happening even as that does not mean that we are left to our own to reverse its trends. But we also don't have to contribute toward global warming simply to help God initiate the global catastrophe we believe is needed to punish everyone else for their wrongdoing. Rather, the call from the beginning has been to steward the creation given into human care (Gen. 1:26), and to resist participation in the destruction of the earth (cf. 11:18b), in order that we can bear faithful, good, and true witness to the one who created all things good. Our capacities to nurture the created environment rather

---

4. See Robby Waddell, "Revelation and the (New) Creation: A Prolegomenon on the Apocalypse, Science, and Creation," in Amos Yong, ed., *The Spirit Renews the Face of the Earth: Pentecostal Forays into Science and Theology of Creation* (Eugene, OR: Pickwick Press, 2009), 30–50.

than inflict damage on it is mitigated by our sinfulness; hence what is needed is the blowing of the winds of the divine spirit that can enable faithfulness amid the blusterings divulged with the first four trumpets.

The interventions of the divine spirit are even more necessary when we see that the effects of and on global warming are anticipated to intensify. As the echoes of the fourth trumpet fade into the distance, John sees (and hears) "an eagle crying with a loud voice as it flew in midheaven, 'Woe, woe, woe to the inhabitants of the earth, at the blasts of the other trumpets that the three angels are about to blow!'" (8:13). The Greek for *eagle* here, *aetos*, also can be translated *vulture* (as in Matt. 24:28; Luke 17:37),[5] which may be more appropriate given that its message is one of further bad and even worse news of judgment regarding the final three trumpets that in turn reconnect to this theme of terrestrial destruction (see section on 11:15–19 later). It is also related to the additional *woe* announced on the earth and the sea "for the devil has come down to you with great wrath, because he knows that his time is short!" (12:12b). Here, we find an anticipated parallel: the darkening of a third of the world as we know it with the fourth trumpet signals just as ominously what is to come with the fifth and sixth blowings, which is the first extended descriptions of truly demonic destruction waged on and against the world.

---

5. Beale, *The Book of Revelation*, 490.

The First Woe and the Torture-Stinging Locusts: Existing in the Shadow of Abaddon/Apollyon

The fifth trumpet, and first of three woes, connects the heavens to the depths of the earth, indeed the unfathomable underworld (of the first-century three-story universe). What descends from above and emerges from below converges on the human plane as the first elaborate description of the realm of the demonic that we have seen only in passing up to now (mentioned as the satan and the devil a handful of times in the letters to the seven churches). We will find that demonic reality here actualized in an army of locusts (that transmogrifies into a massive cavalry with the sixth trumpet). What does this demonic darkness mean for Christian witness in the world?

At the blowing of the fifth trumpet, John writes: "I saw a star that had fallen from heaven to earth, and he was given the key to the shaft of the bottomless pit; he opened the shaft of the bottomless pit, and from the shaft rose smoke like the smoke of a great furnace, and the sun and the air were darkened with the smoke from the shaft" (9:1–2). This is neither part of the multitude of falling stars associated with the sixth seal nor the great falling star of the third trumpet but more like an angelic or demonic figure. Later, the devil, the satan, is "thrown down to the earth" (12:9b), even as these apocalyptic references and related gospel accounts—for example, when Jesus himself said that he "watched Satan fall from heaven like a flash of lightning" (Luke 10:18)—build off earlier prophetic references to the Day Star falling from heaven as a symbol of the downfall of the Babylonian Empire (Isa. 14:12). For now, this star is given the key to the bottomless pit, known also in the wider Jewish literature as the subterranean abyss that, as later visions also confirm (11:7a, 17:8a), was the prison of YHWH's enemy, the dragon, and of fallen angels or demons,[1] and to which the satan and the devil will also be penultimately returned (20:1–3). Upon the unlocking of the pit, "smoke like the smoke of a great furnace" (9:2) billowed from the shaft. Unlike the prayers of incense arising before the throne in heaven (8:3–4), "the sun and the air were darkened with the smoke from the shaft" (9:2b), this time thoroughly it appears, not just blackening only a third of the material world (8:12).

Further, if the incense of prayers brought forth the judgments of the one sitting on the throne, then the columns of thick and dark smoke bring forth killer locusts into purview (9:3a).[2] Hearkening back to the plague of locusts rained down upon the Egyptians or anteceding the prophetic renewing of the Day of the Lord (Exod. 10:1–20; Joel 2:1–11), here their slaying potency is described thrice in relationship to the scorpions of the earth, in particular to the tails of these poisonous arachnids with their deadly stingers (9:3b, 5b, 10).[3] The demonic character of these locusts-cum-scorpions is heightened in their thoroughly mixed natures—appearing like battle-prepared horses, with gold-crowned heads, human faces, women's hair, lions' teeth, scaly breastplates, chariot-sounding wings, etc. (9:7–9)—an amalgamation that violates boundaries in ways the Old Testament views as unclean.[4] These are aberrant beasts (unlike the four living creatures) whose purposes are ultimately to horrify, completely contrary to the God of edifying life. Theirs is to inflict anguish, not on the earth or its grass or its trees but on human creatures without the divine seal on their foreheads (9:4–5; cf. 7:2–3). John observes that their inability to take life means that, "in those days people will seek death but will not find it; they will long to die, but death will flee from them" (9:6). If wild animals turn on humans

---

1. Ford, *Revelation*, 147. Note also that Jude writes of "angels who did not keep their own position, but left their proper dwelling, he has kept in eternal chains in deepest darkness for the judgment of the great Day" (Jude 6).

2. Brian Blount, *Revelation*, 174, writes in this connection: "evil will be unleashed, but evil will be made to act as God's judgment tool."

3. There are many forms of animals in this Apocalypse, including locusts, a lion, birds in midheaven, a dragon/serpent, alongside the earlier mentioned four living creatures; see Resseguie, *Revelation Unsealed*, 117–35, for a consideration of these locusts amid these other animal characterizations.

4. See Ford, *Revelation*, 151; also, Joseph L. Mangina, *Revelation*, Brazos Theological Commentary on the Bible (Grand Rapids: Brazos, 2010), 123.

as part of the massacre from the pale green horse rider (6:8b), here abnormally hideous monstrosities terrify and torment, yet without being able to bring about the death their agonized victims long for. But not only is this capacity to harm and injure people allowed, permitted, and given to them, but also, simultaneously, its extent is constrained in time to five months (9:5a, 10b). This limitation is perhaps a nod to the presumed lifespan of locusts or to the length of the season during which locusts were considered a threat to the annual cycle of crops,[5] but surely the bounded duration is indicative of the divinely regulated nature of judgment.

Unlike locusts in the wild that were known not to have kings (see Prov. 30:27), this army of locusts-scorpions "have as king over them the angel of the bottomless pit; his name in Hebrew is Abaddon, and in Greek he is called Apollyon" (9:11). Abaddon refers in the Jewish cosmology to "the kingdom of the dead . . . , used as a poetic parallel to Sheol . . . , death . . . , the grace . . . , and the abyss."[6] Apollyon appears again later in Revelation as the realm or state of destruction to which the beast from the bottomless pit is destined (17:8).[7] Their combined nomination leaves no doubt: at the helm of the locust-scorpion legion is the abyssal and demonic regent.

As John pauses after naming the king of the locust-scorpion army to say that he has now portrayed only the first woe and to remind us that two more are looming (9:12), perhaps we can ask what messianic disciples can take away from the description of the fifth trumpet sounding. Two considerations commend themselves about living under the shadow of Abaddon/Apollyon, one more straightforward and the other more intricate. First, even within this passage, we are repeatedly informed that while pain and suffering prevail, they remain under divine jurisdiction. Angels have to blow trumpets, keys have to be given, authority has to be delegated, mayhem has to be sanctioned, time's flow and its events are or are not impeded, and even death has to be permitted. At each juncture, then, messianists can bear witness: to the one who enables endurance, to the

---

5. See Keener, *Revelation*, 268; and Ford, *Revelation*, 149.
6. Aune, *Revelation 6–16*, 534; the ellipses in each case exclude strings of Old Testament scriptural references for which interested readers can consult Aune.
7. For more on these demonic figures, see Simon Woodman, *The Book of Revelation*, SCM Core Texts (London: SCM, 2008), ch. 7.

one who comforts the afflicted, to the one who superintends cosmic circumstances, to the one who gives temporal existence, to the one who sustains life. These are testimonies not merely verbal but carnal, borne in bodies and in the power of the divine spirit.

FURTHER REFLECTIONS
Discerning and Confronting Demonic Forces

As these apocalyptic visions disclose, more complex is that there is both a multifaceted interdependence of realities and activities and yet distinguishing forms of particularity and integrity. On the one hand, heaven and earth, the spiritual and the material, the cosmic and the creaturely, even the angelic and demonic, etc., appear discrete yet also manifest as interwoven; these realms and domains blur across each other dynamically. On the other hand, the heavenly sphere includes angels, elders, living creatures, and human beings that retain their distinctiveness, but the sounding of the fifth trumpet bares a throng recognized as demonic in its improperly assorted and muddled hybridity. Human animals have their orientation to the one on the throne due to their being formed in the divine image and, arguably, other animals—living creatures as the seer elsewhere identifies them—have their species-specific roles to play in the ecology of creation. The demonic, as these locust-scorpion ogres reveal, have distorted forms, disordered orientations, and disoriented purposes, consistent with the deceptive character of their destructive monarch, so that the originating features and roles pertaining to the distinctive forms of creaturely participation in the cosmic scheme of things is no longer recognizable or functional. The creation is out of whack as a consequence of human sinfulness, missing the mark of their intended contribution to love God and fellow creatures and the wider creational environment, and the result is that even living creatures devolve from their creational teleologies and express instead convoluted and confused natures directed to destructive ends.

It is unclear if and when there is a point of no return along the path of mutation from living creature to demonic fiend, a matter we will have occasion to further explore in the next section and along the way in the rest of this commentary. For the moment, however, existence in a fallen world means that we may be continually threatened by, if not also be at risk of seduction from, trajectories that are at cross-purposes with our uniquely crafted pathway, both in terms of our human vocation generally understood and our own individual trek within that broader arc of our evolved humanity. The question is how to discern when we are appropriately interfacing with spheres of realities outside of our conventional epistemic horizons and when incongruous mixing within and across these domains bewilders and short-circuits the goal of proper worship of the creator and of fitting participation in that coming reign. If the odds of overcoming torturously stinging and deceptively demonic forces that assail the creaturely realm from every direction—from above and below as unfolded in the wake of the fifth trumpet—sometimes seem unfavorable from where we sit or on the route we are ambling, at least the visions of the seer from Patmos regularly remind us that in the end, nothing transpires apart from the supervision of the one on the throne.

9:13–21

The Second Woe and the Plague-Spewing Hordes: Deliverance from Encroaching Death

So, if we thought the first woe featuring a fallen star/angel and an army of locust-scorpions was bad, then the second woe releases four bound angels/demons and a two-hundred-million troop of cavalry-serpents! In the following we attempt to get some clarity on both of these aspects of the sixth trumpet discharge and then pursue further the question raised in the last section: Is deliverance from the demonic powers demolishing this world possible and, if so, how? We shall see that the conclusion of this vision, while further despairing in one perspective (the world refuses to repent), provide important cues (unlike the end of the preceding vision) for how messianic discipleship can bear witness even in dark times.

The blast of the sixth trumpet is followed by another sound, "a voice from the four horns of the golden altar before God" (9:12b). Recall that the trumpet heptad is launched from out of the prayers of the saints arising with incense from the golden altar (see commentary on 8:1–5 above), but here there is an added reference featuring the four horns that were part of the temple altar in ancient Israel and was also expected in the restored eschatological temple (e.g., Exod. 29:12; Ezek. 43:15, 20). This voice directs an angel to one further activity (besides tooting the horn), saying: "Release the four angels who are bound at the great river Euphrates" (6:14b). Bound angels, as we have already seen in our discussion of the bottomless pit,[1] are equivalent to demons, but in this case, they symbolize additionally the

---

1. See preceding section; also, to reiterate from one of the General Epistles: "God did not spare the angels when they sinned, but cast them into hell and committed them to chains of deepest darkness to be kept until the judgment" (2 Pet. 2:4).

natural boundary that the Euphrates river played in separating both Israel (historically) and Rome (for first century contemporaries) from their enemies (cf. 16:12), including invading armies such as the Assyrians and Babylonians of old and the Parthians for the Greco-Roman and Hellenized regions of Asia Minor. The release of these angels/demons, then, also unchecks the powers of destruction at this divinely appointed time: they "had been held ready for the hour, the day, the month, and the year, to kill a third of humankind" (9:15). If the first four trumpets singed a third of the earth, bloodied a third of the seas, embittered a third of the fresh water supplies, and darkened a third of the skies, then here a third of humankind is also explicitly declared as open targets for the demonic onslaught.

John hears the number of the two hundred million cavalry (it is practically impossible to visually inspect or count such a large mass) but sees these horses. Two aspects of what he envisages are noteworthy. First, like the locust army, these are not normal horses and riders but anomalously deviant quadrupeds: "the riders wore breastplates the color of fire and of sapphire and of sulfur; the heads of the horses were like lions' heads"; and "the power of the horses is in their mouths and in their tails; their tails are like serpents, having heads" (9:17, 19a). Again, practically identical with their locust predecessors, these are monstrous hybrids: part human, part horse, part lion, and with tails, except that with the last, scorpion-like stingers are now serpent-like heads. Both, however, "inflict harm" (9:19b). As Joseph Mangina states, "Revelation 9 offers an early glimpse of a theme that will become increasingly central as the story unfolds, namely, that the proximate agent of humanity's torment is not God but the demonic powers."[2]

In the case of this cavalry, then, damage proceeds from their tails and mouths (9:19a), and this ruin emanates in part from "the fire and smoke and sulfur [that] came out of their mouths" (9:17b). The smoke (and darkness) carrying the locusts before now adds fire and sulfur to their destructive potency. Whereas the unsealed are tortured alive by the locust-scorpions, "By these three plagues a third of humankind was killed" (9:18b). Note also that the breastplates

2. Mangina, *Revelation*, 124.

of the riders are also characterized by fire and sulfur, with a tinge of sapphire, so that the liquidating powers of the cavalry can be said to derive equally from rider and horse or to come forth indistinctly from this demonic hybrid.

Whereas at the end of the vision of the fifth trumpet John transitions by noting the passing of this first of the three woes, at what could be seen as the conclusion of the sixth trumpet apparition John bypasses announcing the closure of the second woe (this appears later after the trumpet interlude, in 11:14, right before the third woe commences)[3] and chooses instead to observe the human response: "The rest of humankind, who were not killed by these plagues, did not repent of the works of their hands or give up worshiping demons and idols of gold and silver and bronze and stone and wood, which cannot see or hear or walk. And they did not repent of their murders or their sorceries or their fornication or their thefts" (9:20–21). The idolatry and fornication plaguing some of the seven churches (2:14b, 20b) is here depicted as part of the problem of the wider human family. Like Pharaoh and the Egyptians of old who hardened their hearts in response to the plagues, the eschatological apocalypse also appears incapable of cultivating repentance among human idolaters, even as their persistence in such idolatry-related activities—murders, sorceries, and thefts, additionally specified here—continue unabated to the point of their final exclusion from the new heavens and new earth, and the New Jerusalem as well (21:8; 22:15). Ironically, perhaps, humankind's obduracy in clinging on to their ancient

> As Stephen Smalley notes, "all four sins mentioned in [Rev. ch. 9] verse 21 (murder, magic arts, immorality and thieving) are at different times connected with idolatry elsewhere in biblical literature."
>
> Stephen S. Smalley, *The Revelation to John: A Commentary on the Greek Text of the Apocalypse* (Downers Grove, IL: InterVarsity Press, 2005), 243.

3. A good argument could also be made that everything from 10:1–11:13 is included in the second woe rather than intervening between the second and third woes. I take the view that the prophetic segment/s of 10:1–11:13 is included narratively within but is not technically part of the second woe, particularly given the practically unanimous view regarding these prophecies serving as an interlude between the sixth and seventh trumpet. See also Murphy, *Fallen Is Babylon*, 269–70, for more discussion of the position taken here.

worship of demons is exposed in this case as the most blatant form of demonic deception: that people will continue to declare their allegiances to impotent idols even as the powers behind such trinkets of gold, silver, bronze, stone, and wood are killing their friends and family members, and one-third of their human species. By prolonging these "works of their hands" (9:20), human creatures are signing their own warrants of judgment and death.

FURTHER REFLECTIONS
The Generations of the World under the Demonic Spell

How then might men and women undo these certifications authorizing their execution at the hands of demonic forces? The seer's observations about human behavior here provide at least a set of rhetorical cues for Christian witness in an age of darkness, death, destruction, and demonic idolatry. These include repentance, which means doing the opposite of what has stayed to the present, and forging new "works of the hands" contrary to or counteractive of the effects of the former works. Murder should be replaced by acts of love that seek what is life-giving and beneficial to others. Similarly, countering sorcery, from the Greek *pharmakon* that refers to the uses of magical potions and incantational poisons in the first century and that may be antecedents for (more distantly) our modern practice of medical pharmacology on the one side or (more closely) the persisting practices of witchcraft especially in indigenous cultures on the other side, may involve today (less likely) refusal to participate in the pharmacological enterprise (like some Jehovah's Witnesses or other fundamentalist groups who reject modern medicine) or (more likely) proclamation of the gospel that delivers people from the fear of the magical arts and of the conjuring powers of wizardry. Not stealing is of course a matter of not taking someone else's belongings, but it is more deeply about recognizing the systemic interdependence of a holist world so that we ought not to exploit creational resources in ways that take from our children what they will need. The point is that most of us obviously would not kill or fornicate or steal in any obvious sense, but we often do not see how our actions are life-suppressing for others—our descendants included—in the big picture of the cosmic long run.

I wish to make one more point here about the demonic to lay further groundwork for later discussions. The characterization of the locust-scorpions and cavalry-serpents is of course gruesome and revolting, but as we are now able to discern, demonic realities are deceptively effective in obtaining creaturely fidelities. Very few of us would consent to worshiping directly a lion-toothed creature with iron scales or one with a fiery mouth on one end and a serpent-headed tail on the other; however, many, if not the majority of us Homo sapiens get caught up in habits of activity that engage in the taking and using of what properly belongs to others, that compromise our purity through assimilation to conventional forms of so-called morality, and that gradually suck out of the verve of our fellow human beings rather than renew and revitalize their lives. Our problem is that we are looking for the demonic according to its apocalyptically symbolic forms, but the reality is that the demonic manifests in the works of *our* hands committed in accommodation to the norms of this world! My community of Asian American Christians are continuously enticed to accede to the various powers that govern and structure our existence. But as a perpetual foreigner, I need to draw on instinctive resources generated within this experience of liminality to call on the power of the divine (seven) spirit(s) to deliver me from being too deferential to what may be demonic powers from which later attempts of extraction may be too late. The problem with our traditional demonologies is their hyper-spiritualized and hyper-supernaturalized character. The first two woes more starkly and emphatically broadcast how menacing the demonic is but more subtly also signal that we can go about our merry nine-to-five work schedule under the demonic spell without realizing that we are worshiping what is apocalyptically revealed as grotesque.

10:1–11

Eating the (Little) Scroll: Commissioning for a Prophetic Vocation

As there was a pause inserted after the sixth seal, one that illuminated two arguably interrelated sizable groups (Rev. 7), so also does the "I saw another mighty angel" here (10:1a) signal a hiatus (10:1–11:13), one that foregrounds John the prophet (10:1–11) and a pair of other prophetic witnesses (11:1–13). This and the next section will cover what I call a *prophetic interlude* to probe two related questions: how we begin and how we complete a prophetic vocation. Here, we will take up the matter according to how John introduces and situates himself vis-à-vis his own prophetic commissioning.

We begin by saying a brief word about the angel that John sees in what he presents as a lull between the last two trumpets. He is described as "coming down from heaven, wrapped in a cloud, with a rainbow over his head; his face was like the sun, and his legs like pillars of fire" (10:1b). In contrast to the locusts shrouded in the smoke of the oversize furnace earlier (9:2), this colossal and magnificent angel recalls the revelation of Jesus himself at the beginning of the book, with the added detail about the rainbow first seen around the throne (4:3) enhancing the dazzling brilliance of the portrait. Further, John sees the angel's location and feels his presence: "Setting his right foot on the sea and his left foot on the land, he gave a great shout, like a lion roaring" (10:2b–3a). The titanic nature of the angel, effectively bridging the heavens, earth, and seas, and his voice that attunes us again to the one revealed earlier also as the Lion of Judah (5:5), have led a number of interpreters to identify this mighty being with Jesus. Yet wherever Jesus unquestionably appears in the Apocalypse, he is clearly known as such, even via a multitude of names and descriptions. It may be safer to conclude that this angel is "a heavenly representative of Jesus, who possesses the characteristics of Christ."[1]

Yet a further possible complicating factor regarding the identity of this mighty angel concerns the "little scroll open in his hand" (10:2a). The question is whether this, which openness is reemphasized (10:8b), is the same as the "written on the inside and on the back" (5:1b), which seven seals have by now been broken by the Lamb. It is thrice repeated that this is a "little scroll," seemingly contrasting with the by now unsealed not-mentioned-as-little scroll, although the other, fourth, reference here is merely to "the scroll that is open in the hand of the angel who is standing on the sea and on the land" (10:8b). Yet linguistically, by the latter part of the first century, *biblion* "is itself a diminutive form," such that it had come to be synonymous with *biblaridion* ("little scroll").[2] Further, that its contents have to do with prophecies "about many peoples and nations and languages and kings" (10:11b) is suggestive that this (little) scroll addresses the fulfillment of the "mystery of God . . . , as he announced to his servants the prophets" (10:7b) in ways consistent with what we have already seen with the opening of the (other) scroll's seals.[3] Circumstantially, then, it would seem appropriate to consider that the earlier scroll and this "little scroll" are the same,[4] and if so, that would reinforce the notion that this mighty angel is none other than the slain Lamb.

Whether this mighty angel is or is not the Lamb, he himself declares that "the mystery of God will be fulfilled" (10:7), which concerns for the seer the entirety of the revelation of Jesus himself, even as this christological understanding of *mystery* is also confirmed in the rest of the New Testament, in particular in letters written to churches around the Mediterranean world, including those associated with the seven churches of the Apocalypse (see Eph. 1:9; Col. 1:26; 4:3; 1 Tim. 3:16). Intriguingly, the Pauline epistle to the Ephesians also clarifies that this mystery of Jesus Christ concerns, more

1. Smalley, *The Revelation to John*, 258.
2. Blount, *Revelation*, 190.
3. Blount, *Revelation*, 194.
4. As concluded by Waddell, *The Spirit of the Book of Revelation*, Journal of Pentecostal Theology Supplement Series 30 (Blandford Forum, UK: Deo, 2006), 150–61 (whose book focuses on Rev. 10–11).

specifically, the formation of one new people of God out of what were formerly two: Jews and non-Jews, or Gentiles (Eph. 3:3–9), and this has implications for considering the "many peoples and nations and languages and kings" referred to in this specific vision (10:11b) but also in other formulas throughout the Apocalypse. Whatever may have been said by the seven thunders that John was prohibited from writing down—the one proscription compared to the dozen other instances that he was told to inscribe what he saw or heard[5]—the point was that this mighty angel swore there would be imminent fulfilment of the divine mystery, "in the days when the seventh angel is to blow his trumpet" (10:7a). If the opening of the sixth seal disclosed that divine justice and judgment were delayed only "a little longer" (6:11a), then now, anticipating the final trumpet, it is definitively declared that, "There will be no more delay" (10:6b). The revelation of Jesus is rapidly approaching its denouement.

Yet in order for us to see what comes next, the seer has to glimpse these developments, and it is here that John provides, for the only time, an account of his own prophetic calling, thereby inserting himself more intentionally into the narrative. Following the paradigm established especially by Ezekiel, who was also instructed to eat the scroll prophesying about the fate of Israel and did so only to find it tasting "as sweet as honey" (Ezek. 3:3), John tells of being commanded to eat the little scroll (10:8–9). Yes, it tastes sweet like honey, as with Ezekiel, but becomes bitter in his stomach (10:10). The distastefulness may be connected to the judgments in the second part of this interlude when the two witnesses are martyred for their testimony (about which there is more in the next section), but most immediately, the unpleasantness may also be linked to the summarized contents of the prophecy, not just "*about* many peoples and nations and languages and kings" (my emphasis) but "over" and even "against" them.[6] This surely has to do with the coming visions

---

5. The prototype here is the final Danielic vision, which was also sealed, at least until the end (Dan. 12:4–10; cf. 8:26b), even as there are other New Testament examples of ecstatic visions remaining private rather than rendered publicly (e.g., 2 Cor. 12:1–5); Mangina, *Revelation*, 130–31, suggests also that writing down the message/s of the seven thunders would require elaboration of a fourth heptad, which the narrative movement from the seven trumpets to the seven bowls impedes.

6. See Blount, *Revelation*, 200–201; also Skaggs and Benham, *Revelation*, 110.

regarding the inhabitants and kings of the earth being judged in the rest of Revelation (e.g., 11:9, 18; 13:7; 14:6, 8; 17:15; 18:3, 23; 19:15), but it must not be forgotten that the great multitude is a diversified humanity that derives from the ends of the earth (5:9; 7:9) and that the kings of the earth—the first and only time they are included in the four-group sequence (at the expense of tribes)—will play a much more important role in the second half of the book[7] and eventually bring their glory into the New Jerusalem (21:24). John envisions the mystery of God revealed in Jesus Christ, certainly, but it is just as assured that this is a story that interfaces with cosmic history, including the economic and political aspects of that world-story.

FURTHER REFLECTIONS
The Prophetic Call and Its Hazards

The appearance of John's vocational calling at this point in his account has led some interpreters to see this intermission as the pivot around which the entirety of this prophecy (cf. 1:3; 19:10; 22:7) turns.[8] However we may adjudicate this question literarily—which pertains to how we see the structure and outline of the book of Revelation about which there are, as already mentioned (in our introductory chapter), too many opinions to catalog—the theological issue is more pertinent for our purposes. There are a number of related questions here, including but not limited to, how did John understand the derivation of his prophetic vocation then, and how might

---

7. See Murphy, *Fallen Is Babylon*, 353; those who are tracking will note that this is the third time we have seen these four categorizations appear together (of a total of seven times across the Apocalypse), but never in the same order and in two cases—one right here—with new groups (italicized) replacing one of the staples; here is the way they line up:

    tribe and language and people and nation (5:9)
    nation, from all tribes and peoples and languages (7:9)
    peoples and nations and languages and *kings* (10:11)
    peoples and tribes and languages and nations (11:9)
    tribe and people and language and nation (13:7)
    nation and tribe and language and people (14:6)
    peoples and *multitudes* and nations and languages (17:15)

    See further comment (on 17:1–18) regarding the appearance of *multitude* instead of *tribe* in Rev. 17:15.
8. Waddell, *The Spirit of the Book of Revelation*, makes this argument.

we comprehend the inauguration of our own prophetic witness today? Are there occasions when prophetic revelations are for personal musing and even edification rather than for public disclosure, and how might we recognize which is when, other than through audible divine voices or mighty angelic manifestations? Can prophetic disclosures be of the more personal (or interpersonal) sort, or do most authentic divine messages relate to the public square, or interface with the realms of the powers, terrestrial and political, maybe also cultural and transnational? Does prophecy always taste bitter, and if so, what are the implications for contemporary prophets in particular and for prophetic speech-acts in general?

No doubt, even knowing to ask some of these kinds of questions beforehand might scare off would-be prophets from responding to or embracing that vocation today. Perhaps that is in part why contemporary Christians are more likely to exercise our prophetic gifts *within* rather than *outside* the church: it may be more conducive to a durationally longer prophetic vocation (as the next section will more forcefully illustrate). So, while in theory the prophetic call or function is one of at least three or four other ministerial or missional vocations—alongside apostles, evangelists, pastors and teachers, with the grammatical construct sometimes allowing a conjoining of these latter two roles (see Eph. 4:11)—the modern separation of church and state, among other reasons, complicates the relationship between the two realms (which prophets in the apocalyptic mode often occupy) and makes it difficult to imagine how those in the more sacred spheres may have anything to contribute to the presumed secular character of the public square (unless they were deemed "crazy" or believed to be in a similar condition that is then more easily dismissed). Especially in pentecostal and charismatic segments of the global church, which are becoming the increasingly dominant forms, one might add, there is more and more discussion of the prophethood of all believers alongside what the Reformation advanced, and which has become widely accepted, of all followers of Jesus as participants of the priesthood of believers.[9] But if many

---

9. E.g., Roger Stronstad, *The Prophethood of Believers: A Study in Luke's Charismatic Theology,* Journal of Pentecostal Theology Supplement Series 16 (Sheffield: Sheffield Academic Press, 1999).

if not most believers would welcome the priestly vocation that represents the divine presence and activity to others, oftentimes in salvifically and redemptively palpable ways—who would not prefer to be such conduits in a hurting world—fewer would be delighted to speak *against* the peoples, nations, and kings of this world. To confront the powers is to be confronted in turn by the powerful. Hence, who would be willing to eat of any prophetic scroll, even one offered by a mighty angel coming down from heaven, or even by Jesus himself, especially if visible as a slaughtered Lamb?[10]

10. After the events of 6 January 2021 when rioters stormed the capitol building of the United States in an effort to overturn the results of the 2020 presidential election, it has also been now more widely recognized how many pentecostal-charismatic Christians have supported Donald Trump and been encouraged to do so by the thousands of prophecies given during his presidency by acknowledged prophets within the movement about his reelection (documented by James A. Beverley, with Larry N. Willard, *God's Man in the White House: Donald Trump in Modern Christian Prophecy* [Pickering, Ont.: Castle Quay Books, 2020]). The hazards of contemporary prophecy engaging the public square have never been more stark; for discussion of the stakes, see Aizaiah G. Yong and Amos Yong, "The Inequitable Silencing of Many Tongues: Political, Economic, and Racialized Dimensions of the Pandemic in American Pentecostal-Charismaticism," in Wonsuk Ma and Opoku Onyinah, eds., *Response of the Global Spirit-Empowered Church to the COVID-19 Pandemic* (Tulsa, OK: ORU Press, 2022), forthcoming.

11:1–14

Prophesying at the Ends of the Earth: Completing the Prophetic Witness

Before diving into what is often viewed as one of the more befuddling chapters of an already obscure book, let us be reminded that this is a kind of second portion of an interlude between the sixth and seventh trumpets (the second and third woes!) that depicts the form of prophetic witness that the book as a whole is presented as, beginning with the commissioning of the seer of Patmos himself and now continuing with the efforts of the two end-time witnesses (or witnesses at the perceived end of time). As John's assignment is to prophesy about "many peoples and nations and languages and kings" (10:11b), he carries that out also in the remainder of this intermezzo, specifically describing how "members of the peoples and tribes and languages and nations" (11:9a) respond to the two witnesses. Although John speaks as a single prophetic voice, his message—of the two witnesses in this case—concerns "the inhabitants of the earth" (11:10).

Although the events surrounding these two witnesses transpire upon the world stage, in that they are witnessed by earthlings the world over, they are situated more abstrusely in Jerusalem, described with symbolic multivocality as "the great city that is prophetically called Sodom and Egypt, where also their Lord was crucified" (11:8b). This location is thus anticipated with the commandment—by God or Christ, it would appear, given the first-person voice at the end of these instructions (11:3a)—that John measure the temple and its altar (11:1), as if in a preservative manner, although he is then instructed not to measure the outer court, which thereby leaves that space exposed.[1] No wonder, then, that the latter "is given over to the nations, and they will trample over the holy city for forty-two months" (11:2b), here consistent with, as we have previously observed (see comments on 6:1–8 above), the apocalyptic sentiments preserved in the Gospel accounts (e.g., Luke 21:24; cf. Dan. 9:26). It is in the space symbolized by this outer court that the two witnesses, representative of the faithful people of God, are attacked and killed, after carrying out their prophetic witness for "one thousand two hundred sixty days" (11:3b). One thousand two hundred sixty days is equivalent to forty-two months, and each appears once more in Revelation (see 12:6 and 13:5), with the former, which is also three-and-a-half years, almost surely an allusion to Daniel's "a time, two times, and half a time" (Dan. 7:25b; 12:7; also Rev. 12:14b). If seven is the number of completion, however, then half of seven years—which is forty-two months, or 1,260 days—represents transitoriness.[2] The point is both that the time given over to the pagans, for them to overcome the holy city and its inhabitants, is a limited one, in part connecting back to the "five months" of locust torment released with the fifth trumpet (9:5a, 10) and in part reinforcing the notion that the remnant will be divinely protected, whether the 144,000 in the seal intermission or those believers associated with the temple and around the altar here (even if they are vulnerable when engaging as witnesses to the outside world).[3] On the other side, what transpires in this space outside the temple and during this designated time is also ordained—"*given over* to the nations" and "*grant*[ed to] my [God's presumably] two witnesses" (11:2, 3, italics added)—and thus further indicative of the divine oversight.[4]

It is when we turn especially to the identity of the two witnesses that we descend into the thickets of interpretative dispute. This is

1. For measurement as provision of divine protection, see Rob Dalrymple, *Revelation and the Two Witnesses: The Implications for Understanding John's Depiction of the People of God and His Hortatory Intent* (Eugene, OR: Resource Publications, 2011), esp. 5–15.
2. Catherine Gunsalus González and Justo L. González, *Revelation*, Westminster Bible Companion (Louisville, KY: Westminster John Knox Press, 1997), 72.
3. On the latter interpretation of the temple and altar symbolizing messianic believers and the outer courts representing the arena of their witness to and engagement/interaction with the unbelieving world, see Aune, *Revelation 6–16*, 597.
4. See Ekkehardt Müller, "The Two Witnesses of Revelation 11," *Journal of the Adventist Theological Society* 13:2 (2002): 30–45, esp. 32n9.

in part because the Dispensational approaches that have dominated much of the more recent (the last century especially) speculations have focused either on how the persecution of these two witnesses is supposed to illuminate the three and a half years of great tribulation, "of unprecedented trauma and persecution for the people of God,"[5] that is central to their scenario of the end times, or on whether these refer to individuals (like Enoch, Moses, Elijah, or other Old Testament figures with exploits phenomenologically similar to what is described in 11:5–6) or to the covenant people and witnesses of God.[6] As John has already alluded to the prophet Zechariah in the seven lampstands (among other symbols), it is not surprising that his description of these two witnesses as "the two olive trees and the two lampstands that stand before the Lord of the earth" (11:4) again appear to draw forward his predecessor's prophecy (Zech. 4:2–3). No matter what is decided, it is safe to say that these are those who maintain prophetic witness to their Lord unto death (11:8b). And as their Lord was raised from the dead, so also does their testimony live on not only in heaven, as evidenced by their ascension, but also on earth, as seen in the apocalyptic events of the related earthquake and its seven thousand victims, the number of completion indicating the accomplishment of justice (11:13).

For our purposes, it bears reiteration that the two witnesses maintain their testimony not only unto death but through death at the hands of the "beast that comes up from the bottomless pit" (11:7) and on the other side, "after the three and a half days" when they are resuscitated and then ascend to heaven in the sight of their enemies (11:11–12). Their adversary's provenance not only links back to the abyss unearthed by the fifth trumpet (9:11) but also situates the assailing of these two witnesses within the broader context of the demonic forces announced by the first two woes. Note also the reactions to the testimony of these witnesses: during the 1,260 days, it is implied that their listeners sought to do them harm (11:5); during the three and a half days when their dead bodies lay visible to the

---

5. Thomas, *The Apocalypse*, 326–27.
6. For an example of a dispensationalist approach, see Daniel K. K. Wong, "The Two Witnesses in Revelation 11," *Bibliotheca Sacra* 154 (1997): 344–54; a dozen or more interpretations of the identity of these two witnesses is surveyed by Aune, *Revelation 6–16*, 598–603.

inhabitants of the earth, the latter "will gloat over them and celebrate and exchange presents" (11:10); and upon their revitalization and ascent to the heavens, the masses of people were terrified (mentioned twice), although those not among the seven thousand victims also "gave glory to the God of heaven" (11:11b, 13b). There is a sense in which the intransigence of those unrepentant despite the death and destruction waged by the demonic cavalry (9:20–21) is replayed in the pigheadedness of those who seek instead to retaliate against these two witnesses, who remain stubborn in rejoicing over their death accomplished by the beast, and whose character seems so warped that even to behold the resurrection and vindication of the witnesses only generates a sense of terror rather than penitence. On the other hand, perhaps there is also a glimmer of hope in that at least some among them are at least ready to glorify the heavenly deity; might there also be remorse among these earth-dwellers?

FURTHER REFLECTIONS
The (Eternal) Implications of Our Testimony

We do not know if our commissioned prophet's attempt to be faithful to his call landed him in political exile in Patmos or whether he eventually was martyred for that testimony like these two witnesses that he tells us about. There have been others, however, like Antipas, who have persisted in their testimony like our two prophets, even at the cost of their lives. It is not how we begin, the old adage goes, but how we end. And even as all will die, these images regarding the two witnesses press the questions regarding the how and why of our death that may be just as important, if not more so, than that human life is transitory. What legacy will we leave? The how and why of our death are part of the witness that our lives proclaim. There is life after death, not just biologically with regard to the divine breath reanimating (our) corpses (see 11:11) but, more important, theologically regarding what our lives and deaths say about the God of heaven. Put another way: everybody dies, but after demise, we are remembered for different things; or, everyone lives on in some way or other, but the question is what carries forward from our lives and efforts? The legacy of these two witnesses hence prompts the query: what will we be remembered for, or what will be the post-mortem effects of our deeds and actions?

Consideration here of the legacy we leave presumes not any (South or East) Asian notion of karmic reincarnation but the eschatological arrow of our apocalyptic narrative. It is fitting that the seer from Patmos invites us to ponder the longer-term, even eternal, ramifications of our lives in light of the announcement at the end of this intermezzo: "The second woe has passed. The third woe is coming very soon" (11:14). The arrival of the third woe, the seventh trumpet, could be understood as the end of the beginning of the end, or the beginning of the end of the end, depending on one's perspective, since, according to our reading, the heptads are recapitulative, meaning that the heptad of bowls brings to a culmination the judgments initiated by the trumpets even as the latter intensified the judgments of the seals. What better time is there to consider the eternal implications of our testimony than when we anticipate the zenith of all things, including the divine judgments?

Worship at the Sound of the Seventh Trumpet: Singing in the Polis as in Heaven?

The seventh trumpet that sounds in this passage, it should be recalled, is the last of the trumpet heptad, which sits between the seal and bowl heptads. Each of the trumpets and bowls both recapitulate and deepen the message of the seals, which means that the blowing of the seventh trumpet brings to the apex what is initiated in the seals earlier but also sets up the pouring out of the bowls later. More theological than chronological (although not necessarily without any historical or sequential implications), the three series of seals-trumpets-bowls provide, if imagery serves us well, a spiraling look at how God brings God's redemptive plans to pass. This passage lifts us back up from the earthly perspective of the trumpet interlude (10:1–11:13) toward a more heavenly vantage point. It invites us to consider the degree to which we can embrace this heavenly posture as Jesus' followers on this historical planet. It poses especially the questions of if and how we can sing with the heavenly choir while enduring earthly oppression.

The blowing of the seventh trumpet is described thus: "Then the seventh angel blew his trumpet, and there were loud voices in heaven, saying, 'The kingdom of the world has become the kingdom of our Lord and of his Messiah, and he will reign forever and ever'" (11:15). Against the backdrop of the recapitulation theory of the seals-trumpets-bowls heptads, this is a significant announcement, one that indicates that the divine judgments are crowning and that the reign of God is ensuing. Yet it is also the case that what happens with the seventh trumpet is "an explanation of the consummation of history, since 10:7 has announced that when the seventh trumpet sounds,"[1] in John's own words, "the mystery of God will be fulfilled, as he announced to his servants the prophets" (10:7b). The hearing of this final trumpet, then, brings us back up to the heavenly throne room where we hear for the first time explicitly about the *messianic* reign (the word *Messiah* appearing only here and in 12:10). The fulfilment of the divine mystery, then, involves making overt what has been intimated before, that although both the Father (1:6; 4:9–10; 7:12; 10:6) and the Son of Man or the Lamb (1:18; 5:13) abide eternally, here their domains are fused so that the slain Lamb, also the crucified Lord (10:8b), will rule heaven and earth forever.

In addition to the "loud voices in heaven," which are common enough so far across the visions (5:2, 7:2), we hear also the twenty-four elders more specifically, whose singing further discloses the fulfillment of the divine mystery. We have already observed and heard these elders casting their crowns before and worshiping the one on the throne (4:10–11; 7:11) and also bowing low before and worshiping the Lamb (5:8, 11–12). Although on occasion (at least one: 7:13), they also break away from their otherwise perpetual worship to engage in conversation with the seer (to clarify the identity of the great multitude), the unveiling of the mystery of God and of his Son includes, reiteratively, further elaboration of their adulation before the throne. In their prostrated posture, they sing: "We give you thanks, Lord God Almighty, who are and who were, for you have taken your great power and begun to reign" (11:17). The seventh trumpet thus signals the beginning of the divine rule inaugurated in the messianic and Pentecost ministries of the Son and the divine spirit. The Lord God Almighty who was and is will now begin to reign through the divine coming.

The elders further intone, however, that "The nations raged, but your wrath has come, and the time for judging the dead, for rewarding your servants, the prophets and saints and all who fear your name, both small and great, and for destroying those who destroy the earth" (11:18). If worshipful chanting ring throughout the heavens, the terrestrial situation is rather different. On the one hand, then, the divine wrath is part of the fulfilling of the mystery of God,

---

1. Beale, *The Book of Revelation*, 609.

judging the raging nations and destroying earth's destroyers. There is much to be said here not only about those who destroy other human lives, socially, economically, politically, and in every other way if not also biologically, but this song also makes clear that those who do not steward the material world, as humankind was vocationally commissioned to in the creation narrative (Gen. 1:26), but destroy what was created good will come under judgment.[2] On the other hand, the completion of God's mysterious plan to redeem the world includes the rewarding of the saints (including those martyred for their witness: 5:8–9; 6:9; 8:3–4), prophets (including the two witnesses), servants (whether those martyred or preserved as a remnant: 6:11; 7:3), and those who fear God (rather than seeking to avoid suffering: 2:20). Herein we behold the message of the rest of the visions of the Apocalypse, and that of the bowls in particular: those raging against God and who destroy God's creation will be judged, while those embracing of God's will and embodying God's redemptive witness to others and to the world will be rewarded. In this context of cosmic conflict, then, the hymns of Revelation take a different hue, being not only doxological but also exhortatory, pastoral, admonitional, and pedagogical.[3]

Yet, the response to the message sung by the elders is additionally and intriguingly pertinent: "God's temple in heaven was opened, and the ark of his covenant was seen within his temple; and there were flashes of lightning, rumblings, peals of thunder, an earthquake, and heavy hail" (11:19). These are apocalyptic indicators that the world itself is responding to the divine revelation, as it has consistently already (6:12–14; 8:5). However, whatever apocalyptic phenomena communicate figuratively and symbolically from a geophysical and earth sciences perspective, we can say that the earth itself is convulsing in response to how human beings pollute and ravage their environment so that earthquakes, volcanos, tremors, continental movements, and tectonic shifts—so-called "acts of God" by our insurance industry—can be understood as the planet's inherent

2. A theme already broached in 8:6–13 (see comments there); for further consideration of the destroyers of the earth vocalized by the elders, see Barbara R. Rossing, "For the Healing of the World: Reading *Revelation* Ecologically," in David Rhoads, ed., *From Every People and Nation: The Book of Revelation in Intercultural Perspective* (Minneapolis: Fortress, 2005), 165–82.
3. See Robert S. Smith, "The Purpose of Revelation's Hymns," *Themelios* 43:2 (2018): 193–204.

mechanisms for renewing itself and the biosphere in an era of global warming and climate change.[4] Hence, natural disasters, so to speak, can also be viewed as divine judgments, in this case, for our own encroachments against the creation and our damaging of what God has formed, shaped, and named as good. The divine redemption of the world thereby involves renewal of the cosmos itself from our damaging actions and activities. So, whereas during the trumpet intermezzo John was instructed to measure the temple on earth (11:1), the final trumpet's blowing opens up the temple in heaven to divulge that God has not forgotten God's covenant with the creation—mediated as the Torah informs us through Noah (see Gen. 9:1–17)—thus also reassuring the saints, prophets, and servants of the Almighty One that those pledges would not be abrogated.

> "There is an indissoluble link between global warming and the rise in violence," writes René Girard, in the context of a broader argument that the human problem is mimetic violence spiraling out of control.
>
> René Girard, *Battling to the End: Conversations with Benoît Chantre*, trans. Mary Baker (East Lansing: Michigan State University Press, 2009), 216.

FURTHER REFLECTIONS
The Redemptive Work of Earthly Worship

By now, we realize that central to these apocalyptic visions is worship that booms, everlastingly and eternally, throughout the heavenlies, emanating from around the throne. Amid all of the chaos and even destruction that human creatures wreak, the heavenly hosts continue their melodic chorale. The seer peers into this transcendent choir from his Patmos standpoint, and the gift of these

---

4. Thanks to my son Aizaiah Yong for reminding me of these geological dynamics. See also Evgeny A. Podolskiy, "Effects of Environmental Changes on Global Seismicity and Volcanism," *Bulletin of the American Meteorological Society* 90:9 (2009): 1263–64; cf. Mark R. Handy, Greg Hirth, and Niels Hovius, eds., *Tectonic Faults: Agents of Change on a Dynamic Earth* (Berlin: Freie Universität Berlin, and Cambridge, MA: MIT Press, 2007); and P. R. Sammonds and J. M. T. Thompson, eds., *Advances in Earth Science: From Earthquakes to Global Warming* (London: Imperial College Press, 2007).

revelations mean that we, his hearers and (more often) readers, also have a portal into the beyond. As Stephen Smalley thereby puts it, "we engage with the theological truths and historical events of the drama from the vantage point of the brink of eternity."[5] In other words, although situated specifically in our own particular places and times, we navigate our personal and collective lives under the heavenly canopy, even within a cosmic auditorium filled with an eternal choir.

The question presses itself upon us: What are we doing in the shadow of eternity and against the backdrop of the harmonies of the heavenly hosts? The sounding of the seventh trumpet prompts what may otherwise be a very crass binary: Are we singing in emulation of the twenty-four elders (in this case), or are we otherwise participating in the destruction of the earth that is carried out by the nations and their inhabitants (us also)? Put otherwise, what are we doing to ameliorate the earthly destruction that has been ongoing since the primordial creation, and is participating in the worshipful singing of the heavenly band part of what is needed to chart an alternative course? These are big questions not least for Asian Americans who often find themselves powerless in their marginal locations but also for all contemporary disciples seeking faithfulness to the God of Jesus Christ. Although the nations rage in futility since the divine reign is imminent, the activities of human creatures have devastating planetary and environmental, if not cosmic, consequences. Might singing the song of the elders realign our deeds away from creational destruction toward restoration and reconstitution of the earth, and the heavens with it?

5. Smalley, *The Revelation to John*, 296.

Excursus C

Between the Trumpets and the Outpouring of the Bowls (Chapters 12–14)

If there was no gap to speak of between the final seal and the first trumpet (8:1–2), there is a substantive narrative distance between the end of the seventh trumpet (11:19) and the outpouring of the first bowl (16:2), even the introduction of the bowl heptad (15:7 specifically, but Revelation 15 as a whole generally). How, then, do we understand this remoteness, not at all like the interludes that occur within the septenary judgments, but a dramatic expanse that seems to defer or postpone the denouement of the judgments expected with the arrival of the reign of God (11:15b) rather than speed things up in accordance with the earlier announcement that "There will be no more delay" (10:6b)? The key is to comprehend that the recapitulative approach of the heptads means not only that the bowls are the apogee following the trumpets but also that the final trumpet, which is exactly the third and final woe (8:13), brings us to the pinnacle of the tensions of the book, and from there on, these pent up pressures are released so that it is, as the colloquial saying goes, all downhill after that. As the seer himself clarifies, if the blasting of the seventh trumpet brings to completion the divine mystery, then what happens after 11:15–19 is precisely the concluding account of what was before cryptically enigmatic. In this sense, then, the end of the eleventh chapter combined with the beginning of the twelfth serves as a pivot around which the book rotates, in effect dividing the visions between a kind of first (prior to and including Rev. 11) and second sector (Rev. 12 and after).[1] Let us explore how this section from Revelation 12–14 reflects this crucial turn along three axes.[2]

First, most immediately, Revelation 12 is a fulcrum correlating chapters 10–11 with chapters 13–14. This hinge can be more clearly seen when structurally delineated:

A—Rev. 10: mighty angel (representative of Jesus)

    B—Rev. 11: two witnesses

        C—Rev. 12: the woman and the dragon

    B′—Rev. 13: the two beasts

A′—Rev. 14: the Lamb and the seven angelic representatives

---

1. Waddell, *The Spirit of the Book of Revelation*, 190–91.
2. John E. Hurtgen, *Anti-Language in the Apocalypse of John* (Lewiston, NY: Mellen, 1993), ch. 4, considers 11:19–15:4 as the climactic center of the book, although to achieve this, he treats 14:6–13 as an interlude rather than its own subsection.

It is true that the swiveling twelfth chapter associates material from the interlude (Rev. 10–11) with visions between the last two heptads (Rev. 13–14). Yet, intriguingly, the inner ring portrays developments on earth (the prophetic ministry of the two witnesses in the great city or "outer court" of the world in Rev. 11 and of the satanic efforts of the two beasts vis-à-vis the inhabitants of the earth in Rev. 13) even as the outer ring connects heaven, earth, and everything in between (via the mighty angel who descends from heaven to plant his feet on the earth and the sea while yet touching the heavens in that mien in Rev. 10, and via the unfolding of scenes in heaven and earth as well as, explicitly, in the midheavens, in Rev. 14). In short, the turning point of the book from the final trumpet onwards is preceded by cosmic and terrestrial developments that find their counterparts, albeit in reverse order, following.

This begs further analysis of how the last trumpet introduces the final unveiling of the mystery of God in Jesus Christ. Let me thereby posit this more general hypothesis: that the three judgment heptads depicting "what must take place after this" (4:1b) unfold in the first part of the book (Rev. 4–11) from a more heavenly perspective, whereas we get another angle from "down under," as it were—"terrestrially oriented," as Josephine Ford puts it[3]— in the second half (Rev. 12–18). What I mean is that the first part's account of that which is to come commences from the throne room (Rev. 4–5) and is anchored from that venue, including but not limited to the opening of the seals and the role of the prayers of the saints within that, the gathering of the 144,000 and the great multitude, the blasting of the trumpets that occur in the heavenly regions (8:2), and the depiction of the anticipatory final celebration (11:15–19). What happens in the second part regarding what is to come is situated instead on earth, beginning with the plight/flight of the woman and her persecution by the dragon and its beasts (Rev. 12–13), and focuses on the visitation of divine bowl judgments on the earth (Rev. 15–16), inexorably devouring the great city, symbolic of the wickedness of the earth under the sway of the dragon's deceptions, and all that are caught up in its mechanisms (Rev. 17–18). Whereas the primary actors in the earlier half are divine, including the Father, the Lamb at right hand of the throne, and his seven spirits, the agents of destruction that are in turn destroyed in the latter portions are demonic, a kind of triadic counterpart to the heavenly figures: the dragon and its two beasts.[4]

This reconfigured reading does not mean that there are no earthly scenes in the first part (the work of the two witnesses being most tangibly so rooted) or that there are no heavenly panoramas in the second (the

---

3. Ford, *Revelation*, 182.
4. James G. Kallas, *Revelation: God and Satan in the Apocalypse* (Minneapolis: Augsburg, 1973), is aptly titled in this regard, although the satan for Kallas is not understood literalistically but rather symbolically as representing the worldly systems that oppose God.

Even if a bit overstated, it is helpful to hear Adela Yarbro Collins's claim that "the primary impact of the book is the movement from persecution to salvation through combat."

The Combat Myth in the Book of Revelation, Harvard Theological Review/Harvard Dissertations in Religion 9 (Missoula, MT: Scholars Press, 1976), 44.

mediating visions between the beastly endeavors and the bowl judgments are clearly portended in heaven). It simply invites consideration, I suggest, of both how the heavenly vindication of the saints remains a divine prerogative (through seals and trumpets on the one hand) and how the final bowl judgments befall earth dwelling sinners who swallow rather than expel the evil deceptions led by the dragon and its beasts (culminating with the bowls and their aftermath vis-à-vis Babylon on the other hand). In both cases, each segment concludes with a heavenly celebration: the singing of the twenty-four elders in anticipation of the final debut of the divine mystery of salvation (11:15–19) and the hallelujahs of the entirety of the heavenly hosts in response to that disclosure (19:1–10).

There is one final observation to be made about how the full and final exposé of the divine mystery sounded off by the seventh trumpet and therefore comprising the second half of the book is designed, at least loosely, to parallel how the first half is introduced. There is an initial introduction of the God of the Apocalypse (1:1–9), it will be remembered, then an initial revelation of Jesus (1:10–20), followed by messages to the seven churches (Rev. 2–3), and then the heavenly scenes (Rev. 4–5), all of which precede the seal and trumpet judgments (Rev. 6–11). The second half of the visions exhibits a similar rhythm. There is an initial framing of the urgent situation involving the preeminent evil source, the dragon, and its threatening of the people of God on earth (Rev. 12), then a manifestation of that behemoth's carnal and beastly regimes (Rev. 13), followed by seven angelic speech-acts (Rev. 14), and a range of heavenly scenes (Rev. 14–15), all of which go before the bowl judgments (Rev. 16–18). The symmetry breaks down in the sense that the final judgments and the emergence of the New Jerusalem at the end of Revelation (19:11–22:5) do not find a correspondence in the first part, but then again, the seer himself frames the visions also in term of "what you have seen, what is, and what is to take place after this" (1:19) that not only do not mandate any strict equivalence of parts but also in some sense lead us to expect the kind of dissimilarity that this framing observes.

Onward, then, to see what the convergence of divine and messianic kingdoms means for the raging nations of the earth and their constituents.

12:1–18

The Woman, the Dragon, and Us: Wondering When and How This War Will End?

We have already seen the satan introduced (if only in passing in the letters to the seven churches), even as we have also already met its presumptive namesake, the "angel of the bottomless pit" (9:11a) and its destructive locust army as well as its affiliated demonic cavalry (in the fifth and sixth trumpets). Here, however, at this midpoint of the book, we are treated to a much more detailed, overarching, and cosmic perspective of the satan as chief adversary of the Lord God Almighty and the people of God. What we have in this chapter is a combination of perspective on past "events" or developments plus the elaboration of present conditions, including about the very real and spiritual war that is raging between the satan and the saints, "those who keep the commandments of God and hold the testimony of Jesus" (12:17b). What, then, might we be able to take away about the Christian and spiritual life from this vision of the woman and the dragon, which, revealed as portents in heaven (12:1a, 3a), are symbolically dense?

Here is what we know about the woman from what John writes. She is "clothed with the sun, with the moon under her feet, and on her head a crown of twelve stars. She was pregnant and was crying out in birth pangs, in the agony of giving birth" (12:1–2). Then, the woman is threatened by the dragon, and her child with her, "a male child, who is to rule all the nations with a rod of iron" (12:5; cf. 2:27a). That this is no less than the Messiah is clear from the allusions to the resurrection and ascension of Jesus in the next sentence: "But her child was snatched away and taken to God and to his throne" (12:5). The woman, however, "fled into the wilderness,

154

where she has a place prepared by God, so that there she can be nourished for one thousand two hundred sixty days" (12:6). More precisely, she "was given the two wings of the great eagle, so that she could fly from the serpent into the wilderness, to her place where she is nourished for a time, and times, and half a time" (12:14). If the dragon's ongoing efforts to destroy (by drowning) the woman are thwarted by the earth—as it "opened its mouth and swallowed the river that the dragon had poured from his mouth" (12:16b)[1]— the serpent then turned its destructive attention in the direction of the woman's descendants, going "off to make war on the rest of her children" (12:17a).

From this composite sketch, a number of summary remarks present themselves. First, the woman is Israel, as the covenant people of God from whom the Messiah comes, but also because her twelve stars are indicative of her constitution via the twelve tribes of the ancient Hebrews (see 7:4–8). Further, she has not only Jewish children, that of the covenant symbolized by the ark in the heavenly temple (11:19), but also other offspring who now come into the dragon's ferocious sights, and these would be the Gentile believers and messianic disciples (in the Apocalypse introduced as the seven churches). Last but not least, Israel, the woman, receives divine protection within a providential wilderness space period for a limited period of time: three and a half years (12:6b, 14b). We shall say more about this temporal duration in the next section, but this reprieve from the murderous intentions of the dragon is provisional, not only for her nourishment but also so that the woman can be "prepared by God" (12:6) for what is to come next.

What do we know about the dragon from our seer from Patmos? Initially, in contrast to the "great portent" that is the woman, the dragon is simply introduced as "another portent" (12:1a, 3a). John more fully describes what he sees thus: "a great red dragon, with seven heads and ten horns, and seven diadems on his heads. His tail swept down a third of the stars of heaven and threw them to the earth" (12:3b–4). But the casting of stars on the earth is followed

---

1. Here the earth protects the woman—the people of God—from destructive waters, contrary to the divinely ordained deluge that covered the earth in primeval history; see González and González, *Revelation*, 83, for this comparative point.

by a war between the dragon and Michael—an archangel renowned
for prior heavenly skirmishes (Dan. 10:13, 21; cf. Jude 8–9)—and
his angels resulting in the dragon being "thrown down, that ancient
serpent, who is called the Devil and Satan, the deceiver of the whole
world—he was thrown down to the earth, and his angels were
thrown down with him" (12:9). Perhaps John here "sees" what is
heard, in the Third Gospel, from Jesus himself: "I watched Satan fall
from heaven like a flash of lightning" (Luke 10:18). Now additionally enraged, not only "because he knows that his time is short!"
(12:12b) but also since its designs on hurting the woman are frus-
trated by the earth (12:13–14), the dragon wages ongoing and des-
perate warfare against the woman and her (ecclesial) children.

What has appeared in the book so far as being only locally situated—e.g., within synagogues in Smyrna and Philadelphia (2:9, 3:9)
or as being resident and even enthroned at Pergamum (2:13)—is
now exposed as the cosmic villain. This rogue's primary mode of
operation is deception, well documented across the New Testament
(John 8:44–45; 2 Cor. 11:3) and evident in its basic description here.
The image of the dragon being "great," effectively straddling the sky
and earth even while attempting to take a stand "on the sand of the
seashore" (12:18), tries to replicate the stance of the mighty angel
with the little scroll (10:2, 5). Further, the seven diadems or crowns
on the heads of the dragon impersonate the twelve-starred crown
on the woman's head. Although, as we shall see, the seven heads and
ten crowns are additionally replicated by the dragon's sea monster
(13:1), these heads and horns being clarified later to be symbolic of
kings past and present (17:9–12) that are fleeting and whose earthly
regimes are transient, unlike the perpetuity of those governments
announced as caught up in the messianic reign (11:15) and in contrast to the legacy of Israel's tribes that are revealed in the end as
inscribed on the gates of the eternal city (21:12).

The last point of import is that besides duplicity and trickery, the
deceiver of the world also engages in accusations against the messianists. This is consistent with the ancient Hebraic understanding
of the satan as a heavenly being with access to the divine council
with a "history" of bringing charges against the righteous, the story
of Job being the most prominent (Job 1–2; also Zech. 3:1). Thus,

the dragon is the ancient adversary not just of the Most High God but also of the people of God, and this is captured in this portentous vision of the monstrous serpent's seeking to devour the vulnerable (female-imaged) people of God. Although including elements of the primordial combat myth involving the oceanic Leviathan's raging against humankind and alluding perhaps even to the Greek myth of the birth of Apollo to Leto, Zeus's wife, who was protected by Poseidon from the menacing deity Python,[2] John's adaptation goes back ever deeper into primeval history. Leaping off the account of the Edenic fall in the first book of Torah, including the curse pronounced on Elohim on the primordial serpent, the seer's narrative brings that antediluvian dispute—in which it was said: "I will put enmity between you and the woman, and between your offspring and hers; he will strike your head, and you will strike his heel" (Gen. 3:15)—into the contemporary horizon. John's vision here confirms the truth of this ancient prophecy. The dragon manages to strike, mortally even, the messianic figure—thus the slain Lamb—but with the subsequent resurrection and ascension this blow turns out to be but akin to a temporary heel injury; on the other hand, the drama here makes explicit the dual counterstrike—first by Michael and his angels in heaven (12:7–8) and then by those servants of the Messiah that the dragon sought to accuse (12:11)—which is said to be dealt to the head, and this will prove deadly by the end of the Apocalypse.

Intriguingly, not only does the Messiah overcome the dragon in part through his angelic and human creatures, but even the latter's weapons were those consistent with that utilized by the Lamb: through being slain. Instead of resisting on the dragon's terms (deploying methods of counteraccusation of "fake news," for instance), the messianic comrades "conquered him by the blood of the Lamb and by the word of their testimony, for they did not cling to life even in the face of death" (12:11). Witness of word and of life via keeping the divine commandments (cf. 12:17b), even to the point of death, not just of any sort but in the messianic footsteps—these are the saints' tools of defiance. As John hears "a loud voice from heaven" declaring, "Now have come the salvation and the power and

---

2. See Collins, *The Combat Myth in the Book of Revelation*; cf. Neil Forsyth, *The Old Enemy: Satan and the Combat Myth* (Princeton, NJ: Princeton University Press, 1989).

the kingdom of our God and the authority of his Messiah" (12:10a). The messianic power is manifest and unleashed through its being slain, and it is precisely this carnage that mediates the divine salvation, power, and reign. Put another way, the Father's defeat of the dragon and its lies is achieved through the Messiah, in particular his gruesome crucifixion. And the saints will triumph over the dragon only by participating in the blood of the Lamb and embracing his testimony.

FURTHER REFLECTIONS
Spiritual Warfare

There are two distinct aspects of 12:1–18 that invite further consideration. First, what might be deemed a minor point from the narrative arc of this passage is significant from my perpetual foreigner location. The dragon is an equal-opportunity devourer, targeting first and foremost the woman as the covenant people of God but also "the rest of her children," those brought into the covenant through messianic grafting. Even if the latter were not directly children of the promise, they are not spared the angry tantrum of the dragon. Similarly, those who find themselves in the hybridic and liminal spaces that characterize the perpetual foreigner experience may identify with the dominant church only marginally, but this does not spare even these peripheral participants from suffering as collateral damage from the dragon's attacks. In other words, the

---

Thus, this passage has been variously received: "In first-century Asia Minor, it was the Christian mimicry of the Dragon Slayer myth (the Leto-Python-Apollo myth) in Revelation 12. In the seventeenth-cent Mexico, it was the Creole mimicry of the Spanish Guadalupan myth located in the works of Miguel Sánchez and Luis Laso de la Vega. And in the twentieth-cent Chicana/o movement, it was the mimicry of U.S. notions of Manifest Destiny in *El Plan Espiritual de Aztlán*, which also employed the counter-iconography of the Virgin of Guadalupe."

David A. Sánchez, *From Patmos to the Barrio: Subverting Imperial Myths* (Minneapolis: Fortress, 2008), 117.

perpetual foreigner as subordinate citizen of the reign of God is not inoculated from the persecution inflicted by the dragon, and hence there is double exposure for these: internally as questioned by the majority ecclesial culture and externally from the dragon's attack.

How can those against whom the dragon and his fallen angels are set respond, defend themselves, and even counter? The messianists'"weapons" are, paradoxically, through embrace of the posture of the slain Lamb, bearing witness to that shed blood, even to the point of their own death. This contrasts with much of the rhetoric of "spiritual warfare" in many pentecostal-charismatic circles around the world today,[3] especially its presumption that triumph over the satanic and demonic involves the avoidance of death and the sustenance of life. What happens if spiritual warfare embraces and embodies this testimony Jesus himself bore witness to in his life *and death*? How might spiritual warfare be waged if believers witness first and foremost to Jesus' life and death? In some contexts, messianic discipleship is just another alternative and no one even cares to question the rights of groups to exercise their religious freedom, even if in other contexts such is quizzically tolerated. But whatever the case, in the cosmic scheme of things—which is the context of this passage—the emphasis lies in following Jesus' teachings and adhering to his living according to the divine commandments. In certain environments, however, like in that where Jesus himself was executed and his devotees were harried and harassed, participation in Jesus' testimony may involve the shedding of blood also. There are sadly many more Antipases across the centuries and around the world than most of us are aware of or care to be counted among.[4] So, for us who are reading this and not in immediate danger of being arrested for our messianic commitments, we can be grateful even as we ought to ask ourselves whether we are bearing full and adequate witness to that for which Jesus lived and died.

3. See James A. Beilby and Paul Rhodes Eddy, eds., *Understanding Spiritual Warfare: Four Views* (Grand Rapids: Baker Academic, 2012).
4. E.g., Paul Marshall, Lela Gilbert, and Nina Shea, *Persecuted: The Global Assault on Christians* (Nashville: Thomas Nelson, 2013).

13:1–10

The Beast out of the Sea: (Nonviolently) Resisting the Politics of Evil

Revelation 13 presents two beasts in the service of the dragon, representing broadly its political and economic arms. In this first part, we will examine how the beast of the sea not only carries out the dragon's agenda but does so in ways that attempt to simulate what God has done in and through the Messiah. The questions for messianists, then and even in the present time, is how to counter the beastly regime, and the answer then and for today may not be a popular one: through nonviolent endurance.

From the shifting sands of the seashore (12:18), the dragon almost appears to call forth reinforcements that appear in the beast "rising out of the sea having ten horns and seven heads; and on its horns were ten diadems, and on its heads were blasphemous names" (13:1).[1] Identically grisly in appearance with the seven-headed and ten-horned dragon,[2] the sea beast is further monstrously hybridic like the demonic locusts and cavalry of the fifth and sixth trumpets: "like a leopard, its feet were like a bear's, and its mouth was like a lion's mouth" (13:2a). Yet if the dragon had jeweled crowns on its seven heads, this sea beast has diadems on its ten horns. This combination, however, points to the dragon's efforts to attain political governance and rule over the whole earth, as if to frustrate the impending divine

---

1. Murphy, *Fallen Is Babylon*, 408, reminds us that the four beasts in Daniel's vision also arise out of the sea (Dan. 7:2–3), even as the fourth beast in the earlier prophet's account also had ten horns (Dan. 7:7b), amid other similarities.
2. Do these seven-headed demonic powers (see also 12:3) contrast with the seven spirits? See the connection suggested by Bogdan G. Bucur, "Hierarchy, Prophecy, and the Angelomorphic Spirit: A Contribution to the Study of the Book of Revelation's *Wirkungsgeschichte*," *Journal of Biblical Literature* 127:1 (2008): 173–94, at 182.

reign. That such domineering ambitions are at least partially realized is later made explicit in the seven heads being the seven mountains, presumably on which the imperial city of Rome sits, and thereby also including seven of its emperors or Caesars more or less contemporaneous with John, while the ten horns are symbolic of a group or network of kings that are yet to emerge (17:9–12). No wonder it is said of the sea beast that, "the dragon gave it his power and his throne and great authority" (13:2). Hence, even if the sea beast were symbolic of a person rather than of any imperial system of government as many would have it, this would be none other than a world leader, someone with great political authority over the whole earth (13:3b).

There are two basic and complementary features of this sea beast's activities: to support the dragon on the one hand and to deceptively caricature the authority and achievements of God on the other. First, it is said of the beast: "One of its heads seemed to have received a death-blow"—by the sword, it is said later (13:14b)—"but its mortal wound had been healed" (13:3). This may allude to the legend of Nero (37–68 C.E.) who was emperor from 54 to 68 CE and supposedly committed suicide but, because of his cruelty and power, was expected to return; or for those who embrace a more collective understanding of the sea beast's miraculous healing, this could also refer to the restabilization of the Pax Romana under the decade-long (69–79 CE) rule of Vespasian (9–79 CE) after the tumultuous year following Nero's death when at least three others in quick succession attempted to secure power but each was violently vanquished by his successor. Yet, however the political correlations are interpreted or understood, it is the mimicry of the resurrection of the Son—the snatching away and elevation to heaven of the male child, in the terms of the cosmic battle (12:5b)—that is the theologically significant matter. So much so that the reanimation of the mortally wounded head leads to the whole earth's amazement and their worship of the dragon and the beast (13:3b–4). If it was asked of the Lamb's wrath, "who is able to stand?" (6:17b), here it is venerated of the dragon's political representative: "Who is like the beast, and who can fight against it?" (13:4b).

So, if the dragon aspires to be a recipient of the worship due properly only to God, then the beast's most extensive activities revolve around galvanizing the state apparatus, most obviously in the imperial cult but not thereby limited, in blaspheming God. Such blasphemous (mentioned four times in this passage: 13:1b, 5, and twice in 13:6) signals and activity are efforts to undermine God's holiness, truthfulness, and righteousness by elevating in place, falsely, that of the dragon and the political regimes captivated and mesmerized by its authority. These blasphemies are extended not only to the heavens and its heavenly creatures but performed against the saints on earth (13:6b–7a), thereby carrying on the dragon's pursuit of those who keep the divine commandments and witness to the truth of Jesus (12:17b). Whereas the (seven) churches are to bear witness to the coming divine reign, here the state is mobilized otherwise as the serpent "authorizes the state as his agent to persecute the church and to deceive the ungodly."[3] The extent of the beast's and dragon's success is measured by their devious seizure of authority—divinely ceded, surely, as mentioned twice (13:7)—over the whole world, so that "all the inhabitants of the earth will worship" the beast (13:8a). Even if the beast's reach "over every tribe and people and language and nation" is divinely granted (13:7b),[4] nevertheless this is another manifestation of the dragon's effort to duplicate the divine redemption that draws "from every tribe and language and people and nation" (5:9; cf. 7:9).

Yet there are additional facets of this vision that register the divine control over the beast's earthly and political powers. First, the hyperbolic "all the inhabitants of the earth" who worship the beast is qualified: "everyone whose name has not been written from the foundation of the world in the book of life of the Lamb that was slaughtered" (13:8b). The Greek could just as well be translated, "whose names are not written in the Book of Life of the Lamb, slain from the foundation of the world" (twenty-first-century KJV)—so that the emphasis here is less a predestination of a group of individuals than of the centrality of the cross in salvation history (although

---

3. Beale, *The Book of Revelation*, 681.
4. Some (e.g., Keener, *Revelation*, 347–48) thus warn of a false multiculturalism, one that is merely politically correct and thereby perhaps idolatrous (see also 17:15–16) rather than is first and foremost committed to keeping the divine commandments and the testimony of Jesus.

17:8 does say that the writing of names in the book of life has been ongoing "from the foundation of the world")—but the important point for our purposes is that only those not so secured are seduced to worship the beast. Put another way: the sway of the beast is not unconstrained.

Second, the duration of the beast's political influence is also limited: to forty-two months (13:5b). We have seen this temporal period of three-and-a-half years or 1,260 days already (11:3; 12:6). There is surely extended discussion especially among Dispensationalist or futurist interpreters that this represents half of the seven-year great tribulation that is prophesied in Israel's Scriptures, especially since Daniel speaks also of the saints being given over to suffering and persecution by a beastly kingdom (and its kings, one in particular) "for a time, two times, and half a time" (Dan. 7:23–25; cf. Rev. 12:14b). Whatever the merits of considering this so-called great ordeal as part of a future last-days scenario, the theological principle regarding the canon as the perennial word of God for the church— also the basic presumption behind the Belief series as a whole and of this commentary within it—means also that this specific text should speak meaningfully both to its original audience (the seven churches in Asia in the last third or less of the first century) and to anyone else who might read or hear this book before the end of time. We will return to consider the specific question about the three and a half years when we comment on Revelation 17, but for the moment, it is important to insist on the limited constraints under which the politics of the beast proceeds.

If the state has been galvanized against the people of God and are oppressing and persecuting them through the deployment of violent measures, to the point of death, what is the appropriate response? The seer anticipates this question and provides a clear, even if difficult to accept, directive: "Let anyone who has an ear listen: If you are to be taken captive, into captivity you go; if you kill with the sword, with the sword you must be killed. Here is a call for the endurance and faith of the saints" (13:9–10). Not quite pneumatically undergirded as in the reprieve at the end of the letters to the seven churches, the injunction is nevertheless consistent both with John's own perseverance (1:9) and the resolve of the Asian congregations, at least at Ephesus, Thyatira, and Philadelphia (2:2–3, 19; 3:9). On the one hand, fortitude is the way forward; on the other hand, and here drawing from Jeremiah's prophecies of judgment against Israel, counterviolence is discouraged if only because "Those destined for pestilence [will go] to pestilence, and those destined for the sword, to the sword; those destined for famine, to famine, and those destined for captivity, to captivity" (Jer. 15:2).

FURTHER REFLECTIONS
Faithful Citizenship

Remember that at the center of the heavenly throne is the slaughtered Lamb, and it is this figure that is found worthy to open the seals. The slain Lamb here counters the antagonistic cosmopolis only by writing the names of the saints down in the book of life, not otherwise. Even if the entire apparatus of the state is roused against the church and arrayed violently against the people of God, to resort to the sword in turn will only exacerbate and perpetuate the spread of death. This is not to absolutize such as a principle of nonviolence in all cases;[5] but it is to take seriously that the Lamb that is murdered in ways sanctioned, if not carried out, by the state is the one whose image calls the saints to endure even when living under a ferociously aggressive and inimical municipality. The seven churches were surely under pressure to participate in the liturgies of the imperial cult, and in their case, the call was to defiance, to resist the lure of or counter whatever is concocted by coercive regimes.

To the degree that late modern believers are confronted with the choice of either worshiping the one on the throne and his Lamb or worshiping the beast and participating in state-sponsored activities that are blasphemous against God, the call to endure in faith remains. On the other hand, generally speaking, the options are not so starkly evident. Instead, our succumbing to the mechanisms of any state is usually more subtle, for instance, when we

---

5. Although a valiant effort to read Revelation pacifistically is Gregory A. Boyd, *The Crucifixion of the Warrior God*, vol. 1 (Minneapolis: Fortress, 2017), esp. appendix 4, "Violence in the Book of Revelation."

The hatred and violence found in certain texts of Revelation express the limit-situation of extreme oppression and anguish that the community is undergoing. Revelation reproduces these feelings in order to produce a catharsis (release and purification) in those listening and thereby transform their hatred into awareness. The violence in Revelation is more literary than real.

Pablo Richard, *Apocalypse: A People's Commentary on the Book of Revelation* (Maryknoll, NY: Orbis Books, 1995), 4.

embrace an uncritical patriotism and nationalism that then invites allegiances that have the potential to compromise our devotional commitments. What happens, for instance, when we swear fidelity to our country and our governments militarize excessively according to the power and authority that we have ceded to them in exchange—so we are promised—for the protection or enhancement of our self (national) interests? If we are willing to die for our country (and human creatures have done that regularly for almost as long as we have been around), are we not rendering our ultimate loyalties to earthly regimes? And how is that different from what the beast seeks to attain, politically, for the dragon? Again, I am not necessarily arguing that military participation is exactly equivalent to worshiping the beast or blaspheming the divine name and dwelling. I am concerned, however, that in troubled times, political leaders who accomplish seemingly impossible tasks for the apparent and at least temporary good of their constituents might garner their adherence in ways that develop idolatrously. Let me be clear: We should be very wary of any readings of Revelation that justify the use of militarized or other violent forces by those in power.

The experiences of Asian Americans attempting to serve in the military of their newly adopted "home" country puts a fine point on the challenges at this juncture. It is not that Asian Americans cannot or do not serve in the military, but their perpetual foreigner status means that even if they were to give themselves wholly for their country, that itself would be noteworthy less because they are Americans and more because of their marginal and hybridic character as *Asian* Americans. No wonder there is ambiguity for such dual-conscious "citizens": Would not the ultimate act of belonging to one's new home country be signified by giving one's life for it? But would not one also still then be forever marked by one's difference, even in this final act of national allegiance? Hence, it emerges that such a liminal and transitional identity is already cautioned against swearing absolute loyalty to any earthly regime. Ought not all messianists whose fidelity is ultimately with the God of Jesus Christ also be at least measured and more tentative in their national, tribal, and various this-worldly fealties?[6]

6. Many Christians believed that storming the United States capitol on 6 January 2021 was warranted to contest what they believed was a stolen presidential election, thus illuminating how nationalistic fervor and religious commitments can converge. Without claiming that Asian American Christians are immune from being captivated by nationalist zeal, the perpetual foreigner posture may provide some tempering of such ardor. With my multiracial son, Aizaiah G. Yong, we name the reckoning needed for Christian disciples and churches at the dawn of the third decade of the third millennium and propose some ways forward from this historical juncture in our essay, "Seeking Healing in an Age of Partisan Division: Reckoning with Theological Education and Resounding the *Evangel* for the 2020s," in Miguel A. De La Torre, ed., *Faith and Reckoning after Trump* (Maryknoll, NY: Orbis Books, 2021), 214–27.

13:11-18

The Beast Out of the Earth: Calculating (within) the Global Economy

John next sees "another beast that rose out of the earth" (13:11a) whose twofold work involves exalting the sea beast and facilitating the imperial economy.[1] It should not be surprising that the dragon's efforts to forestall the impending divine reign involves establishing a counterfeit kingdom replete with its own political economy. We shall see here how the earth beast's organization of the economic domain complements and extends the dragon's political ambitions. The questions for messianists, then and even in the present time, is how to navigate the beastly economy, and the answer, then and for today, may be not only unpopular but also not very practicable or doable: through opting out of the dragon's market and establishing a messianic counter-economics.

The earth beast speaks and sounds dragon-like but appears with "two horns like a lamb" (13:11b). John may be drawing, again, from the prophet Daniel, this time from a two-horned ram that was explained as referring to the then-kings of the Medes and the Persians (Dan. 8:4–7, 20), but in this case, the duplicity of this beast is masked in its lamb-like appearance. Yet the deceitfulness—carried over from that of the dragon (12:9)—is variously effective in misleading earth's inhabitants (13:14): by fostering widespread recognition of the authority of the resuscitated sea beast to the point the latter is worshipped by earth's denizens (13:12); by performing

---

1. Joseph Poon, *The Identities of the Beast from the Sea and the Beast from the Land in Revelation 13* (Eugene, OR: Pickwick, 2017), 157–67, argues thus that the beast of the land is the provincial high priest of the imperial cult whose role is thereby a religio-economic one: to promote the emperor (the beast of the sea) through one of the central economic engines of the Roman Empire.

"even making fire come down from heaven to earth in the sight of all" (13:13), like Elijah of old did upon the putative prophets of Baal on Mount Carmel (1 Kgs. 18:16–40), but also competing with the two witnesses who devoured their foes via fire from their mouths (11:5a); by motivating earthlings to make an idolatrous image of the sea beast (13:14), here reminiscent of Aaron's building the golden calf at the foot of Mount Sinai (Exod. 32), and then miraculously enlivening it as if like the divine supplier of the breath of life in order to cause further creaturely worship, even while ordering "those who would not worship the image of the beast to be killed" (13:15). Although mimicking the (slain) Lamb in its appearance, the earth beast's service of the sea beast means that the former functions more like John the Baptist in relationship to the Messiah. For such reasons related to his disingenuous words and actions, the earth beast is referred to later in the Apocalypse as a false prophet (16:13b; 19:20a; 20:10).[2]

Besides acclaiming the sea beast and stimulating worship of that beast and of its image, indeed, promoting, expanding, and fortifying the blasphemous character of the dragon's imperial tyranny, the earth beast also works on the economic front. John observes that the dragon-sounding earth beast "causes all, both small and great, both rich and poor, both free and slave, to be marked on the right hand or the forehead, so that no one can buy or sell who does not have the mark, that is, the name of the beast or the number of its name" (13:16–17). Befitting the expanse of the imperial Roman state, the earth beast forges a global (Mediterranean) economic system, one that involves *all* persons and classes and categories of people. Any form of participation in the market, whether on the supply or demand side, required the relevant mark on one or the other location. It is perhaps clearer now why the Pentecost outpouring of the divine breath had to be upon *all flesh*, male and female, young and old, slave and free (Acts 2:17–18): not only to catalyze Jubilee

---

2. And in that respect, the earth fiend is "a beastly imitation of the spirit of prophecy," indeed of the divine spirit and the seven spirits of the Apocalypse; see Robert W. Wall, "A Pneumatic Discernment of the Spirit-Beast of Revelation 13:11–17," in Blaine Charette and Robby Waddell, eds., *Spirit and Story: Pentecostal Readings of Scripture—Essays in Honor of John Christopher Thomas* (Sheffield: Sheffield Phoenix Press, 2020), 101–16, at 106.

sharing between all who had need (Acts 2:42–43; 4:32–36),[3] but also to counter the universal reach of the imperial Roman economy by speaking truth in many languages.

As John describes entry into the economy of the Pax Romana as enabled by the marked right hand or forehead, end times speculative eschatologies see realization of this text in the twenty-first-century computer chip now embedded in our credit cards or other forms of payment or identification, perhaps soon to be implanted in our skins or bodies. Even if this might bear sufficient resemblance to be considered as fulfilling such prophecy, I continue to consider what this might have meant to the original readers and hearers and even to every generation in every place who might seek to encounter the divine word in such apocalyptic passages. We have already seen the 144,000 marked on their foreheads (7:5), and these shall soon reappear in Zion (14:2). By contrast, it appears that this insignia, which is "the name of the beast or the number of its name," demarcates the devotees of the dragon from those of the Messiah. In effect, "the followers of Satan escape his anger unleashed against the Church (12.17) by carrying his mark."[4]

The earth beast hereby secures allegiance to the dragon by appealing to the economic well-being of earth's citizens. If buying and selling were the central, if not the only means of physical survival, then human flourishing in any conventional sense required involvement in the imperial economy. The latter, in turn, was procured through manifestation of the appropriately-placed mark. Absent this passport, human well-being according to and amid imperial spaces would be gradually and inexorably strangled. Not being able to buy or sell may mean not being able to eat and live. If deception is anything less than completely effective, then economic coercion becomes the dragon's modus operandi, effected by his earthly sound-alike, the false prophet.

Within this economic sphere of consideration, John addresses his readers and hearers: "This calls for wisdom: let anyone with understanding calculate the number of the beast, for it is the number of a person. Its number is six hundred sixty-six" (13:18). There have

---

3. See also my essay, "Glocalization and the Gift-Giving Spirit: Informality and Shalom beyond the Political Economy of Exchange," *Journal of Youngsan Theology* 25 (2012): 7–29.

4. Smalley, *The Revelation to John*, 349.

been many efforts to decipher what is said here, including what the number might symbolize. Would not all faithful biblical interpreters want to exhibit the called-for wisdom, not least in light of John's invitation to carefully consider, even calculate the mark. For those who see the mortally wounded but restored sea beast as referring to the emperor Nero who was also a fierce persecutor of Christians, they observe that, "The Hebrew consonants used in spelling Nero's name, attested in an ancient document . . . , are *nron qsr*," and the addition "of each consonant's numerical equivalent (nun = 50 + resh = 200 + waw = 6 + nun = 50 + qoph = 100 + samekh = 60 + resh = 200) is 666."[5] Alternatively, the word "'Beast' (*therion*) can be transliterated into Hebrew as '*TRYVN*,' which also comes out to 666," so that "the number 'of the beast' is not surprisingly literally the 'beast'!"[6] Yet we also have to be honest with ourselves that two thousand years of extended computations have brought about more miscalculations than consensus. We are safest when we allow for John's symbolic imagination to provoke multiple significations, but the most theologically relevant is that the number six is one short of seven, which is John's number for perfection and completion. In that case, the tripling of six names futile, deceitful, and iniquitous humanity,[7] John's way of calling attention to both the finitude of the beast's mark and of the limitations of the imperial economy. The wisdom called for then relates not only to cognitive understanding but to practical response: How should Jesus' followers live in light of their (financial) estimations?[8]

FURTHER REFLECTIONS
The Almighty Dollar?

There is certainly nothing wrong with buying and selling insofar as our eating is in some measure predicated on such market

---

5. Wall, *Revelation*, 174–75.
6. Keener, *Revelation*, 356.
7. See Minear, *I Saw a New Earth*, 260.
8. Hence, the invitation to be wise (13:18) involves hearing, specially attending to and considering, and then obeying; see Anne-Mart Enroth, "The Hearing Formula in the Book of Revelation," *New Testament Studies* 36 (1990): 598–608, esp. 607.

exchanges. The issue is whether our market activities are beholden to the anti-christic imperial mechanisms that the earth beast's economic policies are designed to support. Would not any system of market interactions be blasphemous if it resulted in social veneration of the state's salvific capacities (as if political governance could provide that kind of ultimate safety for citizens, unending peace from strife, and conditions nurturing perpetual economic security)? The Roman imperium made such claims as evidenced in the pronouncement of Caesar being lord. The Pax Romana was the state's promise that its citizens could flourish under the Roman regime. The imperial cult in turn fostered worship of the emperors as conduits of such social, political, economic—indeed, civilizational—thriving. Response to any of these questions required discernment and wisdom so that John's call is least of all about solving numerological puzzles and much more about seeing through the world and its economic systems.[9]

Do twenty-first-century global citizens similarly look to their heads of state for such reassurances? Do we presume that our governments can and ought to act in ways that foster economic growth, secure peaceful communities, and enable personal freedoms and prosperity in a global and interconnected world? At the end of the day, is not the dollar or the yen or the euro, etc., almighty? Do not even democratic states sometimes—maybe oftentimes—vote less on principle values of justice, truth, and righteousness, than on the bottom economic line? If that is the case, are we not selling our collective souls to the principalities and powers in exchange for a sense of security at least in the short term? What are the long-term consequences of our bargain in these cases? If we are squeamish to think of our own situation as parallel to or implicated by John's vision of the earth beast, is that because it makes us feel uncomfortable to be so associated?

Here the Asian American location from which I write becomes a growing liability, given that the upward mobility aspired to

---

9. As suggested by John Christopher Thomas, "Pneumatic Discernment: The Image of the Beast and His Number," in S. J. Land, R. D. Moore, and J. C. Thomas, eds., *Passover, Pentecost, and Parousia: Studies in Celebration of the Life and Ministry of R. Hollis Gause*, Journal of Pentecostal Theology Supplement Series 35 (Blandford Forum, UK: Deo, 2010), 106–24.

and striven for by this immigrant group, among every other one, enables its apparently more rather than less successful attainments in pursuing the kinds of educational and related opportunities to excel in this climb, at least relatively speaking in comparison to other minoritized groups. It might be that on this matter we have drawn from the multiple resources of our perpetual foreigner experience to better the immigrant odds than others, but it could also be that we have so assimilated ourselves to the socioeconomic system and bought into its neoliberal and capitalistic rules—e.g., hard work, thrift, and deference to the majority (Eurocentric) culture—that we are merely reaping our just economic rewards. If the latter is the case, then we are more deeply imbricated into the market economy and less able to extract ourselves from its tentacles. We may not even desire to give up our achievements especially if we have decided that the outward marks of affluence in the contemporary global market are both too comfortable and enjoyable. In short, while being phenotypically and linguistically perpetual foreigners, we may be politically and economically indistinguishable from those who heed the earth beast or worship the image of its namesake!

We shall see later on (Rev. 18) that John is seriously concerned that the churches not be trapped in the (earth beast's) imperial economic system. For the moment, he only calls for wisdom, which is the capacity to see the deeper significance of not only what is before us but is the economic environment within which we literally live, move, and sustain our beings. The invitation to calculate the number of the beast anticipates, in a parodic sense, our constant and anxious assessments of our financial situation, particularly as they impinge on our future (retirement!) hopes and aspirations. May we not confuse the latter with what should be our ultimate commitments and hopes.[10]

10. Here, the upward mobility aspired to by all immigrants means that Asian Americans are not invulnerable to what cultural accommodation to the status quo makes possible. This is a particularly subtle form of "fitting in" with complexities that the coronavirus pandemic has exposed regarding the fragility of people of color in majority white societies. In other words, our economic livelihood specifically and our health and well-being more generally may be linked to and correlated with how deeply we are or allow ourselves to be absorbed by the cultural mainstream. The pull is practically invincible unless one can opt for a perpetual foreigner stance and be empowered (at least by the seven spirits) to persist in this vein.

14:1–5

The Lamb and the 144,000:
Being Set Apart as the Redeemed

Most beholders of the last three visions of the dragon and its beasts would in all likelihood come away with a sense of horror, especially since of the urgency with which their collective wrath is being expressed against earth's dwellers (see 12:12b), and not least in the ways in which the satanic triad has been and are mobilizing the political and economic mechanisms of the state for their ungodly purposes. The vision of Mount Zion that follows in 14:1–5 provides a reprieve and seeks to inject encouragement into what might otherwise be a hopelessly defeating reality. Mentioned only here in the Apocalypse, Mount Zion is otherwise a familiar reference in the Old Testament to the glorious city and dwelling place of the name and presence of YHWH, the Lord of Hosts and great king, on occasion identified as immovable against the nations of the world opposing YHWH's rule (Ps. 48:2; 125:1; Isa. 4:5; 8:10; 18:7; 29:8; 31:4; Mic. 4:7).[1] In many respects, this scene of Zion provides further perspective on how the blasphemies and deceptions of the satanic triad, even having galvanized the kingdoms and economic might of this world, are to be controverted. How might the people of God be set apart when they seem otherwise irremediably enmeshed and entangled with the systems of this world?

Here is where the Lamb returns to center stage, this time with the one 144,000 that we had heard sealed and marked before

1. Sometimes associated with Jerusalem (Isa. 24:23; Joel 2:32), Mount Zion is therefore steadfast except when abandoned by YHWH (Lam. 5:18); see also Joseph Jensen, "Mount Zion and Armageddon: A Tale of Two Eschatologies," in Daniel Durken, ed., *Sin, Salvation, and the Spirit: Commemorating the Fiftieth Year of the Liturgical Press* (Collegeville, MN: Liturgical Press, 1979), 134–45.

(7:3b), now more clearly seen as including the Lamb's name "and his Father's name written on their foreheads" (14:1b). While there is much scholarly conjecture about the relationship between these two identically enumerated groups, it is difficult to think that John means two distinct sets and more conceivable that by invoking this number, he is recalling the former scene—the intercalation between the opening of the sixth and seventh seals. Although we have already heard numerous celestial voices by now (e.g., 9:13; 10:4, 8; 11:12; 12:10), at this moment, another resounds from heaven. But this time the voice is more richly described (14:2a), first, "like the sound of many waters," identical to that of the one like the Son of Man in the opening vision (1:15b), and second, "like the sound of loud thunder," resonating in part with that of one of the four living creatures before the throne (6:1), with the booming of the seven thunders in tandem with the shout of the mighty angel (10:1, 3–4) also in the background. Uniquely, though, this voice spanning the heavens and Mount Zion was also harmonious and melodious, "like the sound of harpists playing on their harps" (14:2b).

The harmony and melody are essential in providing the music for the singing of the 144,000. We have already heard the living creatures (4:8) and twenty-four elders sing (4:10; cf. 11:16–17), and not just so-called oldies-but-goodies but also more specifically, at least one "new song" (5:8–9), and we have been privy also to listen in as these two groups have also been joined by the angelic hosts (5:11–12; cf. 7:12–13) and the creational choir (5:13). Here on Mount Zion, John hears the 144,000 "sing a new song before the throne and before the four living creatures and before the elders" (14:3a). This description is perhaps suggestive of Mount Zion's situatedness in the heavenly realm, albeit not necessarily so. Unlike the innovative tune of the latter two heavenly groups earlier (5:8–9), the new song is known only by the former crowd: "No one could learn that song except the one hundred forty-four thousand" (14:3b). Perhaps this is akin to John not being allowed to record or write down what the seven thunders uttered in response to the mighty angel's roar (10:4), but this also draws forward the promise to the church in Pergamum that their overcomers would be given a white stone with a new name that only they as recipients (and no one else) would know (2:17b).

Finally, for our purposes the 144,000 are said to be those "who have been redeemed from the earth" (14:3b). From the earlier seal interlude, we realize that these are the ones who have lived through the havoc and damage wrought by the four angels at and across the four corners of the earth, including its seas and vegetation (7:1–3a). While it is unclear whether their redemption from the world means that they are martyrs—and this obscurity also clouds the earlier vision—the connections in Revelation 7 with the great multitude makes it possible to see the 144,000 in that light. That would also be consistent with the witness borne in the visions of the dragon and beasts since they are given power to take the life of saints (12:11; 13:7b, 10). Suffering death because of their testimonial word, represented by the Father's name sealed on their foreheads, brings the enduring faithful to Mount Zion, into the presence of the Lamb.

Here, we are told further that their redemption has as much to do with the way they have been brought to Mount Zion as with the fact of their being there. More specifically, John writes that "It is these who have not defiled themselves with women, for they are virgins; these follow the Lamb wherever he goes. They have been redeemed from humankind as first fruits for God and the Lamb" (14:4).[2] Such symbolic celibacy surely contrasts with the fornication plaguing the mass of humanity uncovered by the sixth trumpet (9:21) even as it is consistent with the message warning the seven churches against the practice of sexual immorality (2:14b, 20–21). Although their military-like inventory earlier (7:4–8) suggests that these are soldiers of war

---

A gendered hermeneutic observes that, "Revelation rejects, even destroys, the more fully embodied sensuality presented by Babylon in favor of the New Jerusalem's idealized and abstract opulence."

Greg Carey, "A Man's Choice: Wealth Imagery and the Two Cities of the Book of Revelation," in Amy-Jill Levine, *A Feminist Companion to the Apocalypse of John*, 158.

---

2. This vision depicts the paradigmatic saints, those who are faithful in their discipleship after the Lamb; see Keith T. Marriner, *Following the Lamb: The Theme of Discipleship in the Book of Revelation* (Eugene, OR: Wipf & Stock, 2016), 167.

and battle, and this might invite us to read the portrayal here literally with regard to their virginity, the symbolism itself is elaborated
upon: "in their mouth no lie was found; they are blameless" (14:5).
In contrast to the machinations of the deceitful dragon and its
beastly operators, the redeemed of God and the Lamb are antithetical to falsehood, embodying instead truth in their lives and deeds
(the purity that is symbolized by asceticism attesting to this) and in
their words. The blasphemies of the evil triumvirate are countered
through the wholesomeness, truthfulness, and irreproachableness
of the 144,000.

FURTHER REFLECTIONS
Singing and Living the Truth

Living the truth provides us another window into how the saints
not only keep the divine commandments but also retain their testimony to Jesus and his word. If the 144,000 are but "first fruits" of
God and the Lamb's salvific work,[3] then any who follow in their
truthful and blameless footsteps can also experience the redemptive standing of Mount Zion. Such truthfulness is not just a matter
of earning an honest wage within the economic market (although
more on this later) but of authentically embodying the fullness of
the word representative of the Father's name that is emblazoned on
their foreheads. It also involves the faithful and persistent following
of the Lamb, the slaughtered one, regardless of the (economic and
other) costs.

On the one hand, perhaps Asian American believers of minoritized Christian communities can find encouragement that their marginalized experiences are part of the broader and more substantive
historical people of God symbolized by this large 144,000 number.
Followers of the Lamb ultimately are part of an innumerable group

---

3. In the end the 144,000 are part of the people of God and bride of Christ, no matter if they
are related to the martyrs from Rev. 7; see also Paul Middleton, "Male Virgins, Male Martyrs,
Male Brides: A Reconsideration of the 144,000 'Who Have Not Dirtied Themselves with
Women' (Revelation 14.4)," in Garrick V. Allen, Ian Paul, and Simon P. Woodman, eds., *The
Book of Revelation: Currents in British Research on the Apocalypse* (Tübingen: Mohr Siebeck,
2015), 193–208.

gathered from every tribe, tongue, and people, so even when we feel isolated in our circumstances, we can take comfort in our participation in a heavenly choir or orchestra singing and playing blissful instruments directed toward the throne.

On the other hand, perhaps the unknowability of the song of the 144,000 signals that the path charted by the Lamb's footsteps inevitably involves unpredictable twists and unforeseeable turns, and that each of us, individually and even amid the churches that we are constituted by, will have to navigate the Lamb's path extemporaneously in the divine spirit. Thus the template for faithful witness can only be general rather than be reducible to any three- or five-step formula that guarantees success. In other words, redemption and transport to Mount Zion will involve each of us—whether Asian American perpetual foreigners or white Christians—learning what is involved for ourselves, reliant surely on prior (even apocalyptic) maps but still involving new syntheses, discernments, and practices that break away from our culturally established conventions. Will we be steadfast in pursuit of the Lamb's trek, or will we be sidetracked by the allurements of the dragon and his affluent cities?

14:6–20

Seven Angelic Messages-Signs: Apocalyptic Living in the Spirit

It has already been mentioned (excursus C) that the following section of seven angelic messages and signs (Rev. 14) mediate between the unveiling of what may be called the axis of evil (the dragon and its beasts in Rev. 12–13) and the heavenly scene (Rev. 15) precipitating the seven (final) bowls of judgment (Rev. 16), similar to how the letters to the seven churches (Rev. 2–3) mediate between the initial unveiling of Jesus Christ (1:10–20) and the heavenly scene (Rev. 4–5) preceding the (initial) seals of judgment (Rev. 6). If the letters to the seven churches address most directly and exigently the original readers and hearers of this apocalyptic prophecy, then the seven angelic messages and signs—or speech-acts, when taken together—enables this same audience to transition from the evil plight pervasive of their current historical, social, and political-economic experience toward anticipation of the final judgments.[1] Whereas the earlier missives repeatedly remind the hearers that they ought to listen to what the divine spirit is saying to the churches, these angelic communications are punctuated by the only occasion of the spirit's sole and direct edifying word (14:13b).[2] How is life in the spirit understood resonating against this chorus of angelic voices and deeds?

1. *Speech-acts* are utterances that go beyond being informative to accomplishing an action or achieve results or states of affairs. Taken individually, two of the seven angels—the fourth and the sixth being revealed with sharp sickles—are mere signs. Yet, as shall be seen, both when wedded to the next angels that command use of the sickles, accomplish the harvest of grain and of grapes, even as the first three angels, with their sayings, are warning, enacting (judgment), and warning, respectively.
2. The epilogue of the Apocalypse closes with the divine spirit speaking also, but in that case in one voice with the bride of the Lamb (22:17).

The answer to this question cannot emerge except out of attentive consideration of what these angels are saying and doing. The first calls from the mid-heavens to "those who live on the earth—to every nation and tribe and language and people" (14:6b)—what John says is "an eternal gospel" (14:6a), one that is elaborated on thus: "Fear God and give him glory, for the hour of his judgment has come; and worship him who made heaven and earth, the sea and the springs of water" (14:7). We have not long ago been told, twice, that the powers of the dragon have mesmerized (11:9) and effectively subjugated (13:7) these same national/ethnic, tribal, linguistic, and people groups, so it is comforting to know that the creator of the whole cosmos along with its life-giving sources (e.g., seas and springs of water) loves the inhabitants of the earth so much that, rather than abandoning without hope those contaminated by wormwood (in the third trumpet judgment) to the devil's deceptions, instead seeks at this almost final moment to turn their attention to and capture their fidelity for (in worship) the only God that can save them.

The second angel now brings about an admonishment specifically regarding the anti-theistic forces of darkness, including the sociopolitical and economic regimes harnessed for those nefarious purposes. This angel says: "Fallen, fallen is Babylon the great! She has made all nations drink of the wine of the wrath of her fornication" (14:8). This is the first time that Babylon has been mentioned directly, and the seer will provide later a much more expansive version of the dirge bemoaning its fallenness. Yet Babylon, although only a world power for a relatively short period of time (605–539 BCE), had come to loom large in Israel's historical self-understanding since much of the Old Testament had emerged from out of its exile among the Chaldeans. The prophets of old had long ago pronounced judgment on Babylon, in language almost identical to what John hears (e.g., Isa. 21:9b), but it's passing away left not a vacuum but an opening that was filled by later imperial powers. The seer's visions have thus been preparing us variously for this announcement, especially in light of how the Roman regime had since been established with Palestine, among other regions of the known (Mediterranean) world, under its colonizing rule. Most messianic disciples would have recognized Babylon as a reference to Rome (e.g., 1 Pet. 5:13)—especially after the Roman destruction of Jerusalem in 70 CE when this second fall of the holy city would have been compared to its first sacking by the Babylonians in 587 BCE[3]—and not be taken aback by the slew of nations here said to lie in its grip, drunk with the wine of imperial immoralities, to paraphrase John. As John has already alluded to the political maneuverings of the sea beast, this angel now broadcasts her judgment and overturning, to be further explicated below.

The third angel has a lengthy message, as loud as the first angel's, that deepens the divine plot against the Babylonian (Roman) rule. Those who acquiesce religiously to the (Babylonian) dragon and its beasts or collude politically and economically with the dragon and its beasts will "drink the wine of God's wrath, poured unmixed into the cup of his anger, and they will be tormented with fire and sulfur in the presence of the holy angels and in the presence of the Lamb" (14:10). The temporary stupor brought about by the political and economic benefits of the Roman Empire here give way to the eternally grave potions of divine judgments. If the sulfurous plagues of the demonic cavalry inflicted humankind for their appointed year (9:15, 17), these fires from the divine cup of anger will everlastingly and without respite torment idolaters and those who pledge their commitments to the earth beast's commodification system (14:11). As we have already been introduced to the wrath of the Lamb (6:16b), it is not unexpected here to observe its convergence with the anger of God. Those whose sentiments are offended that the holy angels, not to mention the Lamb, here appear so vindictive as to effectively preside over the punishments of the wicked need only to be reminded that there is a major strand regarding retributive justice throughout the Bible that aspects of Revelation's visions accentuate, including when it is said of Israel regarding her oppressors, that "they shall go out and look at the dead bodies of the people who have rebelled against me; for their worm shall not die, their fire shall not be quenched, and they shall be an abhorrence to all flesh" (Isa. 66:24).[4]

At this moment, almost at the midpoint of the seven angelic

---

3. See Joseph Poon, *The Identities of the Beast from the Sea and the Beast from the Land in Revelation 13* (Eugene, OR: Pickwick, 2017), 151.
4. See Prigent, *Commentary on the Apocalypse of St. John*, 444; cf. Murphy, *Fallen Is Babylon*, 324.

messages and signs, the earlier call (13:10b) for the endurance and faith of the saints sounded out in response to the sea beast's politics of idolatry is repeated (14:12), followed by another voice, perhaps as subdued like that of the second angel's (rather than being booming like the first and third angels'), saying to John: "Write this: Blessed are the dead who from now on die in the Lord" (14:13a). Yes, this is indeed the word of the Lord, one that pronounced a blessing on the dead![5] And it is precisely within this frame that the divine spirit chimes in: "Yes, . . . they will rest from their labors, for their deeds follow them" (14:13b). There is a sense in which these are dire words for dire times, and even those depending wholly on the omnipotent creator God are promised by his spirit not deliverance from tragedy but relief after. I will return to this theme before the end of this section.

The fourth angel is probably, in the end, no other than Jesus the Messiah. Having been revealed initially as "one like the Son of Man" (1:13), John now describes "a white cloud, and seated on the cloud was one like the Son of Man, with a golden crown on his head, and a sharp sickle in his hand!" (14:14). On the other hand, while the twenty-four elders have crowns on their heads and the woman assailed by the dragon has a crown with twelve stars on her head, Jesus is nowhere said to have such. Now it is true that this Danielic phrase (Dan. 7:13) could just as correctly be translated "one like a human being,"[6] and taken in this way, a human-looking angel on a cloud could then be more easily comprehended as responding to another angel's command to harvest the earth; further, if Jesus was who John saw, this figure is referred to twice in short order not as this apparent Son of Man but in terms of his seated posture and cloud location (14:15–16). Be that as it may, Jesus here appears also as an angelic figure,[7] the fourth in this sequence of angelic speech-acts.

The fifth and sixth angels both emerge from out of the heavenly temple (recall it was opened earlier: 11:19) and combine to extend

---

5. Mangina, *Revelation*, 177.
6. Aune, *Revelation 6–16*, 801.
7. Loren T. Stuckenbruck, *Angel Veneration and Christology: A Study in Early Judaism and in the Christology of the Apocalypse of John* (1995; reprint, Waco, TX: Baylor University Press, 2017), 242–44, suggests that this one like the Son of Man here has angelic functions even if semantically connected to Jesus in Rev. 1.

and exceed the work of the "one like the Son of Man" just referred to. The former calls on the one on the cloud to reap the ripe harvest of the earth (14:15–16), and the latter arrives also with a sharp sickle (exactly what the one on the cloud also had) to "gather the clusters of the vine of the earth" (14:18b). Just as the fifth angel commands the fourth's harvesting activity, so also is there a seventh angel from the (heavenly, it is presumed) altar that commands the sixth's reaping of grapes to be then thrown "into the great wine press of the wrath of God" (14:19b). This heptad of angelic messages-signs ends with John seeing that "the wine press was trodden outside the city, and blood flowed from the wine press, as high as a horse's bridle, for a distance of about two hundred miles" (14:20). Although perhaps drawn from various prophetic texts—the first part about the wine press from imagery of judgment already voiced by the third angel (14:10a),[8] not to mention prophetically announced on the nations (e.g., Isa. 63:2–6), and the second part about the height of the bloodshed from Israel's having to bury those fallen by God in its battle against God (Ezek. 39:11-14)—the point is that the extent of the carnage is unfathomable, and that the divine judgment that presses obdurately forward "outside the city" means that even the Babylonian imperial powers are bared as impotent against what is no more than a (divinely authorized angelic) sickle.

Together, then, it is suggested that the figure on the cloud gathers the harvest of the righteous while the latter temple angel executes the judgment of the wicked.[9] This division of labor (grain and grape harvests) is prefigured among the prophets (see Joel 3:13) and also alluded to in Jesus' teachings about the ingathering of wheat and chaff or weeds (Matt. 2:12; 13:30). What begins the first angelic messages-sign as the final call and opportunity for repentance granted to the full extent of earth's inhabitants grinds relentlessly to judgment, determining in the process the fated dissolution of the imperial city and economic network undergirding the dragon's deceptions and climaxing with the harvesting of human creatures,

---

8. The great wine press of the wrath of God overflows here in 14:19–20, and recurs through the end of the judgments, e.g., 19:15b; as Aune, *Revelation 6–16*, 834, shows, alternative images are the *cups* of divine anger (14:10a, 16:19b) and the *bowls* of divine fury (15:7b; 16:1).

9. Fee, *Revelation*, 202.

including (presumably) the saints with their rewards (such as rest from their labors: 14:13b), and sinners with their just desserts. The latter will not be overlooked as the divine anger and wrath (14:10, 19b) have been provoked and will be irretrievably poured out and pressed upon.

FURTHER REFLECTIONS
Confronting Death

These are heavenly signs, but they have earthly consequences. For earthlings, in particular for those seeking to remain faithful to the Messiah, the spirit's word is both a blessing and the promise, but in each case, inclusive of rather than involving rescue from death (14:13). Other portions of Scripture might suggest a more triumphant type of life in the holy spirit, but these angelic speech-acts and signs are meant to sustain the disciples of Jesus in and through death. This is not to valorize martyrdom, but it is to name the redemptive plan of God accomplished through death and resurrection, first and foremost through the slain Lamb who is also the Son of Man. If contemporaries are more accustomed to understanding the eternal gospel in terms of good news, these angelic signs combine to admonish any health and wealth interpretation as being more aligned with a Babylon that is fading away. Instead, the apocalyptic rendition of the gospel invites us to expand our notions of what *good* might mean. To the degree that all of us die in any case, the promise of the spirit is that our efforts are not in vain and that our deeds, if aligned with that of the messianic Lamb, will leave a legacy beyond our expiration.

Walking out that kind of life in the spirit may be more radical than the supernaturalistic charismaticism that otherwise permeates segments of the contemporary global pentecostal movement. The power to be witnesses promised through the outpouring of the holy spirit (Acts 1:8) turns out to be true especially insofar as the messianic disciples do so according to the apocalyptic script: "they have conquered him by the blood of the Lamb and by the word of their testimony, for they did not cling to life even in the face of death" (12:11). Asian American experiences in particular and those who find themselves as perpetual foreigners more generally may be more prepared to embrace such an apparently disempowered identity. The truth is, however, that to be betwixt-and-between when we are in Christ is to more restfully enjoy the labor and more fully participate in the works of his spirit that actualize the good news of redemption and judgment. Otherwise, we toil on our own strength following our own ambitions from which come effects that belong with what is trodden in the great wine press of divine wrath.

15:1-8

The End, as at the Beginning: Replaying the Song of Moses

The seven angelic messages and signs give way immediately to another heptad of angels, this time with the seven plagues, "which are the last, for with them the wrath of God is ended" (15:1b). John describes this as "another portent in heaven," not only a "great portent" like the "woman clothed with the sun" earlier (12:1a), but one both "great and amazing" (15:1a). We are on the cusp of the end-of-the-end, then; but before we take this final plunge, we are invited to comprehend these ultimate judgments against the broader scope of God's covenantal and salvation history. For this, John sees and hears Moses's song, and this enables consideration of the final judgments that the church now envisions in relationship to the Egyptian plagues that the ancient Hebrews lived through to witness about. As their liberation was also the judgment of the Egyptians, so here also the final salvation of the people of God will include judgment on the beasts and those who receive their message and mark. What does it mean for us today to also sing and enact the song of Moses?

Just as seven angels blew the trumpet judgments (8:1, 6), so here seven angels, this time "robed in pure bright linen, with golden sashes across their chests" (15:6b)—the latter mirroring that over the chest of the one like the Son of Man in the first vision (1:13b)—enact the seven final wrathful plagues. They are assisted by one of the four living creatures, each of which not only had called forth one of the horses released by the breaking of the first four seals (6:1–7), but also all along holding "a harp and golden bowls full of incense, which are the prayers of the saints" (5:8b). We might further recall that the breaking of the seventh seal introduced the heptad of trumpet judgments that were catalyzed by the "prayers of all the saints on the golden altar that is before the throne" (8:3b), and these prayers appear to continue in efficacy as this appointed living creature in this instance gives the heptad of angels "seven golden bowls full of the wrath of God" (15:7). The judgments of seals and trumpets are now culminating with that of the bowls.

It is within this narrative movement that the great and amazing heavenly portent is even more remarkable and stunning. John sees "what appeared to be a sea of glass mixed with fire, and those who had conquered the beast and its image and the number of its name, standing beside the sea of glass with harps of God in their hands" (15:2). This is no less than the sea of glass before the heavenly throne (4:6) even as the mixture of fire hearkens to the last of the recent beatific messages-signs, which told of the angel that had "authority over fire" (14:18a). More important, the blessing for the dead and promise of the spirit (14:13) given amid the angelic speech acts confirm precisely what the third in that sequence warned against: that whereas worshipers of the beast and its image and recipients of its number and mark would be judged by fire and sulfur in the presence of the Lamb, here those who had neither kowtowed to the beast or its image nor succumbed to being marked by its number or name are not being tormented by fire but are blessedly resting from their labors by a fiery sea of glass and worshiping God and the Lamb.

These conquerors "sing the song of Moses, the servant of God, and the song of the Lamb" (15:3a).[1] The latter has already stimulated a new song, initially from the four living creatures and twenty-four elders (5:8–9) and subsequently, it is strongly implied, from the 144,000 who perhaps echo their heavenly predecessors but do so as strict followers of the Lamb (14:2–4).[2] Even if the Lamb's song here is different from what has been noted before, its retrieval of the song

1. For John's reliance on the Exodus narrative, see HaYoung Son, *Praising God beside the Sea: An Intertextual Study of Revelation 15 and Exodus 15* (Eugene, OR: Wipf & Stock, 2017).
2. If the singers here are the 144,000 from the Mount Zion—Skaggs and Benham give some reasons why (*Revelation*, 158), to which it might also be added that the earlier singing sounded in part like harps (14:2b) even as the current conquering group appears specifically holding harps (15:2b), now complementing the harpist elders and living creatures (5:8)—then the new song sang there is here revealed as the song of Moses remixed or redubbed; further, if the group here who has "conquered the beast and its image and the number of its name" is the same as the 144,000 from Mount Zion, then the triumph of this group would have been achieved through their being marked with the Father's name on their foreheads (7:3–4a; 14:1a) rather than with the number of the beast.

of Moses, which the Torah already identified as servant of YHWH (Exod. 14:31), connects the narrative here with one of the central stories of Israel's self-understanding: the liberation from Egypt.

In the Torah, there are two songs associated with Moses, the first one celebrating deliverance from Egypt, including destruction of Pharaoh and his armies in the Red Sea (Exod. 15:1–18), and the second recited at the end of his life in relationship to the transition of leadership over Israel to Joshua (Deut. 32:1–43). Although drawn more from across the Old Testament than specifically from either of these two songs, the invocation of Moses here not only recollects how God used him to deliver the Hebrews from the grip of Pharaoh through the ten plagues (Exod. 7:14–11:10), but also makes clear that like the people of God who were vindicated from their Egyptian oppressors, so also will the church triumph over their beastly tormentors, including the nations and empires that intentionally collude with or acquiesce to such ecclesial subjugation and harassment. In case it was missed that the bowls and trumpets were eschatological renditions of the plagues that visited ancient Egypt, here the Moses reference solidifies the seer's imaginative vision. Even if not all of the Egyptian plagues are included, the table on the next page reveals how the trumpets and bowls are particularly aligned, and cumulatively, how the three heptads of judgments visit upon the kingdoms of the dragon and its beasts the judgments dispensed against the Egyptians for their tyrannizing the covenant people of God and not heeding their deity's instructions.

The song of Moses and of the Lamb provide occasion for the conquerors to worship God in anticipation of the final judgments. The great and amazing portent of seven angels with seven plagues prompts correlative tributes: "*Great and amazing* are your deeds, Lord God the Almighty!" (15:3a, italics added). Besides eliciting the relevant emotions (fear in the presence of awesomeness) and reactions (that related to glorifying the name of God), the conquerors recognize God's central attributes: "Just and true are your ways. . . . For you alone are holy" (15:3b–4a). And if the nations will trample over the city of God and those striving to be faithful to him (11:2), gloated over the death of the two witnesses (11:9–10), raged against God (11:18a), and fornicated with imperial Rome

Comparison of Revelation's Heptads with Egyptian Plagues				
Number	*Seals*	*Trumpets*	*Bowls*	*Egyptian plagues*[3]
1st	white horse: conquering	fiery hail on earth: grass and trees burnt (1/3)	on earth: painful sores	Nile river turns into blood
2nd	red horse: peace to war	fiery mountain into sea: death and destruction (1/3)	on seas: death	Nile river emits frogs
3rd	black horse: famine (esp. wheat and barley)	fiery star falls on rivers and springs of water (1/3): bitter (death)	on rivers and springs of water: turned into blood	death of livestock
4th	pale green horse: death (1/4)	sun struck: darkness (1/3)	on sun: scorching heat	dust turn into boils on Egyptians and animals
5th	souls under the heavenly altar	demonic locusts	on throne of beast: darkness	hailstorm (destroying flax and barley crops)
6th	apocalyptic phenomena and earthquake	demonic cavalry	on Euphrates: kings of the East and the earth assembled by demonic frogs	devouring locusts
7th	silence in heaven	opening of heavenly temple and celebration of God's judgments	on air; great earthquake and huge hailstones	total darkness over Egypt

3. This column does not include the third (gnats), fourth (flies), and final (death of the firstborn) Egyptian plagues since they do not have a counterpart in the three heptads of Revelation's

(Babylon) (14:8), the conquerors here also recognize the Lord God Almighty as "King of the nations" (15:3b; cf. Jer. 10:7a) and worshipfully announce: "All nations will come and worship before you, for your judgments have been revealed" (15:4b; cf. Ps. 86:9). Just as Israel on the other side of the Red Sea could come to celebrate their redemption (at the expense of the Egyptians), so also these conquering ones worship the just, true, and holy one while realizing he will deal righteously with the nations/ethnicities and they will, through this painful process, come to worship him.

As Jon Morales notes, unlike the earth-dwellers, "In Revelation, *the nations never worship the beast* . . . while the nations are under strong, satanic influence, God is their king, Jesus is their shepherd, and the church is their prophet," guiding them to the eternal city (see comments on 21:22–22:5).

Jon Morales, *Crist, Shepherd of the Nations: The Nations as Narrative Character and Audience in John's Apocalypse,* Library of New Testament Studies 377 (New York and London: Bloomsbury, 2018), 108 (italics his).

With this hymn, the table is set for the final judgments. John thus records, "After this I looked, and the temple of the tent of witness in heaven was opened, and out of the temple came the seven angels with the seven plagues" (15:5–6a). The Greek here is obscure even as the sense is confusing since the tent of witness refers to the period of the sojourn through the Sinai desert whereas the temple belongs to the monarchic period much later. Yet given the appeal to Moses' song in this context, the main point is that the final judgments derive from nowhere else than from the very presence of God, symbolized by the temple and the inner holy spaces. John had already seen something very similar following the blowing of the seventh trumpet and his hearing the voices in heaven and the twenty-four elders announce how the nations (and ethnic groups) of this world will be brought into the messianic kingdom (11:15–18), where and when he wrote: "God's temple in heaven was opened, and the ark of his

---

judgments nor are they alluded to in the final canonical book; in any case, as Ford (*Revelation,* 282) notes, disobedience against and rejection of the divine commandments will bring about the diseases and disasters foisted on the Egyptians (Deut. 28:60), which is precisely what happens here in the final judgments against an idolatrous world obstinately refusing to abide in relationship with their creator.

covenant was seen within his temple" (11:19a). This earlier vision regarding the opening of the heavenly temple is now further specified so that the provenance of the seven angels with their plagues can be discerned. That the conquerors are now standing beside rather than on the fiery glass sea is suggestive since the association of fiery and glassy sea with the seven angels from the temple invokes images of fire being "the stir stick that God uses to whip the sea into a judgmental froth."[4] Contrary to the smoke emanating from the bottomless pit (9:2), here the smoke filling the heavenly temple stems from the divine glory and power (15:8a), perhaps also contributed to by the smoke of incense arising from the prayers of the saints under the altar (8:3–4). From here on, entry back into the temple is inhibited, "until the seven plagues of the seven angels were ended" (15:8b). The divine wrath will be emptied out via the angelic bowls (see 16:1b, 19b), and nothing can stop that.

FURTHER REFLECTIONS
Singing the Song of Moses and the Lamb

According to John, as with Qohelet the preacher, there is not much new under the sun (Eccl. 1:9b). The ends of God are as the beginning: as the Hebrews spent four hundred years under Egyptian domination (Gen. 15:3; Acts 7:6) before they were delivered and vindicated by YHWH and their tormentors judged, so also the church will for a season struggle amid the dominion of the dragon and its imperial constituents before she will be liberated by the one on the throne and the Lamb and her deceiving overlords given to drink of the bowls of divine wrath. As the Hebrews cried out to their God and then celebrated with Moses in the wake of their deliverance, so also can the church today pray to the Almighty one and continue to sing Moses's song, albeit attuned now to the Lamb's new key. Those who are not singing the song of Moses and the Lamb may be worshiping the deceiver instead, acting unjustly, speaking untruthfully, and living in unholy ways. They who are not glorifying the name

4. Blount, *Revelation*, 284.

of the Lord now will not worship before him (now or later) but risk coming under the wrathful judgment of the Lamb.

The key here is the dynamic journey from out of Egypt to the New Jerusalem that is coming. Only those who settle down in any one space (land, nation, etc.) are in danger of assimilating to the dominant culture. To sing the song of Moses and the Lamb is to keep looking ahead, to press betwixt-and-between what is seductive on either side. This means that Asian Americans ought instead to embrace their perpetual foreigner identity and journey in order to be aligned with the Lamb rather than with either Asia or America; this means also that contemporary followers of the Lamb ought to embrace the song of the immigrant Moses rather than the songs of either Egypt or of Sinai. Our earthly comforts and privileges should be held loosely since they are being revealed as transitory by the present divine judgments in anticipation of the time when the sea will turn to glass.[5]

---

5. One of the lessons of the coronavirus may be to impress upon us how life is characterized more by disruptions than by any sense of normalcy. Even after vaccinations are widespread, our world will not revert to some idealized version of what was before, but it will continue to reverberate unpredictably in the wake of the dynamic fluctuations unleashed by the pandemic. Liminality and the constancy of being in-between will be the new norm so agility and adaptability will be what enables flourishing. See my guest editorial introduction to "In Between," *Fuller: Story, Theology, Voice* 20 (spring 2021): 38–39, and the essays in the following pages of this issue.

16:1–21
The Seven Bowls of Judgment:
Staying Awake through the Night

In this central part of the book of Revelation, we have been building since the opening of the seven seals toward these final judgments. But although the seal and trumpet heptads occurred relatively closely together, it's been a while, narratively, since the sounding of the last trumpet. During this time, we have been introduced more explicitly and at length to the ultimate source of the cosmic rebelliousness and its negative impact on human creatures: the dragon and its beasts and the seven angelic speech-acts have also weighed in and found their deeds wanting and deserving of judgment. The seven bowls enact these judgments, albeit without the major digressions that gave pause to the progression of the prior heptads.[1] What we have instead is what amounts to a brief, almost parenthetical, aside during the sixth of these rapidly poured out bowls, and that provides us a window into how the followers of God and the Lamb might or should respond, regardless of whether they will be preserved amid these plagues (as were some of the ancient Hebrews) or be martyred for their commitments.

Since the temple is declared to be empty while the bowls of plagues are being emptied out (15:8b), the "loud voice from the temple telling the seven angels, 'Go and pour out on the earth the seven bowls of the wrath of God'" (16:1) must be that of the Lord

---

1. Thankfully our purposes do not need to adjudicate between the seemingly as many structural frames discerned of these bowls as there are scholarly interpreters of Revelation (e.g., 3+1+1+1+1; 3+2+1+1; 4+1+1+1; 5+1+1); for further discussion, see Pieter G. R. de Villiers, "The Septet of Bowls in Revelation 15:1–16:21 in the Light of Its Composition," *Acta Patristica et Byzantina* 16 (2005): 196–222.

God Almighty.[2] Rather than provide a bowl-by-bowl assessment, we proceed with some summary perspective on the first five of these judgments (16:2–11). First, these bowls are emptied, on the earth, the sea, the rivers and springs of water, the sun, and the throne of the sea beast (see 13:2) respectively. While the first four bowls are aimed at the same targets as their counterpart trumpet judgments, the difference is that whereas in the earlier foray only a third of the seas turned into blood, a third of the sea creatures perished, and a third of the ships were ruined, now "every living thing in the sea died" as the seas "became like the blood of a corpse" (16:3b). Besides the death of these sea creatures, the results of the other outpoured bowls include foul and painful sores "on those who had the mark of the beast and who worshiped its image" (16:2b); the rivers and springs that had become bitterly deadly (8:11b) turn into blood (16:4b); and the sun, darkened from the fourth trumpet (8:12b), here becomes fiercely scorching and heated (16:8–9a) while the kingdom of the beast whose throne is struck is "plunged into darkness" (16:10). How do the inhabitants of the earth respond? After the fourth and fifth bowl, it is repeated that despite their painful sores, people cursed God in heaven, and his name, and persisted in unrepentant obstinacy (16:9, 11), even as the thickness of the darkness, no doubt in part symbolizing the utter alienation of evil hearts not just from God but from one another, brings forth a horrifying pain depicted only by the seer's passing description that those under the beast's regal sway "gnawed their tongues in agony" (16:10b).

After John describes the seas and the rivers and springs of water turning into blood, he writes, "I heard the angel of the waters say, 'You are just, O Holy One, who are and were, for you have judged these things; because they shed the blood of saints and prophets, you have given them blood to drink. It is what they deserve!' And I heard the altar respond, 'Yes, O Lord God, the Almighty, your judgments are true and just!'" (16:5–7). First, as the earth and its elements are being struck as part of these final judgments, we hear here the responses of angelic voices representing or having custody over these creational forces. If there are angelic authorities over the

---

2. See Ford, *Revelation*, 269.

winds, the sun, and fire (7:1, 2; 14:18), this time the keeper of the waters perhaps feels the need to provide an apologetic for their being turned (ubiquitously it seems) into blood: so that those who have shed the blood of saints and prophets will now in turn have their blood shed. If the earth is being destroyed by the dragon's followers (11:18b), then these judgments are divine means of renewing the world.[3] Second, the altar (see also 6:9; 8:3, 5; 9:13; 11:1; 14:18) responds, effectively with an "Amen," to the angel of the waters, no doubt related to its channeling the prayers of the saints whose blood had been shed that in turn brought about the divine judgments. Third, as those singing the song of Moses and the Lamb had declared the King of the nations to be just, holy, and true (15:3b–4a), this triad of assertions are reiterated by what the angel of the waters and the altar say. Last but not least, the Holy One is recognized as being/ existing in the present and in the past, and perpetually having persisted: "are and were"; but rather than repeating the by now expected refrain about also being the one who is coming (the future on its way), that is left out and replaced instead by the fact that it is the divine judgments that we have been waiting for from the future that are now being presently executed.[4]

The sixth bowl is poured out on the Euphrates river from where the sixth trumpet had earlier released the huge demonic cavalry (9:14–19). If before the drying up of the Red Sea facilitated Israel's escape from Egypt (Exod. 14) and the hardening of the Jordan river allowed Israel to cross over to the land of promise (Josh. 3),[5] ironically here an emptying out (of this bowl of judgment) that dries up achieves the opposite effect: that of releasing the (Roman-feared) kings of East to not only be an instrument of divine judgment on the beastly kingdom but also to then gather with "the kings of the whole world, to assemble them for battle on the great day of God the Almighty" (16:14b). Orchestrating this invasion are "three

---

3. Here I follow Curtis Johnson, "The Earth's *Ethos*, *Logos*, and *Pathos*: An Ecological Reading of Revelation," *Currents in Theology and Mission* 41:2 (2014): 119–27, whose argument reminds us that our care for the world ought to follow God's concerns for its renewal and redemption, because God "created *all* things, and by your will they existed and were created" (4:11b, italics added).

4. See Prigent, *Commentary on the Apocalypse of St. John*, 466–67.

5. Ford, *Revelation*, 342.

foul spirits like frogs coming from the mouth of the dragon, from the mouth of the beast, and from the mouth of the false prophet" (16:13). These are "demonic spirits"—a demonic trinity, effectively—who continue in their efforts to lead astray those who are gnawing their tongues in agony not only in and through their many lying words but also in their actions, "performing signs" deceitfully so that worshipers of the beast's image and holders of its mark perceive they can go against the Almighty and prevail (16:14a).

These froggish demons gather the kings of the East and the world and "assembled them at the place that in Hebrew is called Harmagedon" (16:16). Although literally this translates as *mount of Megiddo*, this city in ancient Israel was situated on a plain (2 Chr. 35:22; Zech. 12:11). But if we associate this final battle of worldly kings against the Almighty with those later explicated in the Apocalypse (19:14–21; 20:8–9), then the imagery here can be clarified by those deployed later, including especially the situating of the decisive conflagration vis-à-vis the Gog and Magog (20:8) prophesied by Ezekiel as unfolding in the end against Israel (Ezek. 36–38). In the Ezekielian prophecy, as Pierre Prigent puts it, "God will rise up at the head of his troops to launch an eschatological assault on 'the mountains of Israel' (Ezek. 38:8; 39:2, 4, 17)."[6] We already know from the seer's visions that rather than being a refuge for those who have resisted keeping the divine commandments, the mountains of this world will be radically moved and shaken with drastic consequences for human creatures (6:14–16; 8:8–9), and this is reiterated with what follows after the pouring out of the seventh bowl (16:20; cf. also Ezek. 38:19).[7] From this perspective then, the sixth bowl unveils not the locale of any end-times war but the conclusive demise of the unholy trinity and especially its humanly gathered forces. Will onlookers—hearers and readers of this book—thereby choose to line up with the kings of this world and their demonic leaders on the (figurative) Mount Megiddo, or will they instead anticipate standing

---

6. Prigent, *Commentary on the Apocalypse of St. John*, 475.
7. For more on the role of Ezekiel in John's symbolism of the seven bowls of judgment and their aftermath (16:17–19:10), see Jean Pierre Ruiz, *Ezekiel in the Apocalypse: The Transformation of Prophetic Language in Revelation 16,17–19,10*, European University Studies XXIII, Theology 376 (New York: Peter Lang, 1989), part III.

with the Lamb and those redeemed on the earth on (spiritualized and idealized) Mount Zion?[8]

Before contemplating further this binarily articulated question, we need to see what happens with the final bowl. Poured out "into the air," effectively on the cosmos wholly considered, once again, the (divine) voice calls from the heavenly temple and throne saying, "It is done!" (16:17). The expected apocalyptic phenomena follow— "flashes of lightning, rumblings, peals of thunder, and a violent earthquake" (16:18a)—with two elaborations. Beginning with what appears second, John sees "huge hailstones, each weighing about a hundred pounds, dropped from heaven on people, until they cursed God for the plague of the hail, so fearful was that plague" (16:21). The fiery hail of the first trumpet (8:7a) and the "heavy hail" following the trumpeting of the third woe (11:18b) now are magnified and massified, but this results, as with the Egyptian plagues where Pharaoh and his people further hardened their hearts (e.g., Exod. 7:13, 22; 8:15, 32; 9:7, 34), not in repentance but in the extension of the profane cursing precipitated already by the vastly contrary conditions of scorching heat and agonizing blackness (16:9, 11). More important, the accompanying earthquake's fierceness, furiousness, and ferocity are accentuated: "such as had not occurred since people were upon the earth, so violent was that earthquake," with the result that "the great city was split into three parts, and the cities of the nations fell" (6:18b–19a). Although earlier the "great city" referred to Jerusalem (11:8), the prophet here clarifies that with this vicious earthquake "God remembered great Babylon and gave her the wine-cup of the fury of his wrath" (16:19b). Equally important is that while the great city (so repeatedly called: 17:18; 18:10, 16, 18, 19, 21) of Babylon is judged through this quake, Babylon is symbolic of Rome, which is itself constituted imperially by its reach over the known world. Thus, the quake judgment strikes not one locale but also "the cities of the nations" and in that sense assures that the divine justice has massive terrestrial reach. The implication may also

---

8. I am helped with this contrast by Joseph Jensen, O.S.B., "Mount Zion and Armageddon: A Tale of Two Eschatologies," in Daniel Durken, O.S.B., ed., *Sin, Salvation, and the Spirit: Commemorating the Fiftieth Year of The Liturgical Press* (Collegeville, MN: Liturgical Press, 1979), 134–45.

be that this judgment exceeds in severity any preceding calamities, experienced in a way "such as had not occurred since people were upon the earth," John puts it, which subordinates the horror of prior judgments, including that of Pharaoh and the Egyptians but also that of the worldwide Noahic flood, in comparison with the finality of this seventh and final bowl.[9]

Mention of God's remembering the sins of Babylon at this point opens up naturally to the extended description in Revelation 17–18 of how the outpoured divine wrath executes justice over the city's imperial domain. Before turning there, however, what can be said at this intermediate stage, knowing full well that these final judgments pronounced on the world domination system that is especially hostile to God's servants, saints, and prophets will yet receive much elaboration by the seer of Patmos? We are invited to consider this question by the christologically voiced aside—in this case, the third of seven macarisms in Revelation—inserted toward the end of the sixth bowl, which our English translation depicts parenthetically: "('See, I am coming like a thief! Blessed is the one who stays awake and is clothed, not going about naked and exposed to shame')" (16:15). The Messiah's return is both expected but also unpredictable, "like a thief" (cf. 3:3; Matt. 24:43; 1 Thess. 5:2). The blessing here retrieves both the promises and the warnings (respectively) to the Sardians (3:4–5a) and the Laodiceans (3:18), so that they are not immediately exposed amid the final battle but also, more generally, not shamed in falling away after repeated admonitions.

FURTHER REFLECTIONS
Being Vigilant

Given the awful nature of the final bowl judgments, some of us might simply wish to be safely secured away until the storm blows over. On the other hand, the character of this blessing suggests that no such "easy out" is possible. The faithful are not allowed to sleep

9. See Ralph J. Korner, "The 'Great Earthquake' Judgment in the Apocalypse: Is There an Urzeit for this Endzeit?" *ARC: The Journal of the Faculty of Religious Studies, McGill University* 39 (2011): 143–70.

through the night and awaken safely at dawn. Instead, faithfulness requires vigilance throughout the night, despite the sounds of gnawing tongues and notwithstanding the utterances of blasphemous recalcitrance that these who are undefiled, truth-loving, and blameless would otherwise prefer not to overhear. Conventionally received, then, this blessing is not practically better than being cursed, at least not in the sense that to listen to the outcomes of the outpoured bowls is in some respects to experience those effects. Alternatively, to fall and stay asleep is also to abdicate messianic discipleship and be exposed to different risks, including the kind of stupor that may not allow escape from the deceits of demonic spirits performing signs and all of the divine wrath such incurs.

And the reality is that only those who are "not at home," so to speak, are more likely to remain awake at night, while those who are most secure and comfortable are in turn more likely to sleep soundly until daybreak. Immigrants, outsiders, the marginalized—the perpetual foreigners—may be more vigilant, unless they are exhausting themselves climbing the ladder of upward social mobility toward the center of the dominant culture. The point here is not to inculcate anxiety over being "left behind" but to emphasize that it is only by keeping our eyes on the slain Lamb who is also arisen and coming that we can avoid being seduced by the (false) signs and wonders that are concocted during this era to deceive the inhabitants of the world but that are destined to finally be exposed, condemned, and swallowed up forever and ever.

Excursus D
The Fall of Babylon and the Arrival of the New Jerusalem (Chapters 17:1–22:5)

Having moved through the heart of the book of Revelation with its judgment heptads of seals, trumpets, and bowls, we are coming to the final and concluding part of the book. It is timely, then, that we gather our thoughts about how the seer brings his visions to a close, and we will do that by both looking backward and looking forward. We shall also take the opportunity to reflect more critically on the dominant role of gender that comes to the fore in this last section of the Apocalypse, engaging particularly feminist perspectives on the matter.

In the most immediate vicinity, narratively, the next two visions (broadly construed: Rev. 17–18), elucidate the judgment and fall of Babylon enacted by the final bowl (16:19), which was also previously announced by the second of the angelic messages-signs (14:8). Babylon is here personified as a great whore (17:1–5) even as it in turn stands in for the city of Rome and its imperial powers that are animated demonically by the beastly liege from the bottomless pit (9:11a; 11:7a; 17:8a). The whorish Babylon is exposed, especially its political powers (Rev. 17), and then portrayed as overthrown and devastated, particularly its economic supremacy (Rev. 18). Once completely undercut, the saints, servants, and prophets of the Almighty are vindicated, and the creatures of God, those redeemed from the earth and the heavenly ones also, celebrate the final victory (19:1–10). From this perspective, the vision of the great whore and Babylon's final dismantling followed by the final jamboree are a fitting finale to the three heptads of judgments, and in that sense part and parcel of the central part of the book.

On the other hand, read pneumatologically, the debut of the whore is signaled as distinct by John's own admission that for this vision he is escorted "in the spirit" (17:3a), similarly to when he was moved from addressing the churches into the heavenly throne room (4:2a) from whence the heptads of seals, trumpets, and bowls originated. Thus it makes sense to see Revelation 17 and what follows as related to but disparate from the judgment heptads. Read in this way, the central trunk of the Apocalypse, Revelation 6–16, is fed by a prolonged introductory route (Rev. 1–5) and a protracted concluding section (Rev. 17–22). From this perspective it is thus arguable that the six introductory sections can be read chiastically relative to the six concluding sections, as follows:

A—Prologue: 1:1–9

  B—The Unveiling of Jesus Christ: 1:10–20

    C—Letters to the Seven Churches: 2:1–3:22

      D—The elevated/heavenly throne of God: 4:1–11

        E—The glorious Lamb: 5:1–14

        The central section: three heptads of judgments: 6:1–16:21

        E′—The detestable Babylon: 17:1–18

      D′—Fallen Babylon: 18:1–19:11

    C′—Seven final visions: 19:11–22:5[1]

  B′—The last words of Jesus Christ: 22:6–16

A′—Epilogue: 22:17–21

Looked at from this perspective, the vision of the great whore and her demise is the beginning of the end of the book of Revelation.

A pneumatological reading invites also further comment since John's transportation "in the spirit" moves him from a wilderness scene where he views the great whore to a mountaintop site where he sees the new Jerusalem (21:10), "coming down out of heaven from God, prepared as a bride adorned for her husband" (21:2b). As there is extensive observation about the eventual plight of the great whore (17:1–18:24), so also is there comprehensive portrayal of the bride of the Lamb (21:9b).[2] Additionally, both of these female figures are introduced by "one of the seven angels who had the seven bowls" (17:1a; 21:9a). This means that over half of these closing pages—65 verses (17:1–18:24 + 21:10–22:5) of the 126 left (Rev. 17–22)—and concluding moments (for those who experience the book audibly) of the Apocalypse are taken up with the juxtaposing of two female images: the great whore and the Lamb's bride and wife.

Here it is befitting to consider one of the more critical issues that more recent scholarship on the book of Revelation has generated: the Apocalypse's alleged misogynistic character. There are actually two sides to the criticisms that have surfaced, one approached from a more feminist perspective and the other related to the discussion of the book's masculinities and the violence exhibited in that light. The former has emerged in the last generation, noticing particularly how John not only uses the name of Jezebel to describe the insidious, seductive, and deadly entrapments at work within the church (2:20–23)

---

1. Robert Wall (*Revelation*, 227) identifies these as "each introduced by the apocalyptic formula, 'and I saw'": 19:11–16, 17–18, 19–21; 20:1–3, 4–10, 11–15; 21:1–22:6 (I see the end of this final vision at 22:5 instead); our own discussion will treat each of these visions in order but not sectionally like we did the letters to the seven churches.

2. See Beale, *The Book of Revelation*, 1117–21; see also David E. Aune, *Revelation 17–22*, Word Biblical Commentary 52C (Nashville: Thomas Nelson, 1998), 1020–21 and 1144–46.

but also portrays as a female character the evils of Babylon pressing the people of God from the outside.[3] If Jezebel is personified as leading the people of God astray with her beguiling fornication, such activity is intertwined with the worship of demons and idols in general (9:20–21) and part and parcel of life under Babylonian captivity more particularly (14:8). Throughout the visions, the argument goes, the major threats to the faithfulness of the people of God are depicted in female terms.[4]

The problem crescendos, in this view, in Revelation 17. As Shanell Smith has recently urged, as a great whore, the woman Babylon is marked (sealed and tattooed) as both brothel slave-girl and an imperial city to generate a dual characterization that is not only doubly complex but is also ambivalent at best for women.[5] On the one hand, whore Babylon is a victim, castigated and dominated by empire; but on other hand, woman Babylon is a participant in and beneficiary of imperial power and expansion. Nevertheless, the benefits that she enjoys can always be withdrawn at any time, just as prostitutes can be paid but then discarded. Whore/woman Babylon, then, is both victim and victimizer in various respects but ultimately pitiable since she is at the mercy of, even if she is a conduit for satisfying the beast's (and dragon's) ravenously evil appetites.

Revelation 17 thus depicts "women as subject and object of colonizing discourse," and if not attended to, this in turn "creates not a *Sitz im Leben*, a setting in life, but a *Sitz im Tod*, a context of death."

The two quotations are from Caroline Vender Stichele, "Re-membering the Whore: The Fate of Babylon according to Revelation 17.16," and Amy-Jill Levine, "Introduction," in Amy-Jill Levine, *A Feminist Companion to the Apocalypse of John*, 117 and 9 respectively.

---

3. The initial salvo being Tina Pippin, *Death and Desire: The Rhetoric of Gender in the Apocalypse of John* (Louisville, KY: Westminster/John Knox 1992); for an updated argument, see Pippin, "The Heroine and the Whore: The *Apocalypse of John* in Feminist Perspective," in David Rhoads, ed., *From Every People and Nation: The Book of Revelation in Intercultural Perspective* (Minneapolis: Fortress, 2005), 127–45.

4. Note that Catherine Keller, *Apocalypse Now and Then: A Feminist Guide to the End of the World* (1996; reprint, Minneapolis: Fortress, 2005), especially in her final chapter, urges a pneumatological approach toward what she calls a counter-apocalyptic narrative that seeks to keep open redemptive possibilities from what on the surface seems to be Revelation's binarily fore-closed world. I am sympathetic to many of Keller's proposal, but she addresses an academic theological audience, whereas my own work is mostly directed to the church, especially its evangelical and pentecostal spheres.

5. Shanell T. Smith, *The Woman Babylon and the Marks of Empire: Reading Revelation with a Postcolonial Womanist Hermeneutics of Ambiveilence* (Minneapolis: Fortress, 2014), esp. 154–71.

On the flip side, if the evils confronting the church are presented through feminine imagery, God seems to also appear in very masculine terms.[6] In this reading, the God on the heavenly throne is as great as can be imagined less because it is what John sees and more because it is viewed through the imperial lenses of Caesar's earthly thrones. In other words, the greatness and gloriousness of God is refracted through the power, wealth, might, and honor given to Roman Caesars. From that perspective, the violence with which Rome interacts with the far reaches of its empire is that with which she is judged by the transcendent lord of lords and king of kings. Whereas the church is assailed from within and outside by alluring and bewitching snares, the answer comes from a male figure, from a location higher and more transcendent than the ones on which earthly rulers are enthroned, albeit strikingly more forcefully and destructively than the latter's machinations in order to give them their due.

These feminist and masculinist readings are informed surely by postcolonial perspectives, but one does not need to accept all the latter to appreciate the issues that are being raised. After all, the postcolonial hermeneutic is not just about being anti-colonial, even if that is an important component of its critical approach, but such a stance invites consideration of how socioeconomic and political locations inform our interpretive presuppositions, and these are especially helpful when those of us in European and North American contexts can begin to appreciate how our own affluence have been attained through the colonial enterprise.[7] More important for the issues at hand, however, is the care with which we have to handle the putative violence of the book. To say that mimicry of imperial Rome justifies the use of divine violence is both to forget that images of violence are strewn throughout the Old Testament from which the seer of Patmos so deeply draws and to overlook the central symbol of the slaughtered Lamb: a nongendered symbol, it ought not be understated.[8] Brian Blount proposes that "slaughtered Lamb" is not just a noun but a way of life, even "an action verb" ("sLamb"), which then can be understood as John's antidote to violence, so that the Lion acts as a "slaughtered Lamb" and, thus, "The Lion *sLambs* God's opposition."[9] From this perspective, we shall have to see if the concluding pages of Revelation emphasize more of a vindictive divine violence or if those who are violent and those who destroy the earth

6. See Stephen D. Moore, *Untold Tales from the Book of Revelation: Sex and Gender, Empire and Ecology* (Atlanta: SBL Press, 2014), esp. ch. 4, "Hypermasculinity and Divinity."
7. See, e.g., Wes Howard-Brook and Anthony Gwyther, *Unveiling Empire: Reading Revelation Then and Now* (Maryknoll, NY: Orbis Books, 1999).
8. Loren L. Johns, *The Lamb Christology of the Apocalypse of John*, Wissenschaftliche Untersuchungen zum Neuen Testament 2.167 (Tübingen: Mohr Siebeck, 2003).
9. Brian K. Blount, *Can I Get a Witness? Reading Revelation through African American Culture* (Louisville, KY: Westminster John Knox Press, 2005), 87.

"will drink their own punishment," and whether these demonically inspired "acts of violence and greed are their own punishment."[10]

Yet having hinted at the substance of our own approach, it is not possible to minimize how our sacred texts can be understood as sanctioning our attitudes about and behaviors toward others, in this case, to women. The disparaging use of the great whore symbol at the beginning of this concluding section of the Apocalypse derives from a male-centered perspective, and the latter remains prevalent around the world even two thousand years later. Evil and sexual immorality is feminized and that then justifies the stripping naked, devouring, and killing of the female whore. Is there not a way "to target the evil of empire without exposing women to such rhetorical and potentially real collateral damage," Brian Blount asks?[11]

Two comments are in order. First, more generally, feminist perspectives and concerns ought to be not only welcomed but prioritized in our still male-dominated world.[12] Such interpretations will sensitize especially men to their own biases and enable what is perennially needed: the warding off of inappropriate take-aways from such texts. Second, and more concretely, a few hermeneutical and apocalyptic (Revelation-related) guidelines will be helpful. Most important is to remember that the *two-women* stereotype in ancient Hebrew wisdom, including but not limited to Proverbs 1–9, was familiar enough in the first century to be used by John to contrast Rome/Babylon and the New Jerusalem.[13] Further, and no less significant, is that Revelation ends with a feminine redemptive symbol: that of the church (and people of God) as the bride of the Lamb. The 144,000 virgin males in Revelation 14:1–5 (see comments above on this passage) are now transfigured, effectively, into the Lamb's wife in the Apocalypse's crowning moments. This recognition may enable the church to "envision itself as embodied within the feminine gender [and] rethink the categories of 'masculine' and 'feminine'" along the way.[14] Although this shift in these concluding heavenly scenes should not alleviate our vigilance against anti-women impulses that historic (male-predominant) readings of Revelation

---

10. Mark Bredin, *Jesus, Revolutionary of Peace: A Nonviolent Christology in the Book of Revelation* (Waynesboro, GA: Paternoster, 2003), 216.

11. Blount, *Revelation*, 310.

12. E.g., Lynn R. Huber, *Thinking and Seeing with Women in Revelation*, Library of New Testament Studies 475 (New York and London: Bloomsbury/T&T Clark, 2013).

13. See Barbara Rossing, *The Choice between Two Cities: Whore, Bride, and Empire in the Apocalypse* (Harrisburg, PA: Trinity Press International, 1999), ch. 2.

14. Lynn R. Huber, "Unveiling the Bride: Revelation 19.1–8 and Roman Social Discourse," in Amy-Jill Levine, *A Feminist Companion to the Apocalypse of John*, 178. The epilogue to Schüssler Fiorenza, *The Book of Revelation*, also recommends avoiding a binarily-constructed gendered hermeneutic and suggests instead a rhetorical and political one that I believe is viable for theological interpretation.

continue to perpetuate, let's see how a cautious attentiveness to these matters might generate a more egalitarian understanding of the redemption of history and the end of the world as we work through the last few chapters of John's visions.

17:1–18

The Mystery of Babylon Exposed: Wising Up in the Beastly Cosmopolis

This seventeenth chapter of Revelation gets us into the thickets of speculative grappling with the figures of the woman, the beast, and the seven and ten kings that are central to the vision unraveling of the Babylonian mystery. Recall that up until now, John has already declared Babylon to be ruined (14:8; 16:19). This vision clarifies who and what it is that the seer is seeing judgment rendered upon: Rome and its empire as experienced by John and the seven churches in the latter part of the first century. Amid all of the conjectures about what the various symbols refer to, what does John expect the saints and servants of God to internalize and perform? Nothing less than to distance themselves from and even to live in opposition to what Rome represents. Determining how to do so will require wisdom to discern the minutiae related to the woman, her beastly carrier, and the beast's heads and horns. So into the wilderness of what John sees by the spirit (17:3a) we enter.

What are we told about the woman? She is being judged (17:1); she is "the great whore seated on many waters" (17:1; Jer. 51:13a), which one of the bowl-angels (17:1a, 7a) who is escorting John through this vision later explains "are peoples and multitudes and nations and languages" (17:15b);[1] her activities are likened to fornication, immoralities involving the kings and inhabitants—the waters of peoples, multitudes, and so on—of the earth (17:3); she sits on "a scarlet beast that was full of blasphemous names, and it had seven heads and ten horns" (17:3b); she is seated, also, on seven

---

1. *Multitudes* replace *tribes* in this by now familiar quartet, perhaps to emphasize with *nations* how vast is the reach of the great whore over the world.

mountains, which John's original readers and hearers would have associated with the city of Rome, geographically and topographically, but which are also related to the beast's seven heads and further symbolic of seven kings (17:9); she is alluring in her purple and scarlet clothes, her gold, jewels, and peals (17:4a); her forehead is marked with the mysterious name: "Babylon the great, mother of whores and of earth's abominations" (17:5b); she has devoured the saints and those who have witnessed to Jesus (17:6a); she is, further, "the great city that rules over the kings of the earth" (17:18b); and her appearance amazes John (17:6b–7a).[2] It bears repeating that the many waters that represent the peoples and nations of the earth, the seven-headed-and-horned scarlet beast, and the seven heads-mountains-kings are all ridden by the woman. These are therefore neither mutually exclusive nor synonymous, but how they are related will need to be kept in mind as we continue.

As David L. Barr urges, John's goal in these visions is "to distance the hearer from Rome and from Roman culture. To disillusion the hearers—to destroy their illusion that they can be at home in the Roman world—is the primary performative effect of this story."

David L. Barr, *Tales of the End: A Narrative Commentary on the Book of Revelation* (Salem, OR: Polebridge, 2012), 321.

And our hopes that further clarity may be forthcoming is buoyed when the bowl angel volunteers to explain the mystery of the woman by shifting to the scarlet beast on which the woman is sitting (17:7b). We have actually already met a blasphemous beast with seven heads and ten horns, the one from the sea with the dragon's authority over the tribes, peoples, nations, and inhabitants of the earth (13:1–10). What else are we told about this beast? First, this beast "was, and is

---

2. Is the scarlet woman's mesmerizing capacity related in part to the (John's) male gaze, attractive because of her charm but disgusting due to her undisguised sexuality? A male-dominated church has historically deployed passages like Rev. 17 to keep women in their "proper" places, and in that sense, in many cultures, women are perpetually alienated—with biblical warrant!—to the margins of the church. We will have to tread judiciously in the rest of the book of Revelation in navigating John's rhetorical use of both the great whore (Babylon) and the bridal wife (new Jerusalem); see also discussion in excursus D.

not, and is about to ascend from the bottomless pit and go to destruction" (17:8). While not quite parallel to and hence a parody of the
God who was, is, and is to come, what is said here connects to the
earlier visions warning about the one ascending from the bottomless
pit: the locust king, Abaddon/Apollyon, and the killer of the two witnesses (9:11a; 11:7). Further, the threefold temporal description of
the beast as one who was, no longer is, but coming (17:8a), is twice
repeated albeit in varying terms (in 17:8b, 11), with the second itera-
tion prompting a call for wisdom (17:9a)—the second of two such
calls in the entire book (see 13:18)—related to the seven heads that
provides background for comprehending the coming beast. The
angelic interpretation is that these seven heads also are "seven kings,
of whom five have fallen, one is living, and the other has not yet come;
and when he comes, he must remain only a little while. As for the beast
that was and is not, it is an eighth but it belongs to the seven, and it
goes to destruction" (17:9b–11). Note then that the beast who *is not*
but *is coming* is distinct from the seventh king who is also coming, so
both the seventh head of the beast (the seventh king) and the beast
itself, are said to be coming. Now, that the beast is *not* present (even
if coming) may be confusing since this is the same beast that is said
to be, presently, ridden by the woman. Two considerations are pertinent: that the beast that *is not* but *coming* may be a theological rather
than historical datum, a further parody of God in Christ's death and
resurrection—recall the mortally wounded sea beast and its recovery
(13:3a)—and if so, then the *is not* "refers to the continuing effects
of [the beast's] defeat by Christ at the cross and resurrection."[3] But
to return to the main point: the beast has seven heads which are the
seven kings, so is related to the seven kings but transcends the kings.
The interpreting angel puts it this way: "As for the beast that was and
is not, it is an eighth but it belongs to the seven, and it goes to destruction" (17:11).

Our goal is to understand the scarlet beast on which the woman
sits. Complicating our efforts here are not only its seven heads, representing seven kings, but also its ten horns, representing also ten
future kings (17:12a).[4] They will arise in due course, for a short time

3. Beale, *The Book of Revelation*, 864.
4. Speculation has practically run amok since there are few constraints in this text regarding how

("one hour"; 17:12b), when the beast comes: "These are united in yielding their power and authority to the beast" (17:13) to war against (and be trounced by) the Lamb (7:14a). They are like the ten-horned beast/kingdom in Daniel that also wars against the saints but is defeated by the Most High (Dan. 7:7–8, 19–27). Or, to put it more emphatically in theological terms accentuating God's sovereignty: "God has put it into their hearts to carry out his purpose by agreeing to give their kingdom to the beast, until the words of God will be fulfilled" (17:17). Not only is the time when these ten kings arrive on the scene divinely orchestrated and their defeat divinely ordained, but what they do, in cahoots with the beast, is also predetermined: "the ten horns that you saw, they and the beast will hate the whore; they will make her desolate and naked; they will devour her flesh and burn her up with fire" (17:16).[5] This brings us back full circle to the woman: the great whore who rides the beast will later be consumed by that beast and its ten horns/kings. The graphicness describing the woman's demise is standard to prophetic judgments on ancient cities and nations (e.g., Ezek. 23; Nah. 3).

Let us now recapitulate what we know. The vision of the woman is of a great whore, of Babylon the great city that rules over and exploits the earth and its kings and kingdoms (17:5b, 18). During John's time this can refer only to Rome (the city on seven mountains), its emperors (the seven heads/kings) as symbolic of the centralized imperial powers, and its extended empire of client-kings spread out over the known Mediterranean world (the kings of the earth: 17:2a, 18). The woman's sitting on the seven mountains and the many waters thus conveys that the Roman Empire is both centrally constituted (by its imperial caesars) and regionally enacted

---

to understand the futurity of these kings and so there have been innumerable applications of these kings by as many interpreters to their own times, not least Dispensationalist readers in the last third of the twentieth century (and continuing) who see these ten in the European Union of nations (with complications since there is no established *ten* that fits at any one time); rather than look for historical connections, my own approach is to remain at the theological level that is nevertheless quite clear in the text.

5. This is parallel to the kings from the east coming across the Euphrates (16:12–16), indicated in the description of the sixth bowl to be gathered with other kings against the Almighty but also clearly presented as threatening to their Western (Roman) neighbors and to be used by the Almighty to bring judgment upon the latter; the difference is that the fall and defeat of these kings is not explicitly stated in the sixth bowl scene but is being elaborated upon as part of the seventh bowl (16:17–21) and its aftermath (Rev. 17–18).

(by client-kingdoms/governments ruling over the world's many peoples, tribes, and languages).[6] But the woman is also sitting on the beast (which serves the dragon), and that can be understood as the demonic imperial character at the heart of this transnational regime. This satanic lie both enriches the woman, imperial Rome as a whole, and then engulfs the same: its deception is both unsustainable and ultimately self-destructive.[7] No wonder John is deeply amazed and astonished (17:6b–7a) by this mystery of Babylonian evil—the opposite of the mystery of divine redemption (10:7)—even as the earth's inhabitants who have been seduced by the beastly deceits are also astounded by its (re)appearance (17:8b).

Much ink has been spilled on deciphering historical references to the seven kings or emperors, given the seven mountain and Roman connection, perhaps justifiably so given its introductory remark calling for "a mind that has wisdom" (17:9a). The problem with decrypting who is the living one depends in part both on when we begin and on if and how we count the three emperors-in-quick-succession in the year following Nero's suicide. Two possibilities, among at least a half dozen other candidates, can be laid out to illustrate the issues.[8] For instance, we could begin with Augustus Caesar (27 BCE to 14 CE), in which case he, Tiberius (14–37), Caligula (37–41), Claudius (41–54), and Nero (54–68) are the five of the past; then, ignoring the three in Nero's wake—Galba, Otho, and Vitellius (*c.* 68–69)—we can specify the sixth as Vespasian (69–79), and the seventh who comes for a short while to be Titus (79–81). Or we could begin with Galba and count through to Titus as the five in the past, which means the sixth is Domitian (81–96) and the seventh to come for a short while is Nerva (96–98).

Three quick points can be made. First, depending on when the book was written or, perhaps more apropos, if there are various editions of the text culminating in its final, present form, then not only might both of these interpretations be appropriate but at the

---

6. I get the language of *client-kings* and *client-kingdoms* from Keener, *Revelation*, 411.
7. In this sense, the woman as the great whore is both victimizer (of the imperialized lands) and victim (of the imperial system itself); see Smith, *The Woman Babylon and the Marks of Empire*, 154–71.
8. Ford has a handy chart (*Revelation*, 289) from which primarily I rely; see also Wilson, *Charts*, 95–96, and Aune, *Revelation 17–22*, 947.

evolving moments of the text's history (e.g., at the end of the sixties or in the early nineties), the different alignments would be true.
Second, regardless of how the historicity of these symbols are sorted
out (and no definitive solution appears to be forthcoming after two
thousand years), what seems assured is that the Nero redivivus myth
lies behind both this interpretation of the bowl-angel and the earlier
portrait of the mortally wounded and revived beast (13:3).[9] Third,
the beast that is ascending, returning, and coming is doomed for
destruction (17:8b), and along with it, its seven-headed (17:11) and
ten-horned kingdoms, the latter specifically indicated as being conquered at the hands of the Lamb-king (17:12–14a).[10] Historically
the disintegration of imperial Rome is forecast; but more important
are the theological ramifications for whatever other imperial regi-
mens might arise in and long after its wake.

FURTHER REFLECTIONS
Reckoning with Our Own Imperial Desire

The call for wisdom to discern the seven-headed and ten-horned
beast (17:9) is the second such in the Apocalypse, following the earlier plea to do so vis-à-vis calculation of the number of the beast
(13:18).[11] Elsewhere in Revelation, wisdom is heralded as belonging to the Lamb (5:12) and the one of the throne (7:11–12). Here,
it is those who are "called and chosen and faithful" and with the
Lamb that is also Lord of lords and King of kings (17:14b), who are
appealed to exercise wisdom. Most of us at this point of the vision
exposing imperial Rome as both a whore and a beastly confedera-
tion of nations and peoples may feel sufficiently repulsed so as to
dis-affiliate ourselves, like the perpetual foreigner stance from out

---

9. See Richard Bauckham, *The Climax of Prophecy: Studies in the Book of Revelation* (1993;
   reprint, London and New York: T&T Clark, 2005), ch. 11.
10. Skaggs and Benham (*Revelation*, 174) call attention to the antecedents of this vision's
   imagery, such as the psalmist (74:12–14) singing of YHWH the king breaking the heads of
   dragons and crushing the heads of the sea monster Leviathan.
11. So that the spiritual wisdom needed to discern the economics of 666 is now also needed to
   discern the mystery of Babylon/Rome; see also John Christopher Thomas, "The Mystery of
   the Great Whore—Pneumatic Discernment in Revelation 17," in Peter Althouse and Robby
   Waddell, eds. *Perspectives in Pentecostal Eschatologies: World without End* (Eugene, OR:
   Pickwick, 2010), 111–36.

of which this commentary is being written. Why would we wish to insert ourselves more centrally into and embrace the world's blasphemous fornications and abominations? Yet we also ought to realize that things are never so simple.

Part of the challenge is that, as postcolonial studies have documented, the colonized usually mimic the colonizers. This uncomfortable truth expresses the power of colonization: that colonial power is of such potency as to stir among those subjugated the desire to become like their masters.[12] On the one hand colonized nations are decimated and their cultures destroyed; on the other hand, colonized peoples inevitably resist, at least pockets of them, even if they are often limited to utilizing the tools of the masters and hence, in that respect, there is no avoiding mimicry.[13] Even John's visions, it is clear, deploy imperial imagery to magnify the God of Jesus Christ for the purposes of exposing and undermining, at least rhetorically and imagistically, the power of imperial Rome. So the perpetual foreigner status spawns imperial desire as much as defiance, often two sides of one coin, so that these marginalized stances often both participate in but also remain distant from imperial culture. Yes, there is a sense that, as Stephen Moore warns, "To construct God or Christ, together with their putatively salvific activities, from the raw material of imperial ideology is not to shatter the cycle of empire but merely to transfer it to a transcendental plane, thereby reifying and reinscribing it . . . creating an imperial divine 'essence' that is extremely difficult to dismantle or dislodge";[14] but also, yes, there is another sense in which, as the next section unfolds, the injustices of the colonizers seem to turn upon themselves, devouring those centripetally, from and to the center. Let us see both how we are much more deeply imbricated with Babylon than we might care to admit and how we are given also the wisdom to discern our calling to faithfully forging an alternative (and fraught) path through the mountains, creatures, waters, and enticements of this world.

---

12. See Stephen D. Moore, *Empire and Apocalypse: Postcolonialism and the New Testament* (Sheffield: Sheffield Phoenix Press, 2006), ch. 5, for more on mimicry at work in Revelation.
13. Lynne St. Clair Darden, *Scripturalizing Revelation: An African American Postcolonial Reading of Empire* (Atlanta: SBL Press, 2015), chs. 2–3, explicate this notion.
14. Stephen D. Moore, "The Revelation to John," in Fernando F. Segovia and R. S. Sugirtharajah, ed., *A Postcolonial Commentary on the New Testament Writings*, The Bible and Postcolonialism 13 (London and New York: T&T Clark, 2009), 436–54, at 452.

The Judgment of Babylon Enacted: Constructing a Counter-Imperial Economy?

The immediately preceding has unfolded in great symbolic detail the outward trappings of the beastly structure of evil: namely, imperial Rome imaged as a great whore. This next vision not only announces and depicts the collapse of this imperial administration but also sounds the dirges and laments of the kings, merchants, and ship-masters whose loss of benefits from the regime are a premonition of their own dissolution. Amid the upheaval visited on this world system, the call to the saints and servants of God is to extricate themselves from the sinking ship, so to speak. What are the possibilities for such disentanglement, and how might the challenges inhibiting response to that call be overcome?

The earlier announcement of Babylon's fallenness (14:8) is now repeated in a mighty voice by a bright and splendorous angel from heaven with great authority (18:1–2). Whereas Babylon has been a sort of Grand Central Station—"all the nations have drunk of the wine of the wrath of her fornication, and the kings of the earth have committed fornication with her, and the merchants of the earth have grown rich from the power of her luxury," the angel details (18:3)—it is now being reduced to nothing more than "a dwelling place of demons, a haunt of every foul and hateful bird, a haunt of every foul and hateful beast" (18:2b; cf. Jer. 50:39; 51:8, 37).[1] As the vision unfolds, then, John sees another mighty angel that takes up a great millstone and throws such into the sea (18:21).[2] The uses of past

---

1. Aune, *Revelation 17–22*, 983, identifies at least a dozen allusions to Jer. 51 in Rev. 18.
2. As Skaggs and Benham point out (*Revelation*, 188), there are only two other references to *mighty angels* in the Apocalypse: the one who asks who is worthy to open the seals of the

(at the beginning) and future (here) tenses across this vision might be baffling, although an eschatological perspective can view this Babylonian judgment as both past and coming (future).[3] In any case, the initial threefold reasons given for Babylon's final demise (18:3) are elaborated upon: "for your merchants were the magnates of the earth, and all nations were deceived by your sorcery. And in you was found the blood of prophets and of saints, and of all who have been slaughtered on earth" (18:23b–24). We have been repeatedly reminded that the blood of God's prophets, saints, and servants have been shed (6:10; 16:6; 17:6), and now it is clear that Babylon has played a key role in such persecution and is thereby being punished for her deeds. But the great city's condemnation is also due to its deceptive enchantment of the nations of the world and, perhaps more important for our purposes, to the ways in which its market networks facilitated human trade and industry.

If Babylon represents imperial Rome, as we concluded with the help of the bowl-angel's interpretation in the previous (seventeeth) chapter, then its decline will have worldwide impact. At the heart of this vision of its haunting, then, are three requiems: that of the kings, merchants, and shipmasters/seafarers of the earth. The kings, representing the governmental powers of the nations, are those who through their alliances with Rome—here repeating the initial charge (18:3a)—"committed fornication and lived in luxury with her" (18:9), in short, served the colonizing city and in turn flourished and thrived under Roman rule. These kings "will weep and wail over her when they see the smoke of her burning; they will stand far off, in fear of her torment, and say, 'Alas, alas, the great city, Babylon, the mighty city! For in one hour your judgment has come'" (18:9b–10). The swiftness of Babylon's judgment has been like a thief in the night (3:3; 16:15). The desolation of the distant city leaves its client-kings and governments worrying what their predicament will be.

Next lament the merchants, "since no one buys their cargo anymore" (18:11b). Remember that the earth beast had established

---

scroll in heaven (5:2) and the one who holds the little scroll in his right hand (10:1–2); so it is worth considering that the judgments initially unsealed and then prophesied about from out of John's digestion of the contents of the little scroll (10:9–11) might here also find their culmination in this mighty angel's enactment of Babylon's final sea burial.

3. See Smalley, *The Revelation of John,* 467.

an imperial system of buying and selling (13:16–17), but the fall of Rome means also the breakdown of this scheme of markets and exchanges. And what kind of cargo is now no longer on the move? The list provided no doubt is adapted from that related to the fall of the ancient kingdom of Tyre (Ezek. 27:12–22), albeit updated to more accurately reflect "the trade realities of first-century Rome":[4] "cargo of gold, silver, jewels and pearls, fine linen, purple, silk and scarlet, all kinds of scented wood, all articles of ivory, all articles of costly wood, bronze, iron, and marble, cinnamon, spice, incense, myrrh, frankincense, wine, olive oil, choice flour and wheat, cattle and sheep, horses and chariots, slaves—and human lives" (18:12–13). The last element, human slaves, is notably absent (at least in some English biblical translations) from the exilic prophet's catalog and speaks to the enrichment of imperial Rome from its commodification of human labor. This will not be surprising to those who realize that the cargo involved also is largely "composed of luxuries intended for the wealthy" and that, historically, in this case—and generalizable also to imperial regimes after Rome—"most of this kind of wealth had [and has] been obtained off the backs of the poor and the slaves."[5] Thus, the merchants mourn about Babylon/Rome: "The fruit for which your soul longed has gone from you, and all your dainties and your splendor are lost to you, never to be found again!" (18:14). Like the kings viewing the fall of Rome from afar, so also these merchants wail from a distance: "Alas, alas, the great city, clothed [exactly as was the great whore: 17:4a] in fine linen, in purple and scarlet, adorned with gold, with jewels, and with pearls! For in one hour all this wealth has been laid waste!" (18:16–17). The fall of Babylon/Rome means that its accumulated wealth is not only unable to save the system but will be of no value thereafter.

The final group to cry out, also standing far off from the smoke of Babylon's burning, are the shipmasters, seafarers, and sailors: "What city was like the great city?" (18:18b). Theirs is in part a refrain of the other two (predecessor) groups: "Alas, alas, the great city, where all who had ships at sea grew rich by her wealth! For in one hour she has been laid waste" (18:19b). These who did business at and from the margins of the Roman center nevertheless testify to how

4. Keener, *Revelation*, 430.
5. Fee, *Revelation*, 253; see also Bauckham, *Climax of Prophecy*, ch. 10.

imperial participation also enriches the clients. The implosion of the central node, then, has drastic implications for those outward toward the periphery.

The two angelic messages in this vision (18:1, 21) surround another heavenly voice, one that represents but is distinct from God, referred to in the third person in what is proclaimed: "Come out of her, my people, so that you do not take part in her sins, and so that you do not share in her plagues; for her sins are heaped high as heaven, and God has remembered her iniquities" (18:4b–5). This divine recollection connects back to remembrance related to the great earthquake of the seventh bowl (16:19) and confirms that all that has been disclosed since is an elaboration of the effects of that final bowl judgment. Here, the angelic voice is reassuring about the certainty of this divine verdict, with the call to "Render to her [Babylon] as she herself has rendered, and repay her double for her deeds; mix a double draught for her in the cup she mixed" (18:6), to be taken less quantitatively as indicative of God being extremely vindictive, than qualitatively as registering that and how God will not overlook sin. If Babylon presumptively brandished her impregnability and immortality—"Since in her heart she says, 'I rule as a queen; I am no widow, and I will never see grief'" (18:7b)—God will cause these delusions to come crashing down: "her plagues will come in a single day—pestilence and mourning and famine—and she will be burned with fire; for mighty is the Lord God who judges her" (18:8).

FURTHER REFLECTIONS
A Countercultural Solidarity

The major challenge for those who are called and chosen, however, is how to be faithful to the angelic call from out of this imperial catastrophe. How might the people of God come out of or escape from a system that constitutes the political economy in which they live, move, and have their being, to paraphrase a Greek poet quoted by Luke (Acts 17:28)? This same angel (probably) also calls out:[6]

6. See, e.g., Craig R. Koester, *Revelation: A New Translation with Introduction and Commentary*,

"Rejoice over her, O heaven, you saints and apostles and prophets! For God has given judgment for you against her" (18:20). But how are the people of God to escape when their livelihood depends at least in some part also on the seafarers and merchants and their exchanges? If the latter can no longer buy or sell, even with the mark of the beast, how might the saints, apostles, and prophets— here perhaps comprehensible as referring inclusively to the faithful (saints), including those of the new (apostles) and old (prophets) covenants—and anyone else not so marked, survive? Maybe this will force the kind of sharing of resources featured in the early Christian community (Acts 2:42–45; 4:32–37), but calling the church to come out of the imperial market may be likened to inviting fishes to find their way on land.

Is that too harsh? Let me reframe the matter otherwise. The kings of the earth, its merchants, and the shipmasters and seafarers may be likened to the political and economic systems and their middle-persons, so to speak. In contemporary terms the latter might refer to the digitized global economy. The fall of the entire system means not only that governments are uprooted and the markets are disrupted but that the stock, bonds, and all other financial accounts are literally evaporated and eviscerated. If we are invested in this system, then we would wish that Babylon perseveres luxuriously, as Rome flaunted itself in the first century (see 18:7a). The reality is that our economic power is tied in with our political and even military might and vice versa. Thus, our comforts are interrelationally interdependent on both the "hard power of military force" (kings and governments) and the "soft power of the market and of culture" (merchants and seafarers), as Joseph Mangina observes.[7]

Yet, further complicating our situation, Rome's luxury is what enables, in part, some comforts, even if to lesser degrees, toward the imperial outposts. The higher the standard of living is at the center, the better the quality of life at the outskirts due in part to trickle-down economic disbursements. From this perspective, the cratering of Rome into the chasm of divine judgment will pull down the client-kingdoms with it, and this will impact not just the wealthy

---

Anchor Yale Bible Commentaries (New Haven and London: Yale University Press, 2015), 723, and Smalley, *The Revelation to John*, 460.

7. Mangina, *Revelation*, 207.

but also the not-so-wealthy, the poor, and especially women—who have always done the bulk of the economic work to begin with— even more excessively. Thus, the mighty angel's taunt is doubly foreboding: "the sound of harpists and minstrels and of flutists and trumpeters will be heard in you no more; and an artisan of any trade will be found in you no more; and the sound of the millstone will be heard in you no more; and the light of a lamp will shine in you no more; and the voice of bridegroom and bride will be heard in you no more" (18:22–23a). Yes, the cargoes trafficked in by the elite and the wealthy (8:12–13) will cease, but so also will the more mundane pleasures of life enjoyed by the simple and the most vulnerable also be disturbed.[8] Men will suffer, but least; and women and people of color and the poor will agonize disproportionately. From this perspective, it will be difficult to rejoice at the tanking of the economic system that services human livelihood, and well-nigh impossible to get away altogether from the imperial regime.

Unless there is a way to live that counters the imperial posture but does so multifariously from within rather than attempting to upend the whole shebang.[9] Rather than lording it over as rulers, might we be servants, first of the Lamb and then of each other in the global market? Rather than fornicating indiscriminately with whatever is available, might we live in purity, in truthfulness, and in blamelessness while buying and selling? Rather than thinking we can luxuriate toward and purchase our happiness among the socially elite, might we live instead in solidarity with the subjugated and marginalized on the underside of history? Even if we might not be enthused, in our natural selves, by these possibilities, the option of staying with Babylon leads in any case to eventual demise. Persevering in faithfulness in search of a countercultural socioeconomic modality, however, will bring about ensuing and eternal celebration.

---

8. I owe this insight to González and González, *Revelation*, 122–23.
9. I get this way of framing things from Shane J. Wood, *The Alter-Imperial Paradigm: Empire Studies and the Book of Revelation*, Biblical Interpretation 140 (Leiden and Boston: Brill, 2016), although he is after a slightly different goal. Wood's main thesis is that while John is surely not commending assimilation to the status quo, his text reflects not a straightforward anti-imperial stance, but one that reflects multiple positionalities within an overarching posture that is uncomfortable with the Roman regime. I here make application of Wood's thesis in situating ourselves in the contemporary global economy.

19:1–10
"Hallelujah!" Dressing for the Final Celebration

We now turn to the last of eight hymns in the book of Revelation (4:8–11; 5:12–14; 7:10–12; 11:15–18; 12:10–12; 15:3–4; 16:5–7; 19:1–8), although since each of the judgment heptads conclude with a hymn either right before or as part of its conclusion (seals, 7:10–12; trumpets, 11:15–18; bowls, 16:5–7), we might say that this is the grand hymn of them all, the final celebration, after all of the judgments have been announced. On the other hand, the section also in effect transitions into the final enactment of judgments: the great war (19:12–21), the judgment of the satan (20:1–10), and the judgment of all persons (20:11–15). What might we take away from this hymn given our own location between-the-times, after the ministry, death, and resurrection/ascension of Jesus but before his return and the executing of all judgments announced in this Apocalypse? Singing the hallelujahs—there are four of them here, the only time this psalmic word meaning *praise YHWH* appears in the New Testament—with these heavenly choirs may be suggestive about what it means for us in a twenty-first century global cosmopolis to prepare ourselves for this eschatological gala.

This final celebration is introduced by "the loud voice of a great multitude in heaven" (19:1), which is the second to last of the fifteen other loud voices resounding throughout the book.[1] We have already heard another "great multitude" singing, an innumerable one (7:9–10), although this one may include more specifically the

1. Most loud voices are either by angels (5:2; 7:2; 8:13; 14:6–7, 9, 15, 18) or from heaven (11:12, 15; 12:10, 16:1, 17; 21:3) or heavenlike (1:10), with the one other resounding intonation being from the martyred souls under the altar (6:9–10).

"saints and apostles and prophets" called to rejoice over the falling of Babylon in the prior vision (8:20).[2] This multitude sings, "Hallelujah" twice (19:1, 3a), and they are joined by the twenty-four elders and four living creatures (19:4). The fourth hallelujah rumbles from, for John, what seems also like a "great multitude, like the sound of many waters and like the sound of mighty thunderpeals" (19:6a), and it may have been confused with either the first assembly or with the 144,000 standing on Mount Zion (see 14:2) if its crashing and thunderous applause had not been preceded by a voice from the throne (19:5a; also 16:17) saying, "Praise our God, *all you his servants*, and *all who fear him*, small and great" (19:5b, italics added). This all-inclusive group of God's servants may have included (also) the prophets and saints who earlier were associated with those who feared the Almighty's name (11:18), and perhaps even some drawn from among the nations and ethnic groups who had come to fear and glorify the Lord in recognizing the divine justice, truth, and holiness (15:3–4). In any case, the three groups of laments bewailing the fall of Babylon in the previous vision is drowned out now by the four hallelujahs.

What exactly is the final celebration praising God for? The initial great multitude sings: "Salvation and glory and power to our God, for his judgments are true and just; he has judged the great whore who corrupted the earth with her fornication, and he has avenged on her the blood of his servants" (19:1b–2); and again: "The smoke goes up from her forever and ever" (19:3b). God is here glorified for justly and truly (15:3b; 16:7) judging Babylon—once-for-all and forever and all times as signified by the never-ending rising smoke (cf. 14:11a; 18:9b, 18; Isa. 34:10)—and its corrupting of the world (17:2; 18:3, 9), and for avenging (see also 16:6) the death and bloodshed of his servant martyrs (17:6; 18:24). The twenty-four elders and the four living creatures are in agreement, intoning only, "Amen. Hallelujah!" (19:4b). The final chant by the cumulative gathering of God's servants transitions from a backward-looking celebration of Babylon's fall and judgment to a forward-anticipating festivity that is the marriage of the Lamb and his bride: "Hallelujah!

2. Koester, *Revelation*, 726.

For the Lord our God the Almighty reigns. Let us rejoice and exult and give him the glory, for the marriage of the Lamb has come, and his bride has made herself ready; to her it has been granted to be clothed with fine linen, bright and pure" (19:6b–8a). These four-fold hallelujahs, then, exalt God's just judgments and rejoice that the long-awaited wedding of the Lamb and his bride will now be held.

If the passing of Babylon means that the sounds of weddings will cease (18:23a), it also means that the final marriage between the Lamb and his bride, the church, is now ready to be held (19:7b). The imagery of Christ being the groom and his wife being the church is a familiar Pauline one (2 Cor. 11:2; Eph. 5:23–32) and has been percolating under the apocalyptic narrative all along but now comes into full view.[3] Three facets of this marriage are here registered. First, the bride's readiness is manifest: with her being "clothed with fine linen, bright and pure" (19:8a). The great city of Babylon was so "clothed with fine linen" (18:16), but it is no more. Instead, the bride has donned what the seven angels with the seven last plagues wore (15:6), responding affirmatively to the groom's earlier invitations to not just be clothed (16:15) but to put on, more specifically, white robes (3:4–5, 18). More precisely, such fine, bright, and pure linen is nothing less than "the righteous deeds of the saints" (19:8b). The bride's righteousness is fitting given that this is exactly the character of the groom she is marrying (19:11b).

A feminist approach wonders if "prompting a masculine-identified audience to envision itself as embodied within the feminine gender encourage that audience to rethink the categories of 'masculine' and 'feminine,' especially as they relate to communities?"

Lynn R. Huber, "Unveiling the Bride: Revelation 19.1–8 and Roman Social Discourse," in Amy-Jill Levine, *A Feminist Companion to the Apocalypse of John*, 178.

Second, an angel—the Greek says only *kai legei moi* ("and he said to me"), but this must be an angelic figure since the next verse says that John prostrates himself before this speaker in worshipful

---

3. That Revelation can and should be read nuptially, culminating with the marriage of the Lamb and his bride, is the thesis of Donal A. McIlraith, *The Reciprocal Love between Christ and the Church in the Apocalypse* (Rome: Columbian Fathers, 1989).

adoration, so this may have been the "mighty angel" introduced at the end of the previous vision (18:21)—interrupts with the fourth of seven blessings or macarisms (if we count those in 1:3 as one blessing): "Blessed are those who are invited to the marriage supper of the Lamb" (19:9a). Earlier we were invited to consider that while many may be called and even chosen, would many remain faithful (17:14b)? Here, then, the question lingers for John's original readers and for us today: the invitation may be on offer (see also 3:20), but how many will show up at the wedding dressed and ready for the final consummation (see also Matt. 22:1–14)?

Last but not least, the angel continues: "These are true words of God" (19:9b). The immediate contexts of the angel's affirmations of the truthfulness of these words concerns the heavenly celebration heralding the marriage supper, and this is begun by the great multitude's declaration of God's true judgments (19:2a). Yet this celebration is in some respects the culmination of the narrative arc of this apocalypse, one whose central figures are God and the Lamb, the latter momentarily to be revealed as "Faithful and True" (19:11; cf. 3:7a, 14; 15:3). In short, the heavenly celebration both is happening and will happen, which means that the judgments of God will be finalized and the Lamb's marriage supper will be officiated.

FURTHER REFLECTIONS
Worship God!

The question, variously iterated, needs to be posited again. Will we prove to be saints who live righteously? Will we keep the commandments of God and hold fast to the faith and testimony of Jesus (12:17b; 14:12)? Will we live in the light of divine brightness and splendor (18:1) or in the ever-thickly persisting smoke-filled darkness of the dragon's world and ways (9:2; 16:10; 19:3)? Will we put on white robes and linen (19:14) like the twenty-four elders (4:4) or prefer purple and scarlet and other accessories accompanying Babylon and all who do business with her (17:4; 18:16)? In short, will we do what is appropriate in order to be able to sing with the heavenly choirs now, which enables our fidelity to the Lamb during this season of betrothal, in anticipation of the marriage supper to come, or would we prefer instead to align ourselves with what is unjust and untrue, which means to fornicate with the beast in ways that also target, directly or indirectly, the life and testimony of the saints? In fact, it may well be precisely through such worship that divine ends are accomplished: "Human celebrations in this world are the mysterious moments in which the perfect work of salvation is announced, made known and brought about by way of anticipation, in the expectation that the universal manifestation of it will soon be furnished."[4]

It is at this moment of assured blessing that John confesses: "I fell down at his feet to worship him, but he said to me, 'You must not do that! I am a fellow servant with you and your comrades who hold the testimony of Jesus. Worship God! For the testimony of Jesus is the spirit of prophecy'" (19:10). This is almost exactly what happens (see 22:8–9) after the revelation of the New Jerusalem, which is another reason why many read "the downfall of the harlot and the elevation of the bride"[5] (17:1–18:24 and 21:10–22:5 respectively) as complementary in John's narrative. But, read after Pentecost, as we are attempting to do here in this theological commentary, John's account is additionally noteworthy because the angel asserts that he is no more than John and any of his brothers and sisters—those of the seven churches—who are doing not much more than testifying to Jesus. If God alone is to be worshiped—note that the Greek word for worship, *proskyneō*, is "an act of ritual prostration, common for ancient Eastern rulers, but introduced to Rome by Caligula,"[6] Roman emperor from 37–41 CE—then that worship is extended by his creatures, both human and angelic, even as these same creatures also bear testimony to Jesus through the divine spirit. On the one hand, we are not told here anything different from what we were told at the beginning of the Apocalypse, that angels will bring the revelation of Jesus Christ to John and that John will testify of that revelation (1:1–2); on the other hand, we are now told that the prophetic spirit is what enables our testifying to Jesus. Resituated

4. Prigent, *Commentary on the Apocalypse of St. John*, 653.
5. Murphy, *Fallen Is Babylon*, 417.
6. Murphy, *Fallen Is Babylon*, 7.

across the entire horizon of John's narrative so far, our faithfulness to the divine commandments in general and our capacity to sing and worship the Almighty on this side of heaven are also empowered by the (seven) spirit(s) of God.

19:11–21

The Armies of the White Horse and of the Beast: Cooking Up the Great Supper

The next six visions (counted by the "Then I saw . . ." indicators: 19:11, 17, 19; 20:1, 4, 11) anticipate the final grand vision, that of the New Jerusalem (beginning with 21:1), and in that sense sit between the judgment of Babylon (17:1–18:24) and the establishment of the bride of the Lamb (21:9–22:5). But if the judgment of the great city forecasts the fall of imperial Rome, the fate of its inner beast and the dragon that beast serves have not yet been charted. The three visions that are being covered in chapter 19 begin to address these unresolved matters as part of God's eschatological judgments on not just impenitent imperial forces on this side of history but also unrepentant hearts and creatures on the other side of death, and they do so in part through filling out the details regarding the marriage supper of the Lamb just introduced in the fourth macarism (19:9). Hence, we are provided another set of images regarding the groom and told more about the supper as part of the context for envisioning the judgments of the two beasts.[1] What implications do these very rapidly unfolding triad of visions have for Christian faithfulness?

That we are transitioning from historical to eschatological judgments, that is from judgments regarding Babylon/Rome to judgments of creaturely souls and beings on a cosmic scale, is signaled by

---

1. Interestingly, for all the focus on the coming of Jesus, John's visions do not clearly indicate when this coming takes place within the overall flow of the final judgments and the arrival of the new creation. There is a sense in which the Parousia is symbolized in the coming of the one on the white horse in this passage (19:11–16), but the emphasis here is on completing the judgments of Babylon and in that sense reaching back to the last few chapters. For discussion of these issues relative to the text commented on here, see R. Alastair Campbell, "Triumph and Delay: The Interpretation of Revelation 19:11–20:10," *Evangelical Quarterly* 80:1 (2008): 3–12.

John's seeing heaven being opened (19:11a). This may be seen as the final opening of a movement begun in the main part of John's visions with the unfastening of a door in heaven (4:1a) to the opening of the heavenly temple (11:19) and the heavenly tent of witness (15:5).[2] What appears is a rider on a white horse, clearly Jesus, although never named as such; yet each of the descriptions draw from the preceding visions in myriad ways:

— "Its rider is called Faithful and True" (19:11a): "the faithful witness" (1:5a) and "the faithful and true witness" (3:14);

— "in righteousness he judges and makes war" (19:11b): the dragon and its beast make war on Jesus' followers and on Jesus also (12:17; 13:7; 17:14a);

— "His eyes are like a flame of fire" (19:12a): the one like the Son of May has "eyes were like a flame of fire" 1:14b), and the Son of God also (2:18);

— "on his head are many diadems" (19:12b): in contrast to the limited number of diadems worn by the dragon (seven: 12:3) and its sea beast (ten: 13:1);

— "he has a name inscribed that no one knows but himself" (19:12c): Jesus promises to overcomers in Pergamum that he will give them white stones with "a new name that no one knows except the one who receives it" (2:17);

— "He is clothed in a robe dipped in blood" (19:13a): the one like the Son of Man is clothed with a long robe" (1:13), even as there have been multiple references so far to the "blood of the Lamb" (7:14; 12:11; cf. Isa. 63:1–6, esp. v. 3);

— "his name is called The Word of God" (19:13b): the "Word of God" has been consistently linked with Jesus' testimony (1:2a, 9b; 6:9);

— "the armies of heaven, wearing fine linen, white and pure, were following him on white horses" (19:14): we have just seen that the bride of the Lamb is "clothed with fine linen, bright and pure" (19:8);

— "From his mouth comes a sharp sword with which to strike down the nations, and he will rule them with a rod of iron"

2. E.g., Murphy, *Fallen Is Babylon*, 386.

(19:15): the one like the Son of Man has a "sharp, two-edged sword" coming out of his mouth (1:16; 2:12b, 16), even as overcomers from Thyatira are promised by Jesus that they will be "give[n] authority over the nations; to rule them with an iron rod" (2:26b–27a), and the woman clothed with the sun is said to have "birth[ed] a son, a male child, who is to rule all the nations with a rod of iron" (12:5a);

— "he will tread the wine press of the fury of the wrath of God the Almighty" (19:15c): the seventh angelic sign-message enacted "the great wine press of the wrath of God" (14:19b) and the seventh bowl was about God giving Babylon "the wine-cup of the fury of his wrath" (16:19b);

— "On his robe and on his thigh he has a name inscribed, 'King of kings and Lord of lords'" (19:16): the Lamb who will conquer the beast and its kings and armies is also identified as the "Lord of lords and King of kings" (17:14), even as, initially, Jesus is said to be "ruler of the kings of the earth" (1:5).

All of this is striking confirmation of the unity of the text of Revelation as we have it. Christologically speaking, it is also arresting to observe that Jesus is revealed quadrupedially in three very different respects: initially as the "Lion of the tribe of Judah" (5:5), drawing inspiration from the Torah (see Gen. 49:9–10); variously and repeatedly in many contexts across the book as a (slain) Lamb and (horned) ram (see 5:6); and now here at the end on a white horse.[3] In making this observation I am noting only the richness of the apocalyptic symbolism as applied to the most important theological matters of the book, the person of Christ himself, which has often been overlooked. John is not an ecological theologian in any contemporary sense, but he has already noted that divine judgment is exacted on destroyers of the earth (11:18a) and from that perspective a Lion-Lamb-(rider on)-horse Christology may be more productive than on the surface.

Yet this first of the final eschatological visions merely sets the stage for both holding the marriage and its supper and also finishing off the many wars previously announced as being waged between

3. See Stephen D. Moore, *Untold Tales from the Book of Revelation: Sex and Gender, Empire and Ecology* (Atlanta: SBL Press, 2014), ch. 9, titled "Quadrupedal Christ."

the beasts and its armies and the Lamb. The former is initiated by "an angel standing in the sun" (cf. 7:2) that calls with a loud voice "to all the birds that fly in midheaven"—where from we have heard so far an eagle crying out woes (8:13) and an angel proclaiming the eternal gospel (14:6)—"Come, gather for the great supper of God, to eat the flesh of kings, the flesh of captains, the flesh of the mighty, the flesh of horses and their riders—flesh of all, both free and slave, both small and great" (19:17–18). The congregation of these vultures, then, precipitates the final battle. John thus sees: "the beast and the kings of the earth with their armies gathered to make war against the rider on the horse and against his army" (19:19), and the battle then happens, practically in the twinkling of an eye. The results are immediately reported: the armies of heaven following the rider of the white horse make only a cameo appearance (19:14, 19b) but do nothing; instead, the beast's kings, captains, cavalry, and warriors were all "killed by the sword of the rider on the horse, the sword that came from his mouth; and all the birds were gorged with their flesh" (9:21; cf. Ezek. 39:4, 17–20). Whereas so far John has told us only about the impending demonic cavalry (9:14–16), that the demonically inspired armies had congregated at Harmagedon (16:12–16), and that the ten-kingdom army under the leadership of the beast had gathered to war against the Lamb (17:12–14), in none of those cases are we told of what exactly transpired (except in the last one when it is simply said that "the Lamb will conquer them"—note the future tense—17:14a). These loose ends are now tied together, with the clear implication that the white horse rider's sword is less to be taken as a literal blade and more has to do with his truthfulness (19:9b, 11a) that counters the deceptive lies of the dragon and its modus operandi.

And it is on this note that we also discover what happens with the dragon's two deceptive and beastly adjutants. One moment the beast is at the forefront of the kings, captains, and armies of the earth; the next, John unfolds: "the beast was captured, and with it the false prophet who had performed in its presence the signs by which he deceived those who had received the mark of the beast and those who worshiped its image. These two were thrown alive into the lake of fire that burns with sulfur" (19:20). Here we are reminded (after 16:13b) that the earth beast is a prophet to the sea beast, albeit a false one devoted to misdirecting people to take the mark of the beast and worship its image (13:13–15). As there were not only rich and poor but also "small and great . . . free and slave" caused by the earth beast to take the mark on the right hand or forehead (13:16), so here both spectra of persons, among others, are conned by the false prophet to gather against the rider on white horse. More important, the final fate of both beasts is specified. Their lot has already been predicted in their being conquered by faithful servants of God (15:2a), in the outpouring of the fifth bowl on its throne (16:10), and in the angelic interpretation of the mystery of Babylon that the beast is on its way to destruction (twice-told: 17:8, 11b). Now the final battle clarifies what happens to their armies—served up as meal for the scavenger birds, which is an ironic twist on the great wedding supper—and where they are consigned, once-for-all: to the fire and sulfur previously promised to their followers (14:10–11).

FURTHER REFLECTIONS
Weapons of the Betrothed

Even though the rider on the white horse wages battle with the truth of his words and uses his sword only to dispense of the beast and the false prophet, his followers, long subjugated, persecuted, and yearning for vindication, will rejoice over this final triumph over their foes and perhaps even be motivated by the images of this vision to take up the proverbial swords (or arms) against their oppressors, following in the footsteps (hoofbeats!) of their judge-savior. Contemporary readers who find themselves in minoritized and marginalized sociopolitical locations like those of the seven churches in Asia two thousand years ago may have less access to the tools usually adopted for violent insurrections, but those who are closer to the imperial centers are often less hesitant to deploy the resources at their disposal to retain and extend their power. More problematically, the latter are often less capable (and perhaps less willing) to observe the differences between their social locations from those of the original addressees of this apocalyptic vision and prefer instead to see themselves as faithful disciples participating in executing the judgments of the rider on the white horse. Yet to do so, whether for colonizers or mimicking colonized groups, would be to (conveniently) overlook Revelation's main narrative artery that has the Lion-Lamb-horse-rider overcome not using conventional forms of worldly power but through the witness of death and martyrdom. This is a tall order indeed, which is perhaps why Revelation remains obscure, less because it is opaque and abstruse and more because its primary message is unpalatable and difficult if not dreadful to embrace.

How then can we who seek to be faithful witnesses to the Lion-Lamb-horse-rider prepare for this wedding celebration and its feasts? It depends on who is getting married and who isn't, doesn't it? If that is the case, then the "great supper of God" being thrown for the marriage of the Lamb and his bride, the church, ought to bring out those who are friends of, certainly also family members in, the parties. John's Apocalypse has all throughout been an invitation to the church to act betrothed, meaning to live truthfully, righteously, and purely in accordance with the Word of God even if it means resisting the lies of the dragon and those who operate in its world and risking being killed for their faithful testimony to the ways of God manifest in Jesus. Preparing for the great wedding supper of the Lamb and/as his bride, it turns out, involves wearing white robes and riding white horses but not brandishing military equipment except in a spiritual sense: to expose, ward off, and undermine the untruths propounded by the dragon, his beast, and his false prophet. Part of what that means is that rather than being committed first and foremost to overthrowing the imperial regime at any cost, the ecclesial people will need to embrace a worshipful witness, one that sings and does so prophetically.[4]

4. See Michael J. Gorman, *Reading Revelation Responsibly: Uncivil Worship and Witness Following the Lamb into the New Creation* (Eugene, OR: Cascade, 2011). Added note post-1/6/21: I wrote "violent insurrections" in the initial paragraph of these "Further Reflections" long before the dreadful attack on the U.S. capitol and the congressional confirmation of the 2020 presidential election. It is easy to otherize those we do not agree with and divide the "good" (us) from the "bad" (them), especially when apocalyptic texts like Revelation also seem to justify such segregation. However, we have seen that human lives are more complex than easily placed into two camps and it is surely the case that demonization is deployed by both the right and the left, not to mention everyone situated in-between depending on the issue. How then to be confident in our commitments in light of all this ambiguity on this side of the eschaton? I also cited Gorman's text here when the initial draft was concluded in the spring of 2019, and it is kept as an important reminder that sorting out the proper response to the crises of our public lives requires more than political information but proper worship, which is theological formation at the throne of God, at the feet of the Lamb, with hearts open to the seven spirits.

20:1–10

Millennial Discipleship: Forging the Lake of Fire

As the earth and sea beasts (13:1–18) were initially introduced soon after the appearance of the dragon at the beginning of the second part (12:1–17) of this Apocalypse (see excursus C), now that they have been finally dispatched to the lake of fire (first mentioned in 19:20), it must be time to find out about the fate of their master, the dragon. The next two eschatological visions give us that update in relationship to the one-thousand-year reign of Christ. We will spend some time attempting to understand what has consumed many an interpreter of this book but will keep returning to the theological matter regarding the *end* of the dragon. As we shall see, the crucial issue for us will be less in attempting to establish which millennial position is the right one and more that of discerning how a millennial imagination might shape Christian discipleship in the present aeon anticipating the dragon's final disposition.

With the blowing of the fifth trumpet a key-carrying fallen angel unlocks the shaft of the bottomless pit to release both the smoke of its immense furnace and the locust army king Abaddon/Apollyon (9:1–2, 11). With the incarceration of the two beasts now accomplished, a key-carrying heavenly angel now comes not to unsecure the same unending abyss but to imprison "with a great chain" the fiend and tartar therein, at least temporarily (20:1). There is no doubt about who the target suspect is: "the dragon, that ancient serpent, who is the Devil and Satan" (20:2a), precisely how it was previously identified (12:9a). Whereas in that initial grand entrée "the deceiver of the whole world . . . was thrown down to the earth" (12:9b), now toward the end of the Apocalypse, John sees that the angel has "seized the dragon . . . and bound him for a thousand years, and threw him into the pit, and locked and sealed it over him, so that he would deceive the nations no more, until the thousand years were ended" (20:2–3a).

While John segues here almost immediately into a description of this millennial—meaning: *thousand year*—period when those on earth are allowed to enjoy divine rule unimpeded by the devil's deceptions, let us complete his account of the dragon's fate as that is here unfolded. John notes that after this millennium period, the dragon "must be let out for a little while" (20:3b), and when "released from his prison" (20:7b) the satan will continue to do what it has always done: "deceive the nations at the four corners of the earth" (20:8a). The four corners of the earth have for much of John's Apocalypse been under judgment, unleashed by the four angels when they stopped holding back the winds to and from those figurative corners and ends of the world in anticipation of the opening of the seventh seal (7:1–2). Yet during the millennial respite, the ends of the earth surely will enjoy a blessed time and season—evidenced by the macarism of 20:6 to which we will return in a moment—one undoubtedly correlated with the presence and activity of the divine seven spirits "sent out into all the earth" (5:6b) and now accomplishing God's purposes unhindered by satanic lies. What happens next not only alerts us to the devil's disingenuous powers but also is a sad but urgent warning to John's readers and hearers that even after a thousand years of theocratic rule, human creatures are still susceptible to the dragon's mendacities. Those deriving from "over the breadth of the earth" (20:9a), now represented as "Gog and Magog [and] as numerous as the sands of the sea" (20:8b), allow themselves to be galvanized by the ancient serpent against God and those enjoying his millennial rule (20:9a). Not even the millennial divine rule is able to inoculate human beings from demonic strategies, so ancient and primordial are they in nature. The breadth and depth of lingering human depravity are nowhere more stark than as unfolded in this scenario.

The reference to Gog and Magog now draws explicitly from Ezekiel 38–39, although there have already been multiple allusions in John's previous visions to this section of this exilic prophet's forecast of the final confrontation of the nations hostile to Israel and her God. So, although this postmillennial battle surely seems like a different one than the premillennial (narratively speaking) inferno that resulted in the internment of the two beasts (19:17–21), for John they achieve complementary results.[1] In the former case, the sword of the white horse rider dispatched and the midheaven predators devoured the armies of the beast; in this case, "fire came down from heaven and consumed them" (20:9b; cf. 11:5, 2 Kgs. 1:9–14; Ezek. 38:22, 39:6a). At the "great supper of God" (19:17b), the two beasts are cast, everlastingly, into the lake of fire; now, at this end-of-the-millennium clash, "the devil who had deceived them was thrown into the lake of fire and sulfur, where the beast and the false prophet were, and they will be tormented day and night forever and ever" (20:10). If the earlier historically and cosmically unfolded fire and sulfur judgments of worshipers of the beast and its image and of recipients of the beast's mark occur "in the presence of the holy angels and in the presence of the Lamb" (14:10b), these latter are nowhere to be found vis-à-vis the same eternal afflictions of the dragon and beasts; instead, this hurling down of the dragon is accomplished in the eyes of all the gathered world, as innumerable as the sands of the seashore.[2]

We are now ready, finally, to consider John's millennium. Introduced initially in relationship to and unfolding during this same period of temporal binding of the dragon in the bottomless pit (20:2), John elaborates on this thousand-year period in the fifth of his final seven visions, and does so with regard to the martyrs that have been featured across the Apocalypse: "Then I saw thrones, and those seated on them were given authority to judge. I also saw

1. So complementary that some scholars do not see the narrative insertion of the millennium as introducing a historical time span separating the two "Armageddons" (to use the name John deploys in 16:16) so that these are understood to be the same "event" that cast the dragon and its beasts into the lake of fire simultaneously; see, e.g., Gregory K. Beale, "The Revelation of Hell," in Christopher W. Morgan and Robert A. Peterson, eds., *Hell under Fire: Modern Scholarship Reinvents Eternal Punishment* (Grand Rapids: Zondervan, 2004), 111–34, esp. 129.
2. This also provides a response to *why* the satan is released after a thousand years. If the triumphal processions of the Roman imperial guard during the Flavian dynasty (69–96 CE) publicly solidified the message of Roman rule over the kings of the earth for the peace and benefit of the world's subjects as manifestation of divine favor by including the captive chief enemy leader in the procession as a form of final and public humiliation, then releasing the satan at the end of the millennium and casting into the lake of fire can be understood as part of the culminating triumphant parade through which Jesus Christ finalizes the conclusive defeat of the dragon before a watching world. For details, see Wood, *The Alter-Imperial Paradigm*, ch. 6.

the souls of those who had been beheaded for their testimony to Jesus and for the word of God. They had not worshiped the beast or its image and had not received its mark on their foreheads or their hands. They came to life and reigned with Christ a thousand years" (20:4). The overcomers of the church in Thyatira were guaranteed authority over the nations (2:26), and those of Laodicea were pledged enthronement with Jesus (3:21). But it was Antipas of Pergamum who was martyred for his witness (2:13b), and it is he and others so killed who are the central actors of this millennial period. The question posed by the martyrs under the altar divulged by the breaking of the fifth seal about how much longer more they would have to wait, while preliminarily responded to there as involving only a short while longer (6:9–10), is here definitively answered. Those who have resisted the lies of the dragon with the truth of the Lamb, even through death (12:11, 17), are here inaugurated as justices. Those who have rejected the mark of the beast (13:16)—which buying and selling has already procured divine recompense (14:9–11)—and embraced instead the divine seal and Father's name on their foreheads (7:3–4; 14:1), even at the expense of their lives, are now empowered to reign with Christ. Those who have been crushed to death by imperial Babylon (16:6; 17:6; 18:24) have not only been avenged (19:2) but are raised from the dead to rule with the Lamb.

About this final judgment of the dragon that symbolized all that is ultimately evil and opposed to God, it is rightly said by Adventist Revelation scholar Sigve K. Tonstad, albeit with a directional twist (my crossing out): "Satan is made to stand [fall] alone on stage at the end of Rev's narrative in order to place him in a separate category that is distinct from the human drama."

Sigve K. Tonstad, *Saving God's Reputation: The Theological Function of* Pistis Iesou *in the Cosmic Narratives of Revelation,* Library of New Testament Studies 337 (New York and London: T&T Clark, 2006), 49.

John tells us four more important matters regarding these revived martyrs. First, they are part of the first resurrection, with the rest of the dead not coming back to life until the end of the millennial period (20:5). Whatever the millennium is or however long it endures, its bookends are the first and second resurrections. Second, this initial group of those so raised-from-the-dead are not only blessed but are also holy (20:6a). This fifth of seven macarisms declares the holiness of these raised souls, befitting in light of the triadically declared holy one on the throne (4:8; cf. 15:4; 16:5). Third, those so resurrected here also are exempt from the power of the second death (20:6b), which is momentarily clarified to be residence (with the dragon and its beasts) in the lake of fire (20:14). The second death's impotence and lack of reach is exactly what was assured to overcomers of the church in Smyrna even if, they were warned, their faithfulness would not enable escape from persecution and (the first) death (2:10–11). Finally, what will these martyrs-turned-justices do? They "will be priests of God and of Christ, and they will reign with him a thousand years" (20:6c). While this can be recognized as one expression of the church's provision of priestly services that brings the world into relationship with God (1:6), it is also a direct fulfilment of the heavenly choir's prophetic hymn that the Lamb has redeemed those "from every tribe and language and people and nation . . . to be a kingdom and priests serving our God, and they will *reign on earth*" (5:9–10, emphasis added).

FURTHER REFLECTIONS
Living in the Interim

The question, of course, is how to understand this thousand-year period. Our introductory chapter has elaborated on some of the dominant interpretations of this millennial time. Is it to be taken more literally, as many Dispensationalist and premillennialist readers urge, or does it function more figuratively, ecclesially, and even theopolitically, as those so-called amillennialists might suggest and those who advocate for versions of postmillennial interpretations claim? Interestingly, the prefixes of the pre-, a-, and post-millennial positions have to do with Christ's Parousia vis-à-vis the thousand-year reign, and that detail is of minor if any concern in this passage, completely subordinated to its two major questions: the fate of the dragon and the vindication of those martyred for their faith. Nevertheless, our interaction with this text can benefit from some effort to comprehend the results of these various approaches. Sticking with the details presented in these two visions for the moment—which as we shall see is not a bad idea when there is not much elsewhere in Scripture that addresses John's thousand years—Dispensationalists say that this must be a purely future reality since our current situation features the satan not bound up but out and about and also certainly does not seem like one over which resurrected martyrs are ruling the world with Christ. On the other hand, amillennialists and postmillennialists tend to view the subjugation of the satan as being initially accomplished in the cross and resurrection of Jesus, and the reigning of the martyrs as indicative of the church's spiritual authority during the present age. The difference is that the former tends to map the millennial period onto the time of the church whereas the latter, even if embracing the thousand-years in ecclesial terms, oftentimes also posits that the reign of the saints ought not to be reductively spiritualized but might also be catalytic for the forging of governments that would enact the divine justice and righteousness in historical and earthly time.[3]

However the millennium finally turns out, surely we are making much more of it than John himself did. Appearing only four times throughout the book—all in these few verses—there is scant wider scriptural resources for knowing how John was using this notion. There is the psalmist's poetic ruminations regarding YHWH as the faithful dwelling place for Israel throughout time: "a thousand years in your sight / are like yesterday when it is past" (Ps. 90:4), and this is retrieved in the second Petrine epistle in countering those scoffing the church's belief in Christ's imminent return: "do not ignore this one fact, beloved, that with the Lord one day is like a thousand years, and a thousand years are like one day" (2. Pet. 3:8). Intriguingly, the millennium so translated into an eschatological *day* when God rules the world in and through Christ and the saints would provide a final fulfillment of the seventh *day* of creation when God is said to rest from his creative works. Yet this reading could be defensible without eliminating what the other millennialist considerations proffer.

---

3. For more on what is here so very briefly summarized, see Gregg, ed., *Revelation: Four Views*, part VII.

In the end, then (pun intended!), I would prefer to emphasize what John does: that the millennium is an interim period to both reward the martyrs and to grant reprieve from the dragon's claws, but that it's the passing of these thousand years that is of greater import since that brings about the end of the satan and its promulgated deceptions. Only then can the world find its ultimate rest in the divine presence, no longer anxious about adversaries without or within. Millennial discipleship understood in that sense is not about life in some future one-thousand-year period but concerns serving with Christ in the present time, and this involves, positively, holding fast to the testimony of Jesus and the word of God on the one hand and worshiping God and welcoming his branding in (not the world's marks and symbols on) our lives. Blessed are those who are part of the first resurrection in the sense of being born again in the spirit of Jesus (John 3:1–8; 2 Cor. 5:17; Titus 3:6–7). On the contrary, those who do not experience this second birth and its form of millennial discipleship here on earth will get caught up in the worldly web of lies spun by the dragon, whether now or eschatologically, and those who are fooled may experience the second death in the lake of fire.

20:11–15

The Great White Throne: Writing the Books of Judgment

This sixth of the final heptad of visions (the last being the new Jerusalem in Rev. 21) is the very last of the final judgments and it concerns the rest of humankind against the backdrop of the final assignments of the dragon and its beasts. We will examine the who, how, and whither of this eschatological judgment. How might what is seen shape our own thinking about and living out our lives as part of the (seven) churches to whom this Apocalypse is addressed?

John's line of vision for this final mass judgment is cleared as the "great white throne and the one who sat on it" comes into view, prompting—contrary to the shelter that human creatures called on the world to protect them from the wrath coming from the throne with the breaking of the sixth seal (6:12–17)—the fleeing of heaven and earth "from his presence, and no place was found for them" (20:11).[1] Hence, John now sees "the dead, great and small, standing before the throne" (20:12a). On four other occasions, the "small and great," in that order, are mentioned: as deserving of reward or being rewarded (11:18b; 19:5) or as participating in or doing what is condemnable (13:16; 19:18). These all are now viewed as standing before the just judge, including those regurgitated (20:13a) by the seas (because of improper burials) and by Death and Hades, together symbolizing the realm of the dead (in graves or wandering in what the Old Testament calls Sheol) populated at least in part by the rider of the pale green horse (the fourth seal: 6:8). Some hence view those before the throne (20:12a) as the righteous raised from

1. See Blount, *Revelation*, 376.

the dead on the front end of the millennium (20:4b) and these from the seas and Death and Hades (20:13a) as the unrighteous brought back on the back end of the thousand years (20:5a),[2] thus providing a clearly demarcated scene of sheep and goats (Matt. 25:31–46). Perhaps the one like the Son of Man's holding the keys to Death and Hades (1:18b) means only that those in its grip will still be raised finally for judgment, not that they might be finally saved from out of their captivity. Regardless of how all of this is understood, the point is that this is a conclusive and universal judgment of all: whenever resurrected and however grouped, all of the dead will be reconvened for a final judgment, whether to life or to damnation (see Dan. 12:2; John 5:29).

How does this eschatological judgment ensue? Through the figurative consultation of books. With regard to the ones before the throne, John sees that "books were opened. Also another book was opened, the book of life. And the dead were judged according to their works, as recorded in the books" (20:12b). Then regarding those retrieved from the seas and Death and Hades, he further observes, "all were judged according to what they had done" (20:13b). Those standing before the throne appear to be like the overcomers from Sardis, whose names were preserved in rather than removed from the book of life (3:5), in contrast to the names of others who, like worshipers of the beast, were either never added or so erased from that same book (13:9; 17:8). John appears to be drawing from a long line of biblical references to such divinely kept books or records of judgment (e.g., Exod. 32:32–33; Luke 10:20; Phil. 4:3; Heb. 12:23),[3] not least Daniel's vision of the four beasts and its attendant cosmic judgment overseen by the Ancient One facilitated by many opened books (Dan. 7:8–10; cf. Dan. 10:21; 12:1).

There appear to be two types of determinations made from the consultation of these records. On the one hand, the book of life will include at least names, and those so identified therein presumably are destined to the kind of life that flows from the reign enjoyed by the martyrs (20:4, 6b) and that flows into the new heavens, new earth, and new Jerusalem (21:1–22:5). On the other hand, there is

2. Osborne, *Revelation*, 721–24.
3. See Blount, *Revelation*, 374.

also a judgment of works, both for those standing before the throne, facilitated by multiple books, and for those given up by the sea and by Death and Hades. Both groups, effectively *all* human creatures, are assessed according to their deeds. Some Christian theological traditions might divide the final judgment into two types, with the one side dominated by a Pauline model of salvation wherein notation in the book of life is inscribed by grace rather than merited by works (e.g., Eph. 2:8–9; but cf. 2 Cor. 5:10) so that the latter relate only to the kind of rewards granted to those whose names are gratuitously so recorded, and the other side including all of the other New Testament texts that emphasize works but wherein such are accounted through these other books only for retributive purposes as applied to those whose names are absent from the book of life to begin with (from the foundation of the world, according to 17:8).

John's Revelation itself does not cut such a straightforward line. The letters to the seven churches are replete with commendations for good works related to bearing truthful and persevering witness (2:2a, 19a, 26a; 3:8a), even as Jesus himself said to the Thyatirans: "I will give to each of you as your works deserve" (2:23b; cf. Matt. 16:27). There are also warnings about bad works related to buying into and living out what is later revealed more clearly as the dragon's deceptions (2:5–6, 22b–23; 3:1b–2, 15a), and this is confirmed in the rest of the book leading up to this scene of eschatological judgment (e.g., 9:20; 11:18b; 14:13b; 18:6). In other words, John is interested in not just a supposed state of gratuitously afforded salvation but a way of life, sated with actions, deeds, and conduct. John does not claim to know how names find their way into the book of life from eternity, but as far as he is concerned, our final destination is dependent on how we have behaved and according to what allegiances we have embraced. We "work" and "act out" our way to wherever it is we are headed.

> Instead of belief, the Apocalypse contains exhortations to action: hearers must overcome through repentance, worship, witness, perseverance, and obedience.
>
> Alexander E. Stewart, "*Argumentum ad Baculum* in the Apocalypse of John: Toward an Evaluation of John's Use of Threats," in Collins, *New Perspectives on the Book of Revelation*, 472.

And where is that destination? One possibility is the lake of fire. John puts it this way in summing up how the great white throne judgment concludes: "Then Death and Hades were thrown into the lake of fire. This is the second death, the lake of fire; and anyone whose name was not found written in the book of life was thrown into the lake of fire" (20:14–15). Here Death and Hades join the unholy triad of the dragon and his beasts already in the fiery lake. Although we have already been introduced by the seer of Patmos to the lake of fire imagery, intriguingly, the same Danielic passage that discloses the final judgment conducted through books includes reference to a stream or river of fire emanating from the throne of judgment (Dan. 7:10a).[4] Fire throughout the Apocalypse symbolizes not only the purity of the divine beings and their manifest presence (1:14b; 2:18; 3:18a; 8:5a; 10:1b; 19:12) but also a judgmental power to engulf any impurities in its vicinity (8:7–8; 9:17–18; 11:5; 14:10, 18; 15:2; 17:16; 18:8). That which human beings have feared the most, death itself, now is defeated, once-for-all, in the second death (cf. 1 Cor. 15:54–57).

FURTHER REFLECTIONS
How to Preach Hell and Who To

Note how our text characterizes the possibility, not actuality, of any other final castings into this consuming lake. Beyond the dragon and the two beasts, and besides weighty anxieties that Death and Hades represent, no one can know for sure if or how many names are excluded from the book of life. So how populated the fiery furnace will be for eternity is an open question. And that is precisely John's purpose: to sketch as starkly as possible what the stakes are for our lives and the choices we make. Perhaps those within the seven churches were more sensitive to their seer's rhetorical strategies than our generation, for whom hellish scenes have a revolting rather than motivating affect. But perhaps not: there is little evidence that the seven churches responded to John's imaginative

---

4. See Keener, *Revelation*, 470.

portrayals in accordance with what he hoped to prompt since even a decade later, Ignatius the bishop of Antioch (d. c. 108 CE) indicated that only the churches at Ephesus, Smyrna, and Philadelphia were still faithful, with congregations in the other cities apparently disintegrating or altogether dissolved.[5] But while we can debate how helpful it is to deploy tactics designed to scare people from hell, the bigger picture of these penultimate visions heightens God's sovereignty over the dragon and its beasts. Today's preachers and evangelists, not to mention lay witnesses to the gospel, should proclaim about hell, so to speak, surely (and perhaps only) as the final abode of the satanic triumvirate; more important is to preach heaven, to expound on the New Jerusalem and what such invites us to.

The larger question for John's hearers and readers today, then, is less whether we ought to respond to God in fear and more why we would want to ally ourselves with the one who is the opposite of the truth, holiness, and righteousness manifest in the footsteps of Jesus. Any use of fear in evangelism ought to adhere to Revelation's own guidelines, such as being directed to believers rather than outsiders, advocating and encouraging perseverance, staying within the limits of Scripture itself, and being focused on Christ as providing the wider theological and narrative context.[6] So, without minimizing the fear-based rhetoric that is part and parcel of apocalyptic discourse and imagery, we should also insist that John's visions are designed to open human eyes to the truth of this world's reality but refracted through heavenly lenses. Perhaps his wager is this: that if his readers and hearers come to see the ugliness of the dragon's mechanisms for what they are, they might respond positively to Jesus' knocking on their hearts' door (3:20). And once the latter step is activated, they can begin to confirm, through faithful discipleship, the writing in the book of life that also precedes them.

---

5. See Paul B. Duff, *Who Rides the Beast? Prophetic Rivalry and the Rhetoric of Crisis in the Churches of the Apocalypse* (Oxford: Oxford University Press, 2001), 132.

6. See, e.g., Alexander E. Stewart, "Scaring the Hell Out of You: Scare-Tactics, Christian Proclamation, and the Apocalypse of John," *Journal of Youth and Theology* 16 (2017): 165–84, esp. 176–80; cf. Stewart, "*Ekphrasis*, Fear, and Motivation in the Apocalypse of John," *Bulletin of Biblical Research* 27:2 (2017): 227–40.

21:1-8

The New Heaven and New Earth: Realizing the Divine Presence

This is the last of the heptad of visions unfolding in this conclud-ing section of the book after the fall of Babylon (19:11–22:5), and the final one of the Apocalypse as a whole. For this crowning vision, John saves the new heaven and new earth, and with them also the new Jerusalem. What is seen sets up the ecstatic journey in the spirit through which John then elaborates the magnificence of the coming Jerusalem (21:9–22:5). We will explore how these new aspects of creation are introduced and pay close attention to what is the lon-gest flow of words (21:5–8) coming directly from "the one who was seated on the throne" (21:5a). If it is true to say that, "This vision of transformation, unity, and peace is the hope for our entire planet and the light by which we are called to walk,"[1] then we need to ask how we can participate in realizing this eschatological reality to which the world is aimed.

The passing away of the first heaven and first earth, while figura-tively deployed in the preceding vision vis-à-vis the awesomeness of the great white throne judgment (20:11), is here reiterated but now in the context of indicating how space is opened up for the new heaven and new earth (21:1a). And this new creation includes, cen-trally, "the holy city, the new Jerusalem, coming down out of heaven from God, prepared as a bride adorned for her husband" (21:2). The wedding has been held (19:7) and the supper eaten (19:17–21), so now the new home, anticipated in the promise to overcomers at Phil-adelphia (3:12), is being set up. This is not just a refurbishment of

---

1. Carol J. Dempsey, "Revelation 21:1–8," *Interpretation* 65:4 (2011): 400–2, at 402.

the earthly city that readers of this vision in its final form surely realize had been ransacked by the Romans (in 70 CE; cf. 11:2). Instead,
this new domicile for the groom and his bride derives from heaven
but bridges to earth, not transcendently detached but viewable from
a very high mountain, as John tells us in a moment (21:10). As there
is no more sea (21:1b)—since the sea as historically representing
the chaos has now been domesticated through the locking up of
the anarchic dragon in the lake of fire,[2] although, having said that,
presumably the sea of glass in or at the throne room remains (4:6a;
15:2)—it seems that the new earth and heaven are a re-creatively
and organically interwoven whole.

A loud voice from the throne (21:3a), similar to that heard from
right before the last hallelujah (19:5–6), confirms that the chasm
between heaven and earth is now overcome: "See, the home of God
is among mortals. He will dwell with them as their God; they will
be his peoples, and God himself will be with them" (21:3). Notice
that the covenantal language of the Old Testament linking a transcendent God (in much of the Hebrew Bible canon) with the terrestrial people (singular) of Israel is here not only enlarged to include
the gentiles, the peoples (plural) of the world, but also to indicate
the immanent presence of the divine in an integrated new heaven
and earth. Hence, the creator and lord of the world now enters into
intimate relationship with people from every nation, tribe, and language (see 5:9; 7: 9). The first creation over which God presided has
been renovated into a sea-less and nontumultuous arena where the
divine presence can be coresident with human creatures.

The heavenly voice from the throne also tell us that with the new
heaven and new earth, God has and "will wipe every tear from their
eyes. Death will be no more; mourning and crying and pain will be
no more, for the first things have passed away" (21:4). That there
would be no more tears was already promised to the great multitude that came out of the great ordeal (7:17b) although this also
fulfills the Isaianic promise that crying will not be heard in Jerusalem once it is reestablished within the new heavens and new earth
(Isa. 65:17–19; cf. Isa. 25:8). Death, as we know, has disappeared

2. See Smalley, *The Revelation to John*, 524–25.

once-and-forever in the lake of fire (20:14). Mourning and pain evaporate as the broken first creation is replaced with the new one (cf. Rom. 8:18–22). As creaturely bodies need resurrection that is untouched by the second death so also does the creation itself need transformation for the divine presence amid God's peoples.

At this moment, the deity self-reinserts in a vocal manner. Aside for a very brief self-introduction at the beginning—God says there, "I am the Alpha and the Omega" (1:8)—this is perhaps only the second other time, if the command to John to measure the temple and altar was given by the Father (see the discussion of 11:1–3), that we hear directly from "the one who was seated on the throne" (21:5a). John records eight distinct utterances on this occasion:

1. "See, I am making all things new" (21:5b)—This reinforces and completes, positively, what the voice from the throne has just announced: the first creation passing away (21:4b) allows for the emergence of the second, new creation.

2. "Write this, for these words are trustworthy and true" (21:5c)—With the exception of what he heard from or through the seven thunders (10:3–4), John has been told repeatedly to write: by a trumpet-like voice, to the seven churches (1:11) and by the angels of the seven churches at the beginning of each of the ecclesial epistles (Rev. 2–3); by Jesus himself, about what was, is, and will take place (1:19); and the second and fourth macarisms (by a heavenly voice) blessing those who die in the Lord (14:13a) and (by an angel) inviting guests to the marriage supper of the Lamb (19:9a). On this occasion, God is self-attesting to the trustworthiness of these apocalyptic visions, doubling up on the last instance when the angel's blessing/invitation was corroborated, "These are true words of God" (19:9b).

3. "It is done!" (21:6a)—From the beginning we have known, "the time is near" (1:3b), and the pressure has been building, through the announcement of the seven last plagues (15:1b), to the outpouring of the seventh bowl when a voice from the heavenly temple declared initially, "It is done!" (16:17b). That bowl's pronouncement of what had

been singularly accomplished—literally, "γεγονεν, *gegonen* [singular], 'It is over!'"[3]—involved specifically the overturning of Babylon (Rev. 17–18), even as that was followed by judgment of the city's inner demonic spirits (the dragon and beasts: 19:17–20:10) and their followers, among all others (20:11–15). Hence, the heavenly assertion confirms that all of this—γέγοναν/*gegonan* in 21:6a is actually plural: "they are done"[4]—has now been accomplished and thus we are ready to turn our view toward the new things that are on their way.

4. "I am the Alpha and the Omega, the beginning and the end" (21:6b)—The initial self-identification to John of one who sits on the throne is here repeated, reemphasizing God as the author and goal of all things; the addition of "the beginning and the end" highlights also that the deity oversees the entirety of the process through which creation is directed,[5] which we have seen throughout the visions. We are approaching the end of the visions, and it is appropriate that the author and goal of all things confirms this in his own words.

5. "To the thirsty I will give water as a gift from the spring of the water of life" (21:6c)—The rivers and springs of water have been struck by both the blowing of the third trumpet (8:10–11) and pouring out of the third bowl (16:4). After the devastation of the first world, the thirsty need to be quenched not with literal liquid forms of hydrogen-oxygen but with life-giving water. As the first angelic messages-sign called for people to worship the one who created the first heaven and earth and with that also "the springs of water" (14:7b), so now with the new creation God will provide also living water fit for and capable of nourishing its inhabitants.

6. "Those who conquer will inherit these things" (21:7a)— Promises were made to each of the seven churches,

3. Smalley, *The Revelation to John*, 540.
4. Beale, *The Book of Revelation*, 1154.
5. Smalley, *The Revelation to John*, 541.

encouraging them to be victorious over their circumstances, to be discerning about the lies in their midst, and
to resist participation in the impurities and immoralities
available to them. How these promises will be brought to
pass and the benefits of the entire new creation are made
available to the bride of the Lamb.

7. "I will be their God and they will be my children" (21:7b)—
Whereas Jezebel's children will be struck dead (2:23a),
the children of Israel and of the church who "keep the
commandments of God and hold the testimony of Jesus"
(12:17b) will enjoy the divine paternity in the new heaven
and new earth. The covenant promises to Israel will be fulfilled—in particular the Davidic pledge (regarding Solo-
mon): "I will be a father to him, and he shall be a son to
me" (2 Sam. 7:14a)—but now expanded to adopt all the
faithful. More assuredly, all of the benefits of the Son of
God (2:17a), not least his priesthood and kingship, including sharing the throne with the Father, now accrue to the
people of God as the deity's children.[6]

8. "But as for the cowardly, the faithless, the polluted, the
murderers, the fornicators, the sorcerers, the idolaters, and
all liars, their place will be in the lake that burns with fire
and sulfur, which is the second death" (21:8)—There are
three important facets to this verse:[7] First, these are those
who fail to conquer (21:7a) and therefore will have no part
of the new creation; hence, they are characteristics of sinful unfaithfulness, beginning with those lacking courage to
remain firmly commited to the divine commandments and
the testimony of Jesus, and continuing to include behaviors
emulating not God's justice, holiness, and truthfulness but
the dragon's antithetical unrighteousness, impurities, and
deceptions. Second, this list overlaps with two others: a
prior one regarding those unrepentant despite the effects
of the demonic cavalry (9:20–21), with the exception of

---

6. Smalley, *The Revelation to John*, 542.
7. Keener, *Revelation*, 489–91, is a helpful treatment of each of these categories in light of John's
apocalyptic perspective (from across Revelation).

thefts appearing there but not here, and a later one regarding those excluded from the new Jerusalem (22:15);[8] but the present list is more comprehensive, particularly in its highlighting that cowards and unfaithful individuals are assigned to the second death. Third, John is speaking here prophetically rather than predictably; he is not saying that any specific murderer—David, for instance—will be found in the fiery lake, but he is rather speaking perlocutionarily, attempting to persuade and convince his readers and hearers that they ought to live courageously and faithfully and so on, so that they can be victorious, access the water of life, and be received as eternally adopted children of God into the new creation.[9]

FURTHER REFLECTIONS
Working for the Healing of All

For our purposes, the second death is designed for those who follow the deceptions of the dragon, not those who find themselves marginalized in the here and now for other socially constructed, imperially organized, and racially/ethnically configured reasons. In other words, perpetual foreigners on this side of the eschaton, and those who empathize or find themselves in solidarity with them, may certainly be warned of the impending second death like anyone else but can also be oriented toward the bridal city if they aligned their works with those of the Lamb and the divine commandments. Yet these are not mere addresses to individuals, as Enlightenment sensibilities often reduce meritorious versus punitive assessments to the level of the person; instead they invite consideration about if and how our commitments to the righteousness of the Lamb motivates us to work for the healing of all, addressing along the way the systems of injustice that afflict the poor and the perpetually foreign in more drastic and tragic ways than those otherwise privileged to

---

8. Aune, *Revelation 17–22*, 1130–31, helpfully lays out the three lists side by side.
9. Blount, *Revelation*, 383.

have access to the centers of power. In short, it is not enough to say that I as an individual person am not a murderer or fornicator and so on, but it behooves me to ask if I am working by the power and in the footsteps of the spirit-led Messiah to counter the systems of greed that lead to the taking of lives, or to up-end the networks of consumerism and commercialism that sustain the practices otherwise dubbed as sexually immoral.

The eschatological truth of the Apocalypse is that the old is passing away, although not yet fully gone, and the new is coming, although not yet finally arrived. Put theologically, the divine presence is here in the (seven) spirit(s) but not yet fully and palpably pervasive, even as the divine absence remains intermittently, if not still substantively, insofar as the lies of the dragon and its henchmen (the beasts and their systems) obfuscate the perception of human creatures. The book of Revelation is designed to help the church see through the illusions of the present fallen world, realize that its brokenness is being mended by the one on the throne, and welcome the new creation that promises to fulfill the promise of what is disappearing. As we hear the voice of God anticipate the coming creational transformation, are we inspired to align our lives, behaviors, and actions so as to participate in, and in that sense also bear witness to and realize, however incompletely but no less substantively, the passing of the old and the arrival of the new?[10] Put otherwise, are we motivated to distance ourselves, behaviorally and dispositionally, from what belongs with the dragon and beasts in the lake of fire not only so we can escape its anguishes but more readily orient ourselves in the opposite route? If we are teetering on the edge, there is a final vision elaborating on the new Jerusalem that we can hope will propel us in this direction.

---

10. A further missiological consideration of this passage is Jannie du Preez, "All Things New: Notes on the Church's Mission in the Light of Revelation 21:1–8," *Missionalia* 24:3 (1996): 372–82.

21:9–21

The New Jerusalem: Forming Heaven on Earth

John depicts three dimensions of the new Jerusalem: what I call the architectural, what is related to its reconceptualization of the city's temple, and what might be seen as its urbanized paradisiacal elements.[1] We will focus in this section on the first dimension and keep the latter two for the next and penultimate section of the body of this theological commentary. The goal here is to not only make sense of some of the detail provided regarding the constitution and construction of the new Jerusalem but to appreciate what its envisionment might do for the question raised in the preceding discussion: How might we participate in proclaiming and working for the coming new creation when constrained in the present time by our twenty-first-century imagination?

Two introductory cues connect the revelation of the new Jerusalem to the unveiling of Babylon's judgment. First, as the latter was displayed by "one of the seven angels who had the seven bowls" (17:1a), so is the former so showcased: "one of the seven angels who had the seven bowls full of the seven last plagues came and said to me, 'Come, I will show you the bride, the wife of the Lamb'" (21:9). If the former of these bowl angels then go on to exhibit the great whore, the current bowl angel—possibly but unlikely to be the same one since John could have easily identified such if that had been the case—goes on to convey the Lamb's bride and wife. Second, the earlier bowl angel carried John "away in the spirit into a wilderness" (17:3a) for his demonstration whereas the present bowl angel's

---

1. Fee, *Revelation*, 295, divides these same three sections as the physical, characterological, and Edenic aspects of John's description.

transportational efforts, also "in the spirit," are to "a great, high mountain" (21:10a). The bowl angels work spiritually in both cases, but in different directions: into the wilderness to witness the downfall of the great whore, and into the lofty arenas of the heavens in order to grasp how the Lamb's bride, as a city, connects heaven and earth, similar to but distinct from the mighty angel who had the little scroll (10:1–2, 5–6). Thus, John's intention to compare and contrast the two symbolic female images is made clear. What is before us seeks to orient our hopes and aspirations to the kind of world that God will bring about.

Most important, the new Jerusalem and Lamb's bride/wife "has the glory of God and a radiance like a very rare jewel, like jasper, clear as crystal" (21:11). The Lamb has indeed been glorified (1:6b, 5:12–13), but consistently across the Apocalypse, glory is indicated either as being given or as belonging to God (no less than ten occasions up to this moment: 4:9, 11; 7:12; 11:13b; 14:7a, 15:4a, 8a; 16:9b; 19:1b, 7a). Whereas the great whore attempted to glorify herself (18:7a), here the Lamb's bride is said to simply radiate with the divine glory. Further, if the harlot sought to adorn herself with purple and scarlet clothing and "with gold and jewels and pearls" (17:4; cf. 18:16), then the brilliant translucency of the bride is remarkable, reflecting nothing less than the jasper-like qualities of the one on the throne and the crystal-like sea of glass before him (cf. 4:3a, 6). This dazzling luminosity is what imposes itself on John, and only an imaginative envisionment can appreciate what otherwise pales in written words about the city's walls, gates, and other features. Let us take these in reverse order.

> Since jasper is normally an opaque stone, the description of it being like crystal underlines its purity and value.
>
> Aune, *Revelation 17–22*, 1154.

First, the city is gargantuan, and this is an understatement. We know this because the bowl angel giving John the tour had a "measuring rod of gold" (21:15) and discovers that "the city lies foursquare, its length the same as its width; and he measured the city with his rod, fifteen hundred miles; its length and width and height are equal" (21:16). The city turns out to be a cube, equally lengthy in multiple directions and dimensions, and thus truly inconceivable in its scope.[2] As important is that the city and its main street are both pure gold, clear and transparent as glass (21:18b, 21b). So far, we have seen all kinds of gold items, not only cargo, altars, and even idols (8:3b; 9:13, 20b; 18:12a) but also those worn like crowns, sashes, and other accessories (1:13b; 4:4b; 14:14b; 15:6–7; 17:4a), and those used like bowls, censors, and cups (5:8; 8:3; 16:7; 17:4). But here we glimpse a colossal and entirely golden city, and John's repeated insistence on the new Jerusalem's clarity and its street's incandescence "underscore the resplendent nature of the materials of the city and hence the city's intrinsic trait of reflecting God's glory."[3]

What about the gates of the city? Patrolled by twelve angels, they have as inscriptions "the names of the twelve tribes of the Israelites; on the east three gates, on the north three gates, on the south three gates, and on the west three gates" (12:12–13). The retrieval of the twelve tribes, each named, has already been registered as part of God's eschatological plan for the world (see 7:4–8), but John seems to be following Ezekiel's concluding vision of the restored Jerusalem's city gates carrying the twelve tribal names (Ezek. 48:31–34). John also tells us something else about the gates, that they consist of twelve pearls: "each of the gates is a single pearl" (21:21a). The great earthly city traffics in miniature pearls (18:6, 16), but the heavenly city has gigantic pearls as conduits connecting up any and everywhere to its main street. We shall see in the next section why this is important.

Finally, then, what does John say about the city's walls? Beyond the fact that this is a twelve-gated wall (21:12a), it also "has twelve foundations, and on them are the twelve names of the twelve apostles of the Lamb" (21:14). This is the second time that the apostles have been specifically identified, although here they are referred to specifically as the *twelve* where the earlier mention may have been

2. For North American readers, consider a city running from the northern suburbs of Toronto, Canada, into the waters south of Miami, Florida, which is about 1,500 miles, and then imagine the city extends up into the far outer domains of the earth's atmosphere, past the stratosphere (up to 30 miles up), mesosphere (31 to 50 miles up), and thermosphere (50 to 440 miles up), and well up into the exosphere (the next almost 6,000 miles, as atmospherists define these layers). Now let's cease to think about this literally since the point is simply to come to grips with the incredibility of the new Jerusalem.

3. Beale, *The Book of Revelation*, 1089.

more generically understood (18:20). But the apostolically named foundations plus the tribally named gates suggest that the bride of the Lamb includes both Israel and the church. Further, the wall sized up by the angel with the golden rod is "one hundred forty-four cubits by human measurement" (21:17a), which is about two hundred feet (each ancient cubit being about the approximately eighteen inches from a human elbow to the tip of the forefinger). It is unclear whether this refers to the breadth or the height of the wall, or perhaps the measurement relates to a cube-shaped wall like the city (21:16). Regardless, the wall is ridiculously small relative to the city it encircles, but the point is only that it serves a decorative and imaginative function fit for ancient cities—that are always surrounded by walls—not that the Lamb's bride needs to be protected from enemies (they have all been judged or lodged out of sight in the fiery lake) nor that those in the new Jerusalem need to be demarcated from what is outside (the open gates, we shall soon see, do not reflect that concern). In fact, on the latter point, that the wall "is built of jasper" (21:18b) not only underscores the *that* and the *how* of the entire city's pellucidity but also suggests that the whole notion of being outside or inside is minimized.

There is one more aspect of the city's wall John elucidates. The foundations, named after the apostles, "are adorned with every jewel; the first was jasper, the second sapphire, the third agate, the fourth emerald, the fifth onyx, the sixth carnelian, the seventh chrysolite, the eighth beryl, the ninth topaz, the tenth chrysoprase, the eleventh jacinth, the twelfth amethyst" (21:19–20). Rather than go into details of each stone's symbolism, more relevant here is to note the parallels with the jewels on Aaron's priestly breastplate in the book of Exodus (Exod. 28:17–20; 39:10–13). Even granting the difficulty in agreeing on the appropriate English translations from the Hebrew of Exodus to the Greek of the Septuagint or of Revelation, for that matter, the parallels are arresting, with up to ten of the stones, possibly, carried forward from the earlier lists into John's new Jerusalem.[4] The seven churches have been redeemed to be a kingdom of priests (1:6; 5:10; cf. 20:6), and their service to represent God to the world

---

4. Compare Ford, *Revelation*, 342, with Osborne, *Revelation*, 757, and Koester, *Revelation*, 818; see also the more lengthy discussion in Beale, *The Book of Revelation*, 1080–88.

and vice versa in this regard appears to be built into the new Jerusalem, precisely where the border (the wall) is supposed to separate those within from those outside. The gates not only allow sight from either to the other side (because of its lucidity) but now we see that its foundations reflect the priestly (Aaronic) service of the people of God, illumined in all their jeweled glory.

Taking a step back for a moment to comprehend John's portrayal of the bride of the Lamb, note the multiplicity of the number twelve at almost every turn: twelve gates; twelve angels; twelve tribes; twelve foundations; twelves names; twelve apostles; foursquare cubed; one hundred forty-four cubits (which is twelve times twelve); twelve jewels; and twelve pearls. This doesn't include the twenty-four elders, 144,000, or twelve stars from before, nor the twelve fruits we shall soon see that are part of this urban paradise (22:2). Twelve is surely the number of completion, though, and the angel's showcase of the Lamb's bride confirms that in almost every detail.

FURTHER REFLECTIONS
Reorganizing Margins and Centers

Obviously, no one should build heaven on earth following what the golden rod specifies, even as we currently lack the technology to erect into our exosphere. But what does this preview of the new Jerusalem have to tell us about faithfulness to Jesus in the here and now, or about how to experience a little bit of heaven on our way to the marriage supper of the Lamb and its aftermath? As we are only midway through our tour, this can only be a provisional consideration. There are two important points about the city's architectural features. First, male readers ought to pause at the imagery of being part of the bride of the Lamb. Not only is the "more fully embodied sensuality presented by Babylon [rejected] in favor of the New Jerusalem's idealized and abstract opulence,"[5] but more important, there is no hierarchy of male and female in the coming divine reign:

5. Greg Carey, "A Man's Choice: Wealth Imagery and the Two Cities of the Book of Revelation," in Amy-Jill Levine, *A Feminist Companion to the Apocalypse of John*, 158.

there is only the wife of the Lamb, the people of God, comprised of male and female, young and old, slave and free (Acts 2:17; also Gal. 3:28), from every people, tribe, and nation (ethnicity). All those relegated to foreigner status have now been brought into the center, and their perpetuity on the margins have been cancelled. Those of us used to traversing the margins of church or society might want to consider what it means to be wedded to the Lamb eschatologically, and even now betrothed to the one slain from the foundation of the world; those used to control the margins from any imagined center might want to imagine being the groom's bride and to begin to work in that vein now rather than getting a rude awakening later.

Second, the divine glory reigns. First and foremost, as we have already observed throughout this commentary, this is not a call to mimic the world and erect our own cathedrals, which showcase only our achievements and establish our own imperial identities. Rather, this suggests that any contemporary faithfulness ought to be ordered by and toward God and also suffused with that glory, not by our own efforts (which cannot manufacture this) but by our worship of the one who is glorious. This means also that those who find themselves on the margins, like many who identify as or with perpetual foreigners, can nevertheless be drawn into the city's center following the light of the throne and the Lamb. Finally, the translucency of the city counters the subterfuge that characterizes life in the great worldly city; this invites consideration of how we might structure our churches, not to mention our social relations, truthfully and openly so that illusions are exposed and dishonesties are undermined. Might we thereby begin to erase the worldly conventions that separate the current ecclesial and social centers of power from those marginalized otherwise for whatever reason—us perpetual foreigners being so sidelined for multiple, intersectional even, reasons—so that a new people of God of those from every tongue, tribe, and language can emerge?

There is one more very important insight derivable from the gates that connect to the center of the city, but this awaits further elucidation via the angelic expedition.

21:22–22:5

The Edenic City and the Nations: Being Drawn into Communion with God

Having looked at the materials and structure of the new Jerusalem, we now see what happens to the temple that was in the version that is passing away and observe the Edenic reconfiguration of the city. What we find in these two domains are variously complementary, so much so that we shall see elements from one sphere in the other and vice versa. Here we learn much more about the luminousness of the city walls and the purpose of the pearly gates in facilitating movement into and out of the city. The kings and nations of the world reappear, perhaps unexpectedly, streaming into the city. It turns out that the new Jerusalem represents an always-accessible divine presence for the world. How might these images of the eternal intercourse between the kings and nations/ethnicities of the earth and the Lamb's bride and its inhabitants freshly catalyze thinking about Christian witness and mission in a postcolonial and post-Christendom twenty-first century? Let us proceed through the rest of the angel's guided showing of the new Jerusalem with this question in mind.

First, surely striking for Jewish Christian readers (and hearers) of the seer's words is that he writes: "I saw no temple in the city, for its temple is the Lord God the Almighty and the Lamb" (21:22). The temple was a staple of the Davidic covenant, even as such was elaborated in ancient Israel's most extensive eschatological vision (Ezek. 40–48); and for John, the heavenly throne certainly included such (11:19; 14:15, 17; 15:5–6; 15:8–16:1; 16:17), even the great multitude gathered from out of the great ordeal are said to worship God "day and night within his temple" (7:15). Yet rather than saying the temple and all it represented has disappeared in the new Jerusalem, note that its reality is now taken up by the immanent deity and the Lamb. Whereas the earthly temple was needed since it was the location where a people separated from God could meet the holy and Almighty one through intermediaries (the priests and liturgical cult), there is no longer such absence that needs to be overcome,[1] not when the God of the new Jerusalem is now at home among mortals (21:3), and most assuredly not when "the throne of God and of the Lamb will be in it, and his servants will worship him" (22:3b) directly, rather than through temple-mediated space and activity.

> John presents Jesus Christ as the fulfillment of Ezekiel's temple vision.
>
> Andrea L. Robinson, *Temple of Presence: The Christological Fulfillment of Ezekiel 40–48 in Revelation 21:1–22:5* (Eugene, OR: Wipf & Stock, 2019), xxiv.

So, if religionists might be surprised at the theologically and christologically reconstituted site of worship, naturalists will wonder about the fundamental resourcing of the city's light, the source/s of which make the world, certainly their cities, revolve (so to speak). John writes that "the city has no need of sun or moon to shine on it, for the glory of God is its light, and its lamp is the Lamb" (21:23). Whereas the earth moves around the sun, we could say, if we think of the sun circling the earth (the Ptolemaic perspective prevelant in the first century), that the Apocalypse's revolutionary new creation turns on the presence of the one on the throne and the Lamb. Now, associating the Lamb with the moon is less a matter of subordinating the Son to the Father than of indicating how the service and functions of creation's luminaries are no longer needed in light of (pun intended) the divine glory manifest in the throne now descendant from the heavens (where Father and Son are distinct and yet fused, it will be remembered). Not only that, since the divine presence perpetually pervades the Lamb's bride, John observes, "there will be no night there" (21:24b). This is repeated in a moment for emphasis at the end of when John considers the broader topography of the massive city: "there will be no

---

1. I get the notion of the divine absence in relationship to the temple from Murphy, *Fallen Is Babylon*, 423.

more night; they need no light of lamp or sun, for the Lord God will be their light" (22:5a; cf. Zech. 14:7).

The splendorous luster of the divine light spreads, it appears, far beyond the horizons of the cubed city. We might not expect anything less since this is no natural lighting but the gloriousness of the creator itself. So effulgent is the light emanating from the city that it guides, from beyond the city walls (as John images them), the paths and movements of the nations. This allows "the kings of the earth [to] bring their glory into" the city (21:24b), and "People will bring into it the glory and the honor of the nations" (21:26). Of course, the kings of the nations and their beastly armies, under the sway of and deceived by the serpent's sorcery, have been destroyed (17:28; 18:23b; 19:17–18; 20:8–9), but there have been hopeful indicators throughout the book—e.g., Jesus being declared as "ruler of the kings of the earth" (1:5b) as well as "King of kings" (17:14; 19:16)—that some, from the ends of the earth even, might yet be salvaged and redeemed. The harpists by the sea of glass singing the song of Moses and the Lamb certainly foresaw a time when "all nations will come and worship before" the Lord, that is, once his judgments are revealed (15:4b). Whatever the merchants, seafarers, and shipmasters were lamenting about regarding the losses of trade coming and going into the city on seven hills, here John sees the transnational interchange with the heavenly city: the kings and nations (ethnic groups) of the world bring their glory and honor to the bridal city, and God receives such approvingly from them.[2] John is perhaps merely following his prophetic predecessors in these details, it might be argued, including when it was said: "Arise, shine; for your light has come, and the glory of the Lord has risen upon you . . . . Nations shall come to your light, and kings to the brightness of your dawn" (Isa. 60:1, 3).[3]

John thereby sees a new grand-central station, so to speak, not

2. See Mangina, *Revelation*, 242–43.
3. Scholarship on the nations in Revelation is growing, including, e.g., Ekhard J. Schnabel, "John and the Future of the Nations," *Bulletin for Biblical Research* 12:2 (2002): 243–71; Dave Mathewson, "The Destiny of the Nations in Revelation 21:1–22:5: A Reconsideration," *Tyndale Bulletin* 53:1 (2002): 121–42; and Allan J. McNicol, *The Conversion of the Nations in Revelation*, Library of New Testament Studies 438 (New York and London: Bloomsbury / T&T Clark, 2011).

the old city of Babylon that extorted its patrons and exploited client-kings (the nations and ethnic groups of peoples) but a new Jerusalem that welcomes outsiders and into which those from every tongue, tribe, and language freely and incessantly bring what is honoring to God. This non-stop commerce, less the exchange of goods and more the honorific bestowals of gifts before the throne, is enabled by the continuous luminescence and the constant openness of the pearly gates, which "will never be shut" since there is never any nightfall (21:25). Again, the Isaianic vision has prepared the way: "Your gates shall always be open; day and night they shall not be shut, so that nations shall bring you their wealth, with their kings led in procession" (Isa. 60:11).[4] And if there are any doubts that these foreigners will not soil the bride of the Lamb with their alienness, there is in the center of the city the tree of life with its multiseasonal (again: never-ending) leaf-bearing fruitfulness that serves "the healing of the nations" (22:2b). In other words—and here read after Pentecost—the peoples of God will bring what is unique and particular to their cultures and ethnicities (nations, for John), and these will be purified by the light that draws them so they can enrich the wares and relationships of the bridal city in their multiplicity and pluriformity.[5]

I should say more about the tree of life and the other natural elements of the city's landscape and waterscape, since the angel shows these things to John. The latter sees "the river of the water of life, bright as crystal, flowing from the throne of God and of the Lamb through the middle of the street of the city. On either side of the river is the tree of life with its twelve kinds of fruit, producing its fruit each month" (22:1–2a). Herein is the Edenic paradise regained, albeit incorporated into the bride of the Lamb descended from heaven. The crystal-like character of the walls and city inter-refracts with the brilliance of this central river, somehow intertwining with and even serving as the main street of the cube so that to sojourn on the street and to navigate

4. For further discussion of how the latter parts of the Isaianic prophecy repeatedly signal how the nations of the earth will stream into the restored Jerusalem, precisely the images that here spark John's imagination about the new Jerusalem, see Yong, *Mission after Pentecost*, §§4.2–4.3.
5. See Richard J. Mouw, *When the Kings Come Marching In: Isaiah and the New Jerusalem*, rev. ed. (Grand Rapids and Cambridge, UK: Eerdmans, 2002), esp. chs. 4–5; also, Yong, "Kings, Nations, and Cultures on the Way to the New Jerusalem: A Pentecostal Witness to an Apocalyptic Vision," in S. David Moore and Jonathan Huntzinger, eds., *The Pastor and the Kingdom: Essays Honoring Jack W. Hayford* (Dallas: TKU Press, 2017), 231–51.

down the river would be to equally traverse the central artery of the new Jerusalem (effectively, to walk on water as Jesus did!). More important for John's eschatological urban imagination, however, is that the many trees and rivers in the primordial garden of Eden (Gen. 2:9–14), prophetically foreseen in the renewed and restored kingdom of Israel (Ezek. 47:1–12) but yet ravaged in the meanwhile as collateral damage from the judgments exacted on the earth (the first and third trumpets and in the third bowl), is here effectively transplanted and trans-irrigated—as one collective tree manifest on both sides of the river—into the heart of the bridal city. Victors among the Ephesian Christians will indeed be able to access the tree of life promised to them (2:7b), but more important, to apply the balm of its productive and regenerative leaves.

Perhaps it is in part because of the curative and tonic power of the tree of life's leaves that "nothing accursed will be found there [in the city] any more" (22:3a). Or perhaps it is also because only those who have welcomed the light of the one of the throne and his Lamb will want to be there. John sees it this way: "the throne of God and of the Lamb will be in it, and his servants will worship him; they will see his face, and his name will be on their foreheads" (22:3b–4). Noticeably, by this time, the worship of the one on the throne and the worship of the Lamb are indistinguishable; either case involves worship of *him*, of both. It will be recalled that the promise to the overcomers at Philadelphia suggests the Jesus' new name is interconnected with the name of his God, of the city of his God, and of the new Jerusalem (3:12b). Those whose foreheads are otherwise marked by the beast and the number of his name, however, have long been subject to everlasting and smoky and fiery judgment, either that of Babylon's (14:9–11) or as a result of the great white throne accounting rendered to those who were part of the second resurrection (20:4–5, 13–15). These will never experience the divine presence, but the saints will, even unlike Moses (see Exod. 33:18–23), see *his face*, the two-in-one appearance of the one on the throne and the Lamb.

One more point John makes about the new city that we may prefer to ignore but should not: "But nothing unclean will enter it, nor anyone who practices abomination or falsehood, but only those who are written in the Lamb's book of life" (21:27). This might be the flip side of John's anticipating how the medicinal powers of the leaves from the tree of life will remove any curses lingering upon the city (22:2–3a), and imagining the scenario that way suggests that the unclean, abominable, and prevaricators remain that way only because they either refuse to or are not able to be drawn by the light of the city into its therapeutic transformation. More exact is that John is calling out and uncovering *practitioners* of abominations and deceptions; those who are behaviorally active in these ways will not be found in the city. Put another way, John is less interested in developing the demographics of the rural areas outside the city than in clearly delineating that those so calcified in their ongoing habits and actions are not those whose names have been recorded, from eternity or whenever (17:8), in the book of life.

FURTHER REFLECTIONS
Redeeming Diversity

From a perpetual foreigner perspective, it is important to realize that inscription in the Lamb's records proceeds not discriminatorily, based on the color of one's skin or on one's ethnic, gendered, or class status, but according to whether our behaviors embody his commandments or follow his counterpart's lies and falsehoods. Double clarity is needed: the arrival of the kings and nations and ethnicities mean not that there is simplistic allegiance to national powers or tribal identities but that cultural values and resources are finally redeemed for declaring the glory of God. To repeat: The primordial condemnation of Babel confirms in the eschatological judgment of Babylon that a self-centered pluralism for humanity's own sake is the idolatry that will be swallowed up by the earth, buried under the sea, and consumed in the lake of fire. Instead, Pentecost renews the capacities of human peoples to utter the truth, perform the good, and exemplify the beauty of cultural diversity for the wondrous and powerful works of God (Acts 2:11). Those who have experienced perpetual liminality will finally be able to sing and perform confidently in their own language and culture.

So how does the bride—including the kings, nations, peoples, tribes, and languages of the world—prepare herself so that she can be adorned for the wedding and marriage that serves as the eternal context and environment for these blessed activities? By heeding the words of this revelation, as the final part of this book now restates. On the one hand, yes, the kings and nations/ethnicities exercise some agency in strolling through the city gates with their wares; but on the other hand, also, yes: they do so only as guided by the lamp of divine light (2:24a). John's vision of the new Jerusalem emphasizes throughout God's initiative, not only in the privilege granted the seer to overview the city's descent but also in how all of the city's activities are possible only through the divine provision of light, water, grooves of transportation, produce, and medicine (its infrastructure and nourishment, indeed). There is no commerce, travel, or transaction—no weddings or markets (18:23)—without God's presence. This final heavenly home is secure for all creatures precisely as perfected and sanctified in the Lamb.

22:6–17

The Spirit and the Bride Say, "Come":
Welcoming the World

There are three parts to this concluding segment of John's Apocalypse: one that signals he is bringing the vision/s to a close (22:6–9), one that gathers around, arguably, a number of Jesus' personal last messages (22:10–17), and one that adds John's own final thoughts (22:18–21). We shall save the third and final part of these verses for our final thoughts below and focus here on the first two sections of the book's ending. John is addressing the seven churches, yet as I read these closing words as part of the church to which he has been writing, I am left to wonder also about its implications for us in relationship to others who might be over-hearing or over-seeing our engagement with this text. If we are invited to enter into John's world, what are the implications for our own interactions with others who for the moment are outside of the (seven) church(es)? Let us explore this question by considering Revelation's closing words.

One of the challenges to this initial portion of this apocalyptic conclusion is that there are at least three voices or writers across the span of our four verses: the "he" of verses 6a and 9a, presumably that of an angel, perhaps that of the bowl angel that introduced John to the heavenly city (see 21:9); Jesus (22:7); and John himself (22:8).[1] There are at least three thrusts in this collection for our purposes. First, the words bring us back to the opening of the book, as if to indicate that we have come full circle and to reinforce the message: the revelation of Jesus Christ that began with its urgency and mediated

---

1. Grant Osborne (*Revelation*, 799) thus suggests that the John's ambiguity about who the speakers are may be in order to get his readers "to focus on the message rather than the one speaking it."

character—being about "what must soon take place . . . made . . . known by sending his angel to his servant John" (1:1b)—underlines that "these words are trustworthy and true, for the Lord, the God of the spirits of the prophets, *has sent his angel* to show his servants *what must soon take place*" (22:6, parallels italicized).[2] Part of the difference is that now, at the end of the book, the trustworthiness and truthfulness of these words, asserted almost in these exact terms not long ago—by God and no one else in the context of announcing the descent of the divine presence among creatures in the new Jerusalem (21:5b)—are now restated to cover everything that has been written since the opening verses. If at the start God is emphasized as the ultimate source of the revelation, here that is strengthened with the emphasis on the role of the divine spirit, in particular the prophetic aspects of the divine spirits—notice the plural, consistent with the images of the *seven* spirits present in John's visions (1:4b; 3:1a; 4:5b; 5:6b)—and their work, in this case to communicate trustworthy and truthful words.

Second, Jesus himself reaffirms, "I am coming soon!"—a point to which we shall return shortly—and then practically repeats the first macarism of his Revelation, or at least the second part of that first benediction: "Blessed is the one who keeps the words of the prophecy of this book" (22:7). This not only buttresses John's claim about the prophetic character of the Apocalypse but also links to the first part of the first blessing, which reads in full, "Blessed is the one who reads aloud the words of the prophecy, and blessed are those who hear and who keep what is written in it" (1:3). Jesus' point is not only to inform but to persuade, to encourage the members of the (seven) church(es) to obey the prophecy, especially because his imminent coming means that the time is short.

The third accent extends that of the second, which has to do with ensuring John and the members of his churches are the kind of creatures "who keep the words of this book," especially because they heed the angel's instructions to: "Worship God!" (22:9b). Now this directive comes because, for the second time, John falls to worship at the feet of an angel (22:8b). John names himself here (22:8a), the

---

2. This and other parallels between 1:1–3 and 22:6–9 are charted in Aune, *Revelation 17–22,* 1148–49.

first time since the opening vision (1:4a, 9a), as if to ratify that he who was chosen as final mediating link for the Revelation—from God through angels to him (1:1)—actually "heard and saw [all of] these things" (22:8a), and it was the realization of the massiveness of this revelation, in hindsight as it were, that caused him to prostrate himself again. As it might be thought that our seer protagonist would have learned from the first correction he was to worship only God (19:10), that both scenes conclude visions of women figures—the great whore in the first case (17:1–18:24) and the bride and wife in the second (21:1–22:5)—suggests that what is repeated may serve two interrelated purposes: first to ensure that John's hearers and readers are realizing the point about comparing and, especially, contrasting the evil Babylon and the holy (new) Jerusalem, and second to doubly emphasize that the whole point of these disclosures is not for entertainment's sake but for directing our worship, which represents the culmination of our loves, lives, hopes, and desires, toward the one on the throne. That the angel John tried to worship the first time already said, "These are the true words of God" (19:9b), the angel in this instance avers and adds that beyond their truthfulness, the words, those other ones about the fall of Babylon and everything else, before and since, are also trustworthy (22:6a).[3]

The second part (22:10–17) of these concluding words of the book of Revelation are dominated by Jesus, at least if we read the central portion of these (22:12–16) as an uninterrupted flow of his sayings.[4] Whereas the opening vision of Jesus lifts up the gloriousness of his appearance with his words recorded but playing a supporting role (1:12–20), here at the close of the revelation, it is perhaps appropriate that Jesus' words take center stage. It may be precisely in light of Jesus' insistence, again, that "I am coming soon" (22:12a)—the second of three times in this concluding section, actually (also 22:7a, 20a)—that the angelic words mediating the first concluding segment and these final words of Jesus emphasize both that these prophetic words ought to be left unsealed and open

3. Murphy, *Fallen Is Babylon*, 433–36, includes more extensive commentary on the recurrence of this scene regarding John's worshiping angels; see also Aune, *Revelation 17–22*, 1202–03.
4. Some might believe that 22:14 inserts another voice into what is clearly Jesus' speaking in 22:12–13 and 22:16, but it makes just as much sense to read these continuously in my estimation; I follow here Koester, *Revelation*, 841.

since "the time is near" (22:10b), and that there may not even be enough time to repent: "Let the evildoer still do evil, and the filthy still be filthy, and the righteous still do right, and the holy still be holy" (22:11). Surely the end of Revelation is meant to contrast with the end of the prophetic book of Daniel, for whom "the words are to remain secret and sealed until the time of the end," and for this reason said: "Many shall be purified, cleansed, and refined, but the wicked shall continue to act wickedly. None of the wicked shall understand, but those who are wise shall understand" (Dan. 12:9–10). Hence, Jesus returns "to repay according to everyone's work" (22:12b; cf. 20:12–13).

> This is how Skaggs and Benham understand 22:11 and its rhetorical point: "for the seer in Revelation the end is so near that there is no time to alter the behavior of people on earth."
>
> Skaggs and Benham, *Revelation*, 232.

But Jesus' words also bring together various threads revelatory of divinity throughout the book. He self-identifies, "I am the Alpha and the Omega, the first and the last, the beginning and the end" (22:13). God has already been denoted as Alpha and Omega (1:8) as well as the beginning and the end (21:6), but here the divine creator-and-consummator and all-inclusive guarantor of the entire cosmic process (which is how we understood these phrases as our discussion of 21:1–8 above shows) is also applied to Jesus, with one additional characteristic: that he is first and last, meaning, also at the points of cosmic beginning and ending.[5] Further, he also says, "I am the root and the descendant of David, the bright morning star" (22:16b). The first part recalls one of the elder's naming of the slain Lamb (5:5) while the second confirms how Jesus could have promised to victors from Thyatira the gift of the morning star (2:28b).

It is this Jesus, the one slaughtered for the redemption of the world and who is also concerned enough to encourage his followers to persevere through to final overcoming, who gives the readers and hearers of this book some hope. Perhaps softening the pessimism of the angel about the unchangeableness of the ways of the evildoer and

5. Again, see Smalley, *The Revelation to John*, 541.

the impure (22:11), he pronounces a second blessing (see 22:7b) in
this closing section (and third overall of the book—also 16:15b—
that we will attend to further in the final thoughts section below):
"Blessed are those who wash their robes, so that they will have the
right to the tree of life and may enter the city by the gates. Outside
are the dogs and sorcerers and fornicators and murderers and idolaters, and everyone who loves and practices falsehood" (22:14–15).
We will return to the macarism momentarily, but surely the latter
mention of those outside the city ought to be taken, as were the earlier references to these groups and categories of people (e.g., 21:8),
less as descriptive or predictive than as prophetically exhortative
and rhetorically perlocutionary: to encourage those in the (seven)
church(es) to desist from behavioral patterns (practices) taking
after the deceiver of the world, the dragon. John's point has been,
repeatedly, not to reduce lives to single acts—since, as already mentioned, that would have excluded a murderer like David from being
covenanted to God—but to warn against developing entire ways of
life, including habitual practices, that are polluted and unclean.[6] Perpetual foreigners to the powers that be on this side of the eschaton
can become eternal foreigners to the heavenly city if they persist dispositionally and behaviorally with the dragon rather than the Lamb.

Yet, besides warning against imitation of the dragon's character
and behaviors, there is also a positive urging, which is the seventh
and final macarism of the book (22:14) that leaps off the invitation
to the Laodiceans to purchase white robes so they can have access to
the divine throne (3:18, 21). In this case, those so robed get access to
the tree of life, like the Ephesians (2:7b) inside the bridal city. Some
(especially those drawn to a universalistic theology that considers
the possibility that all are saved by God in the end) imagine that like
kings and nations who can be guided into the city by its divine light,
others who are outside, including those so named here—namely,

---

6. The *polluted* use here hearkens back to the list of those reserved for the lake of fire (21:8),
even as the *unclean* connects back to what is excluded from the new Jerusalem (21:27), and
these would be associated with what Jesus begins this list with: *dogs*, that have perennially
symbolized ritual and moral impurity in the Jewish world (Matt. 7:6; Luke 16:21; Phil. 3:2;
see also Blount, *Revelation*, 409, and Smalley, *The Revelation to John*, 574–75). The key here is
not to predetermine outsiders as *dogs* and in doing so relegating them to perpetual foreigner
status on the basis of conventional wisdom as opposed to Jesus' apocalyptic criteria.

"sorcerers and fornicators and murderers and idolaters" (22:15)—
will always have time to repent, enter the city which gates are continually open (21:25a), and receive the healing available from the
tree of life and its leaves.[7] This seems to rely on an overly literal consideration of the eschatological city's architecture and geography.
John would probably not recognize the question about whether a
universalistic soteriology is plausible, even if he would surely have
affirmed that the call of the gospel has universal extent and reach.[8]

And that is precisely what brings us to the denouement of the
book: "The Spirit and the bride say, 'Come.' And let everyone who
hears say, 'Come.' And let everyone who is thirsty come. Let anyone
who wishes take the water of life as a gift" (22:17). There are some
readings that see the first invitation, by the seven spirits and the
church anticipating the wedding to the Lamb and the arrival of the
new Jerusalem, to hasten the coming of Jesus who has already said
twice here at the end alone (22:7a, 12a) that he is on his way quickly.
That could be the case without also the call playing a dual role,[9] the
other consistent with the next two invitations, which would be to
hearers and readers of the book that they should keep their eyes on
the new heaven and new earth and all that is promised with the new
creation, not least the living water and its medicinal tree of life in
the bridal city. Yet the missiological dimension of the Apocalypse is
perhaps most clearly pronounced in these invitations, in particular
the middle plea that calls out to "*everyone* who hears," which now
includes all those who the witnesses in the churches bear testimony
to that have not yet transferred their allegiance from the dragon to
the Lamb. Again, John is switching back and forth from the future
blessed promises to addressing members of the seven churches in
their imperial environs. The latter include onlookers and on-listeners
who are here also invited to "come!"

---

7. E.g., Bradley Jersak, *Her Gates Will Never Be Shut: Hope, Hell, and the New Jerusalem* (Eugene, OR: Cascade, 2009), esp. ch. 12.

8. Ronald Herms, *An Apocalypse for the Church and for the World: The Narrative Function of Universal Language in the Book of Revelation*, Beihefte zur Zeitschrift für die neutestamentliche Wissenschaft und die Kunde der älteren Kirche 143 (Berlin and New York: Walter de Gruyter, 2006), argues from a literary and narrative perspective that John's universalistic language is rhetorical and hortatory, consistent with much of apocalyptic literature, to encourage the faithful onward in anticipation of final vindication.

9. See here Blount, *Revelation*, 412–13.

FURTHER REFLECTIONS
An Open Invitation

We know that the seven spirits have been effectively patrolling "all the earth" (5:7b), even from before the seals of judgment were broken. These spirits have also been speaking to the seven churches, urging their attentiveness to the words of Jesus (in Rev. 2–3). Here, among the last words of the book, the divine (seven) spirit(s) now make clear, with the supportive witness of the churches to whom they have been speaking all along, that the invitation to the new Jerusalem is for all, anyone who is thirsty and needs or wishes to be quenched by the divine wellsprings of water (cf. John 7:37–38). Whereas much of the Apocalypse sets the church off from and against the world, this final invitation suggests that the lines between the two are more blurred, at least missiologically and eschatologically speaking.

And it is here that I wish to address my Asian American colleagues once more, and then also all who stand in solidarity with us by embracing our liminal and marginal experience. Perhaps those of us who find ourselves always betwixt-and-between are in the best position to speak faithfully and truthfully in both directions: toward the ecclesial center on the one side and to those outside the fold on the other side. There is no boundary of separation other than us as the porous membrane that allows for the world to hear and respond to the call of the bridal spirit. Thus, precisely through such liminality and marginality, there is an ongoing invitation to those outside the people of God to participate, and the ones who respond, even if perpetually foreign to all centers of power on this side of the eschaton, can find home with the Lamb and his comrades—fellow servants—when heaven touches down to meet earth in the end.

Final Thoughts:
22:18–21 and Beyond

The last four verses of the book of Revelation suggest three basic considerations: the apocalyptic message for a twenty-first-century audience, the costs and benefits of the visions' rhetorical urgency, and the overall exhortative and pastoral intent of the Apocalypse.

The Power of Apocalyptic
Two Thousand Years Later

John's final substantive words draw from the Torah (cf. Deut. 4:2; 12:32): "I warn everyone who hears the words of the prophecy of this book: if anyone adds to them, God will add to that person the plagues described in this book; if anyone takes away from the words of the book of this prophecy, God will take away that person's share in the tree of life and in the holy city, which are described in this book" (22:18–19). Appearing here at the end not only of the book of Revelation but also, given the location of the Apocalypse, of the biblical canon, John's warning oftentimes is applied not only to his visions but to the whole of the scriptural collection. It is clear by now that John not only considers himself a divinely (spirit-) inspired prophet, but his words are also prophetic (1:3; 10:11; 22:6, 9–10), and thus they deserve careful consideration. His concluding warnings are thus starkly put: either adding to this book or accessing the tree or life; either taking away from this book or inhabiting the holy city; either adhering to this book or suffering the plagues described therein. There is no middle ground in John's mind.

And there is no *via media* in the apocalyptic genre either. Throughout the visions, John poses rigidly demarcated choices: to heed his
words or the lies of the dragon; to be faithful within the churches or
to embrace the agenda of the world; to worship God and the Lamb
or to follow the beast and the false prophet; to be in a position to
receive the blessings of the book or to be troubled by the plagues
enumerated therein; to attain access to the tree of life or to be cast to
the second death; to find habitation in the holy city or to be judged
as part of the great earthly city; to attain heavenly bliss or undergo
eternal damnation, and so on. John assuredly sought to be persua-
sive and compelling to his hearers and readers, desiring that those in
the seven churches would be incited in their faith commitments in
order to persevere in bearing witness to the testimony of Jesus. From
his perspective, the situation was urgent: the people of God needed
to be alert to what was at stake. The language of apocalyptic served
these purposes well, brokering no compromises that would nurture
laxity in perilous times.

> All of this is consistent with John's apocalyptic language as "an anti-exegesis of
> contemporary society . . . . The tension that the anti-language creates . . .
> between God and the dragon, beast and Lamb, good angel and bad angel,
> earth-dweller and saint. At the heart of the tension is the perception and
> experience of persecution by Christians at the hands of the evil Roman empire.
> The 'back talk' . . . of the Apocalypse of John . . . evinces a satiric tragic mode of
> formal argument, emplotment, and ideological implication."
>
> John E. Hurtgen, *Anti-Language in the Apocalypse of John* (Lewiston: Mellen Biblical Press, 1993), 139–40.

There are a number of challenges with John's approach today.
First, contemporary readers are far removed from the late first-
century West Asian context and thus do not easily comprehend
the existential situation, at least as John saw it. Second, prolonged
exposure to the Scriptures may have also numbed current readers to the jarring message of John's Apocalypse. Initially, efforts to
come to grips with a difficult text may lead to reading strategies
designed to ease if not eliminate the cognitive dissonance, and over
time, familiarity with such texts makes it more likely that readers

domesticate its message or at least empathize with those they can envision as being protagonists within rather than consider themselves to be critically targeted. Third, especially in a late modern era, the binaries of modernity are constantly being interrogated. Fluidity and dynamism are displacing immobility and essentialism. In this climate, even scriptural binaries—us and other, in particular—are less convincing. John's black-and-white world—pun not intended in a white-(Euro-American)-normative yet postcolonial world—may prove difficult to engage. This is especially the case when scriptural authority, including John's strategies of othering and his either-or rigidity, are used by those in power to undergird or advance their position,[1] in which case, John's original marginality is itself overlooked and his criticisms of the dominant cultures of his time are conveniently deployed to shore up the contemporary status quo.

In reading Revelation, then, any way forward, especially for perpetual foreigners like me but also for others in developed Western democracies, has to both adopt a posture of humility in front of a text that speaks the words of God and Jesus and also adapt a hermeneutic of multiple and shifting positioning in historical hindsight. As a perpetual foreigner is a hybridic subjectivity, we are insiders in some respects but outsiders in others, and faithfulness to Jesus means we are both his subjects (and subjected to his admonitions) and agents (participating in his witness), variously, sometimes simultaneously albeit in different directions. I do not know that there is any other option to charting such a via media that reads with John but perhaps also in a cautious manner vis-à-vis historic and now conventionalized retrievals of his Apocalypse. With regard to John's dominant anti-imperialism, the book of Revelation reveals a God who is holy, righteous, and true, and who desires to redeem and transform a world distorted by impurity, unrighteousness, and deception. Faithful appropriation of John's book in our time, then, cannot but foreground the redemptive holiness of God and

---

1. See, for instance, how Revelation's utopianism was used by early modern colonial settlers to advance their projects, in Jacqueline M. Hidalgo, *Revelation in Aztlán: Scriptures, Utopias, and the Chicano Movement*, The Bible and Cultural Studies (New York: Palgrave Macmillan, 2016), esp. ch. 3; Hidalgo's broader project seeks to empower indigenous Americans vis-à-vis the colonial and white Euro-American enterprise, as does David A. Sánchez, *From Patmos to the Barrio: Subverting Imperial Myths* (Minneapolis: Fortress, 2008).

denounce the exclusivistic cleansings perpetrated by the dragon and his divisive lies. This means that we are ordered according to the purity of the Lamb that draws those from every people, language, and nation/ethnicity into the new Jerusalem rather than reliant on this world's ways of categorizing or ranking people. And if the binary rhetoric of this book of Revelation, which appears at the end of the Bible, can help sensitize us to the injustice done in the name of national patriotism, then perhaps there are redemptive possibilities for listening and reading this text once again today.

Further, John is concerned not only that we read and hear but that we also act, that we live out what we have read or heard in accordance with Jesus' way of life. The world's ways, by contrast, destroy the earth and lead, ultimately, to a second death. This is because the great city/cities of the world have been caught up in the delusive falsehoods of the dragon and are captive to its destructive agenda. But what if we were oriented instead to the reparative and restorative new Jerusalem to come and therefore sought to work redemptively and prophetically in the world today—in its political, economic, and social spheres—toward that end? What if the binary rhetoric of great whore and bridal wife jar us into the realization that to uncritically enjoy the comforts of any status quo is to endorse the purposes of the dragon and that in order to engage appropriately in spiritual warfare we ought to see clearly how the mechanisms of the world are destroying the earth, killing the vulnerable, and perpetuating injustice in the name of progress? If John's apocalyptic either-or discourse shocks us into political and economic awakening, perhaps there are redemptive outcomes for considering the book of Revelation in the present.

"... Soon!"
Revelation's Rhetorical Urgency Today

For his penultimate word, John writes: "The one who testifies to these things says, 'Surely I am coming soon.' Amen. Come, Lord Jesus!" (22:20). Here, he overlays his own testimony with that of Jesus; or put another way, he undergirds his visions with the authority of Jesus but now intensifies its urgency with Jesus' insistence regarding his imminent return. Now this is actually the third time that Jesus has said he is coming soon in this concluding section (see also 22:7a, 12a), even as on two other occasions here at the end of the Apocalypse, there is angelic reiteration that what has been disclosed "what must soon take place" (22:6b) and that this book's pages ought to be open for regular consultation "for the time is near" (22:10).

John is clearly concerned that those among the seven churches might become too groggy and therefore unprepared for the Parousia. Remember that in his addresses to the seven churches, on no less than three occasions, Jesus sounds the alarm on his soon return (emphases added):

— to Pergamum: "Repent then. If not, *I will come to you soon* and make war against them with the sword of my mouth" (2:16);
— to Sardis: "If you do not wake up, *I will come like a thief*, and you will not know at what hour I will come to you" (3:3b);
— to Philadelphia: "*I am coming soon*; hold fast to what you have, so that no one may seize your crown" (3:11).

Further, Jesus included a seventh personal announcement—besides the three to the churches and the three in the concluding section—about his looming arrival at the end of the sixth bowl judgment: "See, I am coming like a thief!" (16:15). This version of Jesus' admonition works in tandem with that of the mighty angel during the trumpet intermission: "There will be no more delay" (10:6b–7), even as John himself—if Jesus' seven warnings and the three angelic versions do not successfully sound the alarm—thrice insists that the final judgments about which he discloses are "coming very soon" (11:14) and "must soon take place" (1:1a), "for the time is near" (1:3b).

It seems incontrovertible that John sincerely believed that the end of the world, including Jesus' return, was right around the corner, and since we are here two thousand years later, it is difficult to say it any other way: he was incorrect. There are two issues here. First, there is the matter of the return of Jesus itself. How might we continue to believe in his soon coming if it appears to have been delayed as long as it has? The second Petrine letter puts the question pointedly in this way: "in the last days scoffers will come, scoffing and indulging their own lusts and saying, 'Where is the promise of his coming? For ever since our ancestors died, all things continue as they were from the beginning of creation!'" (2 Pet. 3:3–4). We might not quite be scoffers and skeptics, but it is difficult not to consider the underlying question: Is Jesus coming back, or perhaps his coming can be understood only spiritually rather than expected to usher in the end of this cosmic age? The other matter is no less weighty. For some, to conclude that John was mistaken raises profound questions about the reliability of everything else he envisioned and wrote down. How can we trust what we find in the book of Revelation if on this important point of Jesus' Parousia, the author was misguided? Even if we wanted to honor John's warning to neither add to nor take away from his words, our efforts to comprehend and explain the delay of Jesus itself would inevitably add to or remove from what John has written down, and in that sense the deferral risks the trustworthiness of the whole that comes with that specific promise.

Here I do not wish to repeat some of what was said in the opening section of this book regarding this problem. I will add only two thoughts, the first leaping off John's own response to Jesus' words: "Amen. Come, Lord Jesus!" (22:20b). Clearly, the revelation of Jesus Christ invites our response, and in this case, the broadcast of his return summons our own yearning for that return. John may be read predictively, but doing so only in that sense eliminates his eschatological understanding that fuses the future with the present and that links who Jesus is and what he is doing or will do with who we are (as the people of God) along with what we are doing or should do. In other words, the words of Jesus, mediated through his angels and through John, are designed to orient us properly in the present. Put differently vis-à-vis the issue at hand: the promise of Jesus to return is intended to enable our alignment in the current moment toward that future expectation.

In that sense, John's is a fully orbed prophecy, not meant to merely foretell the future but more importantly to strengthen the resolve of the people of God in their and any other time toward the divine re-creation to come. Those who are caught up with the literalness of John's words are unable to appreciate or be encouraged by his

symbolic rhetoric; those looking for historical or chronological correlations will not be able to see their own lives as subjectively involved
with the unfolding events of this world's beastly systems; those looking for Jesus appearing in the sky are less likely to be living the presence of Jesus through the power of his (seven) spirit(s) in the near and
far political, social, and economic corners of the present world.

To be disciplined by this apocalyptic prophecy, on the other
hand, is to realize that the future promises of God have begun with
the life and teachings of the one slaughtered from the foundation of
the world and slain historically under Pilate and the imperial Roman
system. "The fundamental eschatological reality of Revelation is not
therefore the end of the world but rather the resurrection of Christ
in the present history of our world," writes liberation theologian
Pablo Richard.[2] To adhere to John's christological testimony, in turn,
is to be ready to be filled with the (seven) spirit(s) of Jesus in order
that we can bear witness to how his righteousness, holiness, and
truth is embodied in ecclesial communities whether in West Asia
or to, at, or from the ends of the earth. "The seven Spirits represent
the fullness of God's Spirit in the Church's witness to the nations. . . .
The Spirit conquers the Church to be God's eschatological people in
their prophetic witness, and the seven Spirits enable the Church to
fulfill its prophetic ministry to the world, convincing the nations of
God's kingship on earth as it is in heaven."[3] To live eschatologically,
in short, is to anticipate the coming of Jesus while being engaged
deeply in the here and now of this convoluted world with his life and
words by the power of his (seven) spirit(s).

Grace
The Final Word—Then and Now

In the end John writes: "The grace of the Lord Jesus be with all the
saints. Amen" (22:21). For all the words of judgment elaborated, the
final word is about divine graciousness. Whereas the Lion of Judah

---

2. Pablo Richard, *Apocalypse: A People's Commentary on the Book of Revelation* (Maryknoll, NY: Orbis, 1995), 171.
3. Jan A. du Rand, "'. . . Let Him Hear What the Spirit Says . . .': The Functional Role and Theological Meaning of the Spirit in the Book of Revelation," *Ex Auditu* 12 (1997): 43–58, at 56.

roars in his holiness and righteousness, in the end the slain Lamb also encourages and nourishes. John wishes not to finally use a rod or cudgel with the seven churches but to edify and bless them.

Given that two of the macarisms occur here at the end, one by Jesus himself, it is worthwhile putting all seven of them together at this juncture, to reemphasize what kinds of blessings have been pronounced for the readers and hearers of this book:

1. John: "Blessed is the one who reads aloud the words of the prophecy, and blessed are those who hear and who keep what is written in it; for the time is near" (1:3)
2. Voice from heaven: "Blessed are the dead who from now on die in the Lord" (14:13b)
3. Jesus: "Blessed is the one who stays awake and is clothed, not going about naked and exposed to shame" (16:15b)
4. Mighty angel: "Blessed are those who are invited to the marriage supper of the Lamb" (19:9b)
5. John: "Blessed and holy are those who share in the first resurrection. Over these the second death has no power, but they will be priests of God and of Christ, and they will reign with him a thousand years" (20:6)
6. Jesus: "Blessed is the one who keeps the words of the prophecy of this book" (22:7b)
7. Jesus: "Blessed are those who wash their robes, so that they will have the right to the tree of life and may enter the city by the gates" (22:14)

It is appropriate to revisit these macarisms here at the end of the book, in fact just after our discussion of the question regarding Jesus' imminent Parousia. The blessings are replete with eschatological imagery, from the urgency of Christ's return to being first raised from the dead and reigning during the millennium to enjoying the new Jerusalem's tree of life and other amenities of the holy city. Yet notice also that these macarisms are addressed to the members of the seven churches amid the intricacies of their late first-century West Asian historical, social, political, and economic circumstances. The blessings point to the future, but they are designed to enable faithfulness in that, and any historical, present.

This final word of grace is particularly energizing for those of us on the margins.[4] I have written this theological commentary from a position that some readers might deem to be one of double-marginality: a pentecostal perspective on the one hand (whose arrival in the theological academy has been rather recent) and an Asian American social and ethnic location on the other hand (which is presumed to be subordinated to the majority white and Eurocentric cultural norm). Yet I realize that I have been invited to write for this series in part because I have successfully assimilated into the theological academy, minimizing my Asian American identity and commitments in the process. Writing this commentary has helped me to experience afresh the grace that enables recognition of my own acculturation, and that in turn has helped me to realize first steps in resisting the seductiveness of the status quo. Grace is needed for us to see that the status quo not only will not persist forever but might also be redeemed in accordance with the revelation of Jesus Christ. Grace helps us to envision and work for a most just order. Grace grants perspective that our alienness and exclusion will not be in perpetuity but will be centered in the slain and resurrected Lamb.

Grace enables me as an Asian American theologian to live in solidarity with those from across the broad scope of the people of God, from many peoples, languages, nations, and ethnicities. And it is precisely the Pentecost perspective of many tongues glorifying God that has also inspired my own Asian American witness in this commentary. Reading Revelation after Pentecost has suggested that the West Asian testimonies to and from the seven churches resonates across space and time with the East Asian and diaspora witnesses such as those of my own migrant (Malaysian) Chinese American community struggling for authenticity amid the contemporary pax Americana. It is precisely such a perpetual foreigner experience that has provided both hermeneutical and theological lenses to appreciate and find meaningful John's revelatory apocalypse to the early Christians across Asia Minor. Grace has gifted such connectedness, one that this volume offers to all readers, inviting our allegiance to Jesus

4. Hence complementing and extending what I had previously written in another book about pneumatology (a theology of the spirit) and grace; see *Spirit of Love: A Trinitarian Theology of Grace* (Waco, TX: Baylor University Press, 2012).

Christ, rather than to any nation, tongue, tribe, or people. Yet grace also enables such allegiance to the slain Lamb in and through—not apart from—the specificity of our ethnic, social, cultural, and political experiences. Grace inspires imaginative hope for transformation for our own sociohistorical realities in anticipation of the transcultural and multilingual holy city that is coming.

And all of this is true because grace comes through the divine future invading or undergirding our present. Grace orients all of us in our troubled immediacy, no matter how we self-identify, toward hope. Grace lifts up all of our strengthless hands, regardless of how others may categorize us, to do thankless work. Grace enables the worship and celebration of the church catholic, in all of its differences and diversity, during times of discouragement and challenging circumstances. Grace grants courage when we in our common humanity are otherwise fearful, when anxious in the midst of opposition, when feeling alone in a hostile environment. Grace inspires and manifests wisdom when we from our various wisdom traditions remain confused and disoriented. Grace nurtures discerning and engaging faithfulness when the world calls us, with all of our multiplicity and hybridity, in contrary directions. This is all because grace is the presence of the risen and coming Jesus in the power of his (seven) spirit(s), leading us to the throne of life that overcomes (the second) death.

Bibliography

Adams, Edward. *The Stars Will Fall from Heaven: Cosmic Catastrophe in the New Testament and Its World.* Library of New Testament Studies 347. London and New York: T&T Clark, 2007.

Archer, Melissa L. *"I Was in the Spirit on the Lord's Day": A Pentecostal Engagement with Worship in the Apocalypse.* Cleveland, TN: CPT Press, 2015.

Ascough, Richard S. "Religious Coexistence, Co-operation, Competition, and Conflict in Sardis and Smyrna." In *Religious Rivalries and the Struggle for Success in Sardis and Smyrna,* edited by Richard S. Ascough, 245–52. Studies in Christianity and Judaism/Études sur le christianisme et le judaisme 14. Waterloo, Canada: Wilfred Laurier University Press, 2005.

Aune, David E. *Revelation 1–5.* Word Biblical Commentary 52A. Nashville: Thomas Nelson, 1997.

———. *Revelation 6–16.* Word Biblical Commentary 52B. Nashville: Thomas Nelson, 1998.

———. *Revelation 17–22.* Word Biblical Commentary 52C. Nashville: Thomas Nelson, 1998.

Barr, David L. "Beyond Genre: The Expectations of Apocalypse." In *The Reality of Apocalypse: Rhetoric and Politics in the Book of Revelation,* edited by David L. Barr, 71–89. SBL Symposium Series 39. Atlanta: Society of Biblical Literature, 2006.

———. *Tales of the End: A Narrative Commentary on the Book of Revelation.* Salem, OR: Polebridge, 2012.

Bauckham, Richard. *The Climax of Prophecy: Studies in the Book of Revelation*. 1993; reprint, London and New York: T&T Clark, 2005.

———. *Living with Other Creatures: Green Exegesis and Theology*. Waco, TX: Baylor University Press, 2011.

———. *The Theology of the Book of Revelation*. Cambridge: Cambridge University Press, 2003.

Beale, G. K. *The Book of Revelation: A Commentary on the Greek Text*. The New International Greek Testament Commentary. 1999; reprint, Grand Rapids: Eerdmans; and Carlisle, UK: Paternoster, 2013.

———. *John's Use of the Old Testament in Revelation*. Library of New Testament Studies 166. 1998; reprint, London and New York: Bloomsbury T&T Clark, 2015.

———. *The Use of Daniel in Jewish Apocalyptic Literature and in the Revelation of St. John*. Lanham, MD: University Press of America, 1984.

———. "The Revelation of Hell." In *Hell under Fire: Modern Scholarship Reinvents Eternal Punishment*, edited by Morgan Christopher W. and Robert A. Peterson, 111–34. Grand Rapids: Zondervan, 2004.

Beilby, James A., and Paul Rhodes Eddy, eds. *Understanding Spiritual Warfare: Four Views*. Grand Rapids: Baker Academic, 2012.

Blount, Brian K. *Can I Get a Witness? Reading Revelation through African American Culture*. Louisville, KY: Westminster John Knox Press, 2005.

———. *Revelation: A Commentary*. The New Testament Library. Louisville, KY: Westminster John Knox Press, 2009.

Boesak, Allan A. *Comfort and Protest: Reflections on The Apocalypse of John of Patmos from a South African Perspective*. Philadelphia: Westminster John Knox Press, 1987.

Boring, M. Eugene. *Revelation*. Interpretation: A Bible Commentary for Teaching and Preaching. Louisville, KY: John Knox Press, 1989.

Boyd, Gregory A. *The Crucifixion of the Warrior God*. Vol. 1. Minneapolis: Fortress, 2017.

Bredin, Mark. *Jesus, Revolutionary of Peace: A Nonviolent Christology in the Book of Revelation.* Waynesboro, GA: Paternoster, 2003.

Bucur, Bogdan G. "Hierarchy, Prophecy, and the Angelomorphic Spirit: A Contribution to the Study of the Book of Revelation's *Wirkungsgeschichte.*" *Journal of Biblical Literature* 127:1 (2008): 173–94.

Cadoux, Cecil John. *Ancient Smyrna: A History of the City from the Earliest Times to 324 A.D.* Oxford: Basil Blackwell, 1938.

Campbell, Gordon. "Findings, Seals, Trumpets, and Bowls: Variations upon the Theme of Covenant Rupture and Restoration in the Book of Revelation." *Westminster Theological Journal* 66 (2004): 71–96.

Campbell, R. Alastair. "Triumph and Delay: The Interpretation of Revelation 19:11–20:10." *Evangelical Quarterly* 80:1 (2008): 3–12.

Carey, Greg. *Elusive Apocalypse: Reading Authority in the Revelation to John.* Macon, GA: Mercer University Press, 1999.

———. "A Man's Choice: Wealth Imagery and the Two Cities of the Book of Revelation." In Levine, with Robbins, *A Feminist Companion to the Apocalypse of John*, 147–58.

Carter, Warren "Accommodating 'Jezebel' and Withdrawing John: Negotiating Empire in Revelation Then and Now." *Interpretation* 63:1 (2009): 32–47.

Charette, Blaine, and Robby Waddell, eds. *Spirit and Story: Pentecostal Readings of Scripture—Essays in Honor of John Christopher Thomas.* Sheffield: Sheffield Phoenix, 2020.

Chevalier, Jacques. *A Postmodern Revelation: Signs of Astrology and the Apocalypse.* Toronto and Buffalo: University of Toronto Press, 1997.

Collins, Adela Yarbro. *The Combat Myth in the Book of Revelation.* Harvard Theological Review / Harvard Dissertations in Religion 9. Missoula, MT: Scholars Press, 1976.

———. *Crisis and Catharsis: The Power of the Apocalypse.* Philadelphia: The Westminster Press, 1984.

———. "Feminine Symbolism in the Book of Revelation." In Levine, with Robbins, *A Feminist Companion to the Apocalypse of John*, 121–30.

————, ed. *New Perspectives on the Book of Revelation*. Bibliotheca Ephemeridum Theologicarum Lovaniensium CCXCI. Leuven: Peeters, 2017.

Dalferth, Ingolf. "The Stuff of Revelation: Austin Farrer's Doctrine of Inspired Images." In *Hermeneutics, the Bible and Literary Criticism*, edited by Ann Loades and Michael McLain, 71–95. New York: Palgrave Macmillan, 1992.

Dalrymple, Rob. *Revelation and the Two Witnesses: The Implications for Understanding John's Depiction of the People of God and His Hortatory Intent*. Eugene, OR: Resource Publications, 2011.

Daniels, T. Scott. *Seven Deadly Spirits: The Message of Revelation's Letters for Today's Church*. Grand Rapids: Baker Academic, 2009.

Darden, Lynne St. Clair. *Scripturalizing Revelation: An African American Postcolonial Reading of Empire*. Atlanta: SBL Press, 2015.

Davis, Dale Ralph. "The Relationship between the Seals, Trumpets, and Bowls in the Book of Revelation." *Journal of the Evangelical Theological Society* 16:3 (1973): 149–58.

de Smidt, Kobus. "Hermeneutical Perspectives on the Spirit in the Book of Revelation." *Journal of Pentecostal Theology* 7 (1999): 27–47.

De Villiers, Pieter G. R. "The Septet of Bowls in Revelation 15:1–16:21 in the Light of Its Composition." *Acta Patristica et Byzantina* 16 (2005): 196–222.

De Waal, Kayle B. *An Aural-Performance Analysis of Revelation 1 and 11*. Studies in Biblical Literature 163. New York: Peter Lang, 2015.

Dempsey, Carol J. "Revelation 21:1–8." *Interpretation* 65:4 (2011): 400–402.

deSilva, David A. *Seeing Things John's Way: The Rhetoric of the Book of Revelation*. Louisville, KY: Westminster John Knox Press, 2009.

Du Preez, Jannie. "All Things New: Notes on the Church's Mission in the Light of Revelation 21:1–8." *Missionalia* 24:3 (1996): 372–82.

Du Rand, Jan A. "'. . . Let Him Hear What the Spirit Says . . .': The Functional Role and Theological Meaning of the Spirit in the Book of Revelation." *Ex Auditu* 12 (1997): 43–58.

Duff, Paul B. *Who Rides the Beast? Prophetic Rivalry and the Rhetoric of Crisis in the Churches of the Apocalypse.* Oxford: Oxford University Press, 2001.

Dutcher-Walls, Patricia. *Jezebel: Portraits of a Queen.* Collegeville, MN: Liturgical Press / Michael Glazier, 2004.

Enroth, Anne-Mart. "The Hearing Formula in the Book of Revelation." *New Testament Studies* 36 (1990): 598–608.

Fairchild, Mark R. "Laodicea's 'Lukewarm' Legacy: Conflicts of Prosperity in an Ancient Christian City." *Biblical Archaeology Review* 43:2 (2017): 31–39 and 67–68.

Farrer, Austin. *A Rebirth of Images: The Making of St. John's Apocalypse.* 1949; reprint, Albany: State University of New York Press, 1986.

Fee, Gordon D. *Revelation.* New Covenant Commentary Series. Eugene, OR: Cascade Books, 2011.

Fekkes, Jan III. *Isaiah and Prophetic Traditions in the Book of Revelation: Visionary Antecedents and Their Development.* Journal for the Study of the New Testament Supplement Series 93. Sheffield: Sheffield Academic Press, 1994.

Finamore, Stephen. *God, Order and Chaos: René Girard and the Apocalypse.* Milton Keynes, UK, and Colorado Springs, CO: Paternoster, 2009.

Ford, J. Massyngberde. *Revelation: A New Translation with Introduction and Commentary.* The Anchor Bible 38. Garden City, NY: Doubleday & Company, 1975.

Forsyth, Neil. *The Old Enemy: Satan and the Combat Myth.* Princeton: Princeton University Press, 1989.

Fox, Kenneth A. "The Nicolaitans, Nicolaus and the Early Church." *Studies in Religion/Sciences Religieuses* 23:4 (1994): 485–96.

Francis, Richard Shiningthunder. *The Apocalypse of Love: Mystical Symbolism in Revelation.* N.p. Bookman Publishing, 2004.

Friesen, Steven J. *Imperial Cults and the Apocalypse of John: Reading Revelation in the Ruins.* Oxford: Oxford University Press, 2001.

———. *Twice Neokoros: Ephesus, Asia and the Cult of the Flavian Imperial Family.* Leiden: Brill, 1993.

Frilingos, Christopher A. *Spectacles of Empire: Monsters, Martyrs, and the Book of Revelation.* Divinations: Rereading Late

Ancient Religion. Philadelphia: University of Pennsylvania Press, 2004.

Gallien, Louis B., Jr. "Crossing over Jordan: Navigating the Music of Heavenly Bliss and Earthly Desire in the Lives and Careers of Three 20th Century African American Holiness-Pentecostal 'Cross-over' Artists." In *Afro-Pentecostalism: Black Pentecostal and Charismatic Christianity in History and Culture*, edited by Estrelda Y. Alexander and Amos Yong, 117–37. Religion, Race, and Ethnicity Series. New York: New York University Press, 2011.

García, Lourdes. "The Book of Revelation: A Chromatic Story." In Collins, *New Perspectives on the Book of Revelation*, 393–419.

Gause, R. Hollis. *Revelation: God's Stamp of Sovereignty on History*. Cleveland, TN: Pathway Press, 1998.

Gilbert, Paul Marshall, Lela Gilbert, and Nina Shea. *Persecuted: The Global Assault on Christians*. Nashville: Thomas Nelson, 2013.

Girard, René. *Battling to the End: Conversations with Benoît Chantre*. Translated by Mary Baker. East Lansing, MI: Michigan State University Press, 2009.

Goldsworthy, Graeme. *The Lion and the Lamb: The Gospel in Revelation*. Nashville: Thomas Nelson, 1985.

González, Catherine Gunsalus, and Justo L. González. *Revelation*. Westminster Bible Companion. Louisville, KY: Westminster John Knox Press, 1997.

González, Justo L. *For the Healing of the Nations: The Book of Revelation in an Age of Cultural Conflict*. Maryknoll, NY: Orbis Books, 1999.

Gorman, Michael J. *Reading Revelation Responsibly: Uncivil Worship and Witness Following the Lamb into the New Creation*. Eugene, OR: Cascade Books, 2011.

Graham, Billy. *Approaching Hoofbeats: The Four Horsemen of the Apocalypse*. New York: Avon, 1985.

Gregg, Steve. ed. *Revelation: Four Views—A Parallel Commentary*. Nashville: Thomas Nelson, 1997.

Gumerlock, Francis X., trans. *The Seven Seals of the Apocalypse: Medieval Texts in Translation*. Kalamazoo, MI: Medieval Institute Publications, 2009.

Handy, Mark R., Greg Hirth, and Niels Hovius, eds. *Tectonic Faults: Agents of Change on a Dynamic Earth.* Berlin: Freie Universität Berlin; Cambridge, MA: MIT Press, 2007.

Hansen, Ryan Leif. *Silence and Praise: Rhetorical Cosmology and Political Theology in the Book of Revelation.* Minneapolis: Fortress, 2014.

Hemer, Colin J. *The Letters to the Seven Churches of Asia in Their Local Setting.* Journal for the Study of the New Testament Supplement Series 11. Sheffield: JSOT Press, 1986.

Herms, Ronald. *An Apocalypse for the Church and for the World: The Narrative Function of Universal Language in the Book of Revelation.* Beihefte zur Zeitschrift für die neutestamentliche Wissenschaft und die Kunde der älteren Kirche 143. Berlin and New York: Walter de Gruyter, 2006.

———. "Invoking the Spirit and Narrative Intent in John's Apocalypse." In *Spirit and Scripture: Exploring a Pneumatic Hermeneutic,* edited by Kevin L. Spawn and Archie T. Wright, 99–114. London and New York: T&T Clark, 2012.

Hidalgo, Jacqueline M. *Revelation in Aztlán: Scriptures, Utopias, and the Chicano Movement.* The Bible and Cultural Studies series. New York: Palgrave Macmillan, 2016.

Horsley, Richard A. *Revolt of the Scribes: Resistance and Apocalyptic Origins.* Minneapolis: Fortress, 2010.

Howard-Brook, Wes, and Anthony Gwyther. *Unveiling Empire: Reading Revelation Then and Now.* Maryknoll, NY: Orbis Books, 1999.

Huber, Lynn R. *Thinking and Seeing with Women in Revelation.* Library of New Testament Studies 475. New York and London: Bloomsbury / T&T Clark, 2013.

———. "Unveiling the Bride: Revelation 19.1–8 and Roman Social Discourse." In Levine, with Robbins, *A Feminist Companion to the Apocalypse of John,* 159–79.

Humphrey, Edith M. *And I Turned to See the Voice: The Rhetoric of Vision in the New Testament.* Grand Rapids: Baker Academic, 2007.

Hurtgen, John E. *Anti-Language in the Apocalypse of John.* Lewiston, NY: Mellen, 1993.

Isaacs, T. Craig. *John's Apocalypse: A Study in Dream Interpretation.*
Eugene, OR: Cascade Books, 2016.

Jensen, Joseph. "Mount Zion and Armageddon: A Tale of Two
Eschatologies." In *Sin, Salvation, and the Spirit: Commemorating
the Fiftieth Year of the Liturgical Press*, edited by Daniel Durken,
134–45. Collegeville, MN: Liturgical Press, 1979.

Jersak, Bradley. *Her Gates Will Never Be Shut: Hope, Hell, and the
New Jerusalem.* Eugene, OR: Cascade, 2009.

Jeung, Russell. *At Home in Exile: Finding Jesus among My Ancestors
and Refugee Neighbors.* Grand Rapids: Zondervan, 2016.

Johns, Loren L. "Facing Revelation's Beasts: The Opportunities and
Challenges of Pastoral Ministry at the Edge of History." In
*Apocalypticism and Millennialism: Shaping a Believer's Church
Eschatology for the Twenty-first Century*, edited by Loren L.
Johns, 364–79. Kitchener, ON: Pandora Press; Scottdale, PN:
Herald Press, 2000.

———. *The Lamb Christology of the Apocalypse of John.*
Wissenschaftliche Untersuchungen zum Neuen Testament
2.167. Tübingen: Mohr Siebeck, 2003.

Johnson, Curtis. "The Earth's *Ethos, Logos*, and *Pathos*: An
Ecological Reading of Revelation." *Currents in Theology and
Mission* 41:2 (2014): 119–27.

Johnson, David R. *Pneumatic Discernment in the Apocalypse: An
Intertextual and Pentecostal Exploration.* Cleveland, TN: CPT
Press, 2018.

Jung, C. G. *Answer to Job.* Translated by R. F. C. Hull. 2nd ed. 1969;
reprint, Princeton: Princeton University Press / Bollingen
Foundation, 1973.

Jung, Young Lee. *Marginality: The Key to Multicultural Theology.*
Minneapolis: Fortress, 1985.

Kallas, James G. *Revelation: God and Satan in the Apocalypse.*
Minneapolis: Augsburg, 1973.

Keener, Craig S. *Revelation.* The NIV Application Commentary.
Grand Rapids: Zondervan, 2000.

Keller, Catherine. *Apocalypse Now and Then: A Feminist Guide to the
End of the World.* 1996; reprint, Minneapolis: Fortress Press,
2005.

Kirkland, A. "The Beginnings of Christianity in the Lycus Valley: An Exercise in Historical Reconstruction." *Neotestamentica* 29:1 (1995): 109–24.

Koester, Craig R. "The Message to Laodicea and the Problem of Its Local Context: A Study of the Imagery in Rev. 3.14–22." *New Testament Studies* 49:3 (2003): 407–24.

———. *Revelation: A New Translation with Introduction and Commentary.* The Anchor Yale Bible Commentaries. New Haven and London: Yale University Press, 2015.

Korner, Ralph J. "The 'Great Earthquake' Judgment in the Apocalypse: Is There an Urzeit for this Endzeit?" *ARC: The Journal of the Faculty of Religious Studies, McGill University* 39 (2011): 143–70.

Kovacs, Judith, and Christopher Rowland. *Revelation.* Blackwell Bible Commentaries series. Malden, MA: Blackwell, 2004.

Kraybill, J. Nelson. *Apocalypse and Allegiance: Worship, Politics, and Devotion in the Book of Revelation.* Grand Rapids: Brazos, 2010.

———. *Imperial Cult and Commerce in John's Apocalypse.* Journal for the Study of the New Testament Supplement Series 132. Sheffield: Sheffield Academic Press, 1996.

Lee, Hee Youl. *A Dynamic Reading of the Holy Spirit in Revelation.* Eugene, OR: Wipf & Stock, 2014.

Lee, Sang Hyun. *From a Liminal Place: An Asian American Theology.* Minneapolis: Fortress, 2010.

Lester, Olivia Stewart. "Jezebel: A Study in Prophecy, Divine Violence, and Gender." In Collins, *New Perspectives on the Book of Revelation,* 509–21.

Levine, Amy-Jill, with Maria Mayo Robbins, eds. *A Feminist Companion to the Apocalypse of John.* Feminist Companion to the New Testament and Early Christian Writings 13. London and New York: T&T Clark, 2009.

Levison, John R. *Filled with the Spirit.* Grand Rapids: Eerdmans, 2009.

Lumsden, Douglas W. *And Then the End Will Come: Early Latin Christian Interpretations of the Opening of the Seven Seals.* New York and London: Garland Publishing, 2001.

Macchia, Frank D. "The Spirit of the Lamb: A Reflection on the Pneumatology of Revelation." In *But These are Written . . . : Essays on Johannine Literature in Honor of Professor Benny C. Aker*, edited by Craig S. Keener, Jeremy S. Crenshaw, and Jordan Daniel May, 214–20. Eugene, OR: Pickwick, 2014.

MacKenzie, Robert K. *The Author of the Apocalypse: A Review of the Prevailing Hypotheses of Jewish-Christian Authorship*. Mellen Biblical Press Series 51. Lewiston, NY: Mellen, 1997.

Maier, Harry O. *Apocalypse Recalled: The Book of Revelation after Christendom*. Minneapolis: Fortress, 2002.

Malina, Bruce J. *On the Genre and Message of Revelation: Star Visions and Sky Journeys*. Peabody, MA: Hendrickson, 1995.

Mangina, Joseph L. *Revelation*. Brazos Theological Commentary on the Bible. Grand Rapids: Brazos, 2010.

Marriner, Keith T. *Following the Lamb: The Theme of Discipleship in the Book of Revelation*. Eugene, OR: Wipf & Stock, 2016.

Mathews, Susan F. "The Power to Endure and Be Transformed: Sun and Moon Imagery in Joel and Revelation 6." In *Imagery and Imagination in Biblical Literature: Essays in Honor of Aloysius Fitzgerald, F.S.C.*, edited by Lawrence Boadt and Mark S. Smith, 35–49. Washington, DC: Catholic Biblical Association of America, 2001.

Mathewson, Dave. "The Destiny of the Nations in Revelation 21:1–22:5: A Reconsideration." *Tyndale Bulletin* 53:1 (2002): 121–42.

Mayo, Philip L. *"Those Who Call Themselves Jews": The Church and Judaism in the Apocalypse of John*. Eugene, OR: Pickwick, 2006.

McIlraith, Donal A. *The Reciprocal Love between Christ and the Church in the Apocalypse*. Rome: Columbian Fathers, 1989.

McNicol, Allan J. *The Conversion of the Nations in Revelation*. Library of New Testament Studies 438. New York and London: Bloomsbury / T&T Clark, 2011.

Middleton, Paul. "Male Virgins, Male Martyrs, Male Brides: A Reconsideration of the 144,000 'Who Have Not Dirtied Themselves with Women' (Revelation 14.4)." In *The Book of Revelation: Currents in British Research on the Apocalypse*, edited by Garrick V. Allen, Ian Paul, and Simon P. Woodman, 193–208. Tübingen: Mohr Siebeck, 2015.

Minear, Paul S. *I Saw a New Earth: An Introduction to the Visions of the Apocalypse.*1968; reprint, Eugene, OR: Wipf & Stock, 2003.

Moore, Stephen D. *Empire and Apocalypse: Postcolonialism and the New Testament.* Sheffield: Sheffield Phoenix, 2006.

———. "The Revelation to John." In *A Postcolonial Commentary on the New Testament Writings,* edited by Segovia Fernando F. and R. S. Sugitharajah, 436–54. The Bible and Postcolonialism 13. London and New York: T&T Clark, 2009.

———. *Untold Tales from the Book of Revelation: Sex and Gender, Empire and Ecology.* Atlanta: SBL Press, 2014.

Morales, Jon. *Christ, Shepherd of the Nations: The Nations as Narrative Character and Audience in John's Apocalypse.* Library of New Testament Studies 377. New York and London: Bloomsbury, 2018.

Moţ, Laurenţiu Florentin. *Angels and Beasts: The Relationship between the Four Living Creatures and the Four Riders in Revelation 6:1–8.* Eugene, OR: Wipf & Stock, 2017.

Mouw, Richard J. *When the Kings Come Marching In: Isaiah and the New Jerusalem.* Rev. ed. Grand Rapids and Cambridge, UK: Eerdmans, 2002.

Moyise, Steve. *The Old Testament in the Book of Revelation.* 1995; reprint, New York and London: Bloomsbury T&T Clark, 2015.

Müller, Ekkehardt. "The Two Witnesses of Revelation 11." *Journal of the Adventist Theological Society* 13:2 (2002): 30–45.

Murphy, Frederick J. *Fallen Is Babylon: The Revelation to John.* The New Testament in Context. Harrisburg, PA: Trinity Press International, 1998.

Newton, Jon K. *Revelation Reclaimed: The Use and Misuse of the Apocalypse.* Milton Keynes, UK: Paternoster, 2009.

———. *The Revelation Worldview: Apocalyptic Thinking in a Postmodern World.* Eugene, OR: Wipf & Stock, 2015.

Niebuhr, H. Richard. *Christ and Culture.* New York: Harper, 1951.

O'Hear, Natasha, and Anthony O'Hear. *Picturing the Apocalypse: The Book of Revelation in the Arts over Two Millennia*. Oxford: Oxford University Press, 2015.

Oropeza, B. J. *Apostasy in the New Testament Communities*. Vol. 3, *Churches under Siege of Persecution and Assimilation: The General Epistles and Revelation*. Eugene, OR: Cascade, 2012.

Osborne, Grant R. *Revelation*. Baker Exegetical Commentary on the New Testament. Grand Rapids: Baker Academic, 2002.

Pate, C. Marvin. "Revelation 6: An Early Interpretation of the Olivet Discourse." *Criswell Theological Review* 8:2 (2011): 45–55.

———, ed. *Four Views on the Book of Revelation*. Grand Rapids: Zondervan, 1998.

Paulien, Jon. *Decoding Revelation's Trumpets: Literary Allusions and the Interpretation of Revelation 8:7–12*. Andrews University Seminary Doctoral Dissertation Series 11. Berrien Springs, MI: Andrews University Press, 1987.

Perkins, Pheme. "Apocalyptic Sectarianism and Love Commands: The Johannine Epistles and Revelation." In *The Love of Enemy and Nonretaliation in the New Testament*, edited by Willard M. Swartley, 287–96. Louisville, KY: Westminster/John Knox Press, 1992.

Perry, Peter S. *The Rhetoric of Digressions: Revelation 7:1–17 and 10:1–11:13 and Ancient Communication*. Wissenschaftliche Untersuchungen zum Neuen Testament 2:268. Tübingen: Mohr Siebeck, 2009.

Phan, Peter C. "Betwixt and Between: Doing Theology with Memory and Imagination." In *Journeys at the Margin: Toward an Autobiographical Theology in American-Asian Perspective*, edited by Peter C. Phan and Jung Young Lee, 113–33. Maryknoll, NY: Orbis Books, 1999.

Philpott, Daniel, and Timothy Samuel Shah, eds. *Under Caesar's Sword: How Christians Respond to Persecution*. Law and Christianity. Cambridge: Cambridge University Press, 2018.

Pippin, Tina. *Death and Desire: The Rhetoric of Gender in the Apocalypse of John*. Louisville, KY: Westminster/John Knox Press, 1992.

———. "The Heroine and the Whore: The Apocalypse of John in Feminist Perspective." In Rhoads, *From Every People and*

Nation: The Book of Revelation in Intercultural Perspective,
127–45.

Podolskiy, Evgeny A. "Effects of Environmental Changes on
Global Seismicity and Volcanism." *Bulletin of the American
Meteorological Society* 90:9 (2009): 1263–64.

Pollard, Leslie N. "The Function of Λοιπος in the Letter to
Thyatira." *Andrews University Seminary Studies* 46:1 (2008):
45–63.

Poon, Joseph. *The Identities of the Beast from the Sea and the Beast
from the Land in Revelation 13.* Eugene, OR: Pickwick, 2017.

Portier-Young, Anathea E. *Apocalypse Against Empire: Theologies
of Resistance in Early Judaism.* Grand Rapids: Eerdmans,
2011.

Prigent, Pierre. *Commentary on the Apocalypse of St. John.* Translated
by Wendy Pradels. Tübingen: Mohr Siebeck, 2001.

Ramsay, W. M. *The Letters to the Seven Churches of Asia and Their
Place in the Plan of the Apocalypse.* London: Hodder &
Stoughton, 1904; reprint, Grand Rapids: Baker Book House,
1963.

Reddish, Mitchell G. "Hearing the Apocalypse in Pergamum."
Perspectives in Religious Studies 41:1 (2014): 3–12.

Resseguie, James L. *Revelation Unsealed: A Narrative Critical
Approach to John's Apocalypse.* Biblical Interpretation 32.
Leiden and Boston: Brill, 1998.

Rhoads, David, ed. *From Every People and Nation: The Book of
Revelation in Intercultural Perspective.* Minneapolis: Fortress,
2005.

Richard, Pablo. *Apocalypse: A People's Commentary on the Book of
Revelation.* Maryknoll, NY: Orbis Books, 1995.

Robinson, Andrea L. *Temple of Presence: The Christological
Fulfillment of Ezekiel 40–48 in Revelation 21:1–22:5.* Eugene,
OR: Wipf & Stock, 2019.

Rohr, Richard. *Silent Compassion: Finding God in Contemplation.*
Cincinnati: Franciscan Media, 2014.

Rossing, Barbara R. *The Choice between Two Cities: Whore, Bride,
and Empire in the Apocalypse.* Harrisburg, PA: Trinity Press
International, 1999.

———. "For the Healing of the World: Reading Revelation Ecologically." In Rhoads, *From Every People and Nation: The Book of Revelation in Intercultural Perspective*, 165–82.

Royalty, Robert M., Jr. "Etched or Sketched? Inscriptions and Erasures in the Messages to Sardis and Philadelphia (Rev. 3.1–13)." *Journal of the Study for the New Testament* 21 (2005): 447–63.

———. *The Streets of Heaven: The Ideology of Wealth in the Apocalypse of John*. Macon, GA: Mercer University Press, 1998.

Ruiz, Jean Pierre. *Ezekiel in the Apocalypse: The Transformation of Prophetic Language in Revelation 16,17–19, 10*. European University Studies XXIII Theology 376. New York: Peter Lang, 1989.

Ryan, Sean Michael. *Hearing at the Boundaries of Vision: Education Informing Cosmology in Revelation 9*. Library of New Testament Studies 448. London and New York: T&T Clark, 2012.

Sammonds, P. R., and J. M. T. Thompson, eds. *Advances in Earth Science: From Earthquakes to Global Warming*. London: Imperial College Press, 2007.

Sánchez, David A. *From Patmos to the Barrio: Subverting Imperial Myths*. Minneapolis: Fortress, 2008.

Schnabel, Eckhard J. "Early Christian Mission and Christian Identity in the Context of the Ethnic, Social, and Political Affiliations in Revelation." In *New Testament Theology in Light of the Church's Mission: Essays in Honor of I. Howard Marshall*, edited by Jon C. Laansma, Grant R. Osborne, and Ray F. Van Neste, 369–86. Eugene, OR: Cascade, 2011.

———. "John and the Future of the Nations." *Bulletin for Biblical Research* 12:2 (2002): 243–71.

Schüssler Fiorenza, Elisabeth. *The Book of Revelation: Justice and Judgment*. 2nd ed. Minneapolis: Fortress, 1998.

Seel, Thomas Allen. *A Theology of Music for Worship Derived from the Book of Revelation*. Studies in Liturgical Musicology 3. Lanham: Scarecrow Press, 1995.

Şimşek, Celal. *Church of Laodikeia: Christianity in the Lykos Valley*. Translated by Inci Türkoğlu. Denizli, Turkey: Denizli Metropolitan Municipality, 2015.

Skaggs, Rebecca, and Priscilla C. Benham. *Revelation*. Pentecostal Commentary Series. Blandford Forum, UK: Deo Publishing, 2009.

Smalley, Stephen S. *The Revelation to John: A Commentary on the Greek Text of the Apocalypse*. Downers Grove, IL: InterVarsity Press, 2005.

Smith, Mark S. *God in Translation: Deities in Cross-Cultural Discourse in the Biblical World*. 2008; reprint, Grand Rapids and Cambridge, UK: Eerdmans, 2010.

Smith, Robert S. "The Purpose of Revelation's Hymns." *Themelios* 43:2 (2018): 193–204.

Smith, Shanell T. *The Woman Babylon and the Marks of Empire: Reading Revelation with a Postcolonial Womanist Hermeneutics of Ambiveilence*. Minneapolis: Fortress, 2014.

Son, HaYoung. *Praising God beside the Sea: An Intertextual Study of Revelation 15 and Exodus 15*. Eugene, OR: Wipf & Stock, 2017.

Sorke, Ingo Willy. "The Identity and Function of the Seven Spirits in the Book of Revelation." PhD diss., Southwestern Baptist Theological Seminary, 2009.

Stefanovic, Zdravko. "The Angel at the Altar (Revelation 8:3–5): A Case Study on Intercalations in Revelation." *Andrews University Seminary Studies* 44:1 (2006): 79–94.

Steinmann, Andrew E. "The Tripartite Structure of the Sixth Seal, the Sixth Trumpet, and the Sixth Bowl of John's Apocalypse (Rev 6:12–7:17; 9:13–11:14; 16:12–16)." *Journal of the Evangelical Theological Society* 35:1 (1992): 68–79.

Stewart, Alexander E. "*Argumentum ad Baculum* in the Apocalypse of John: Toward an Evaluation of John's Use of Threats." In Collins, *New Perspectives on the Book of Revelation*, 463–73.

———. "*Ekphrasis*, Fear, and Motivation in the Apocalypse of John." *Bulletin of Biblical Research* 27:2 (2017): 227–40.

———. "Scaring the Hell Out of You: Scare-Tactics, Christian Proclamation, and the Apocalypse of John." *Journal of Youth and Theology* 16 (2017): 165–84.

Steyn, Gert J. "The Order of the Twelve Tribes of Israel and Its Reception in Revelation 7." In Collins, *New Perspectives on the Book of Revelation,* 523–43.

Stichele, Caroline Vender. "Re-membering the Whore: The Fate of Babylon according to Revelation 17.16." In Levine, with Robbins, *A Feminist Companion to the Apocalypse of John,* 106–120.

Stronstad, Roger. *The Prophethood of Believers: A Study in Luke's Charismatic Theology.* Journal of Pentecostal Theology Supplement Series 16. Sheffield: Sheffield Academic, 1999.

Stuckenbruck, Loren T. *Angel Veneration and Christology: A Study in Early Judaism and in the Christology of the Apocalypse of John.* 1995; reprint, Waco, TX: Baylor University Press, 2017.

Tanner, Cullen. "Climbing the Lampstand-Witness-Trees: Revelation's Use of Zechariah 4 in Light of Speech Act Theory." *Journal of Pentecostal Theology* 20 (2011): 81–92.

Thimmes, Pamela "'Teaching and Beguiling My Servants': The Letter to Thyatira (Rev. 2.18–29)." In Levine, with Robbins, *A Feminist Companion to the Apocalypse of John,* 69–87.

Thomas, John Christopher. *The Apocalypse: A Literary and Theological Commentary.* Cleveland, TN: CPT Press, 2012.

———. "The Mystery of the Great Whore—Pneumatic Discernment in Revelation 17." In *Perspectives in Pentecostal Eschatologies: World without End,* edited by Peter Althouse and Robby Waddell, 111–36. Eugene, OR: Pickwick, 2010.

———. "Pneumatic Discernment: The Image of the Beast and His Number." In *Passover, Pentecost, and Parousia: Studies in Celebration of the Life and Ministry of R. Hollis Gause, edited by* S. J. Land, R. D. Moore, and J. C. Thomas, 106–24. Journal of Pentecostal Theology Supplement Series 35. Blandford Forum, UK: Deo, 2010.

Thomas, John Christopher, and Frank D. Macchia. *Revelation.* Two Horizons New Testament Commentary. Grand Rapids and Cambridge, UK: Eerdmans, 2016.

Thompson, Leonard L. *The Book of Revelation: Apocalypse and Empire*. Oxford: Oxford University Press, 1990.

Tonstad, Sigve K. *Saving God's Reputation: The Theological Function of Pistis Iesou in the Cosmic Narratives of Revelation*. Library of New Testament Studies 337. New York and London: T&T Clark, 2006.

Trebilco, Paul. *The Early Christians in Ephesus from Paul to Ignatius*. 2004; reprint, Grand Rapids: Eerdmans, 2007.

Trementozzi, David. *Salvation in the Flesh: Understanding How Embodiment Shapes Christian Faith*. Eugene, OR: Wipf & Stock, 2018.

vănThanh, Nguyễn. "The Final Testimony of *Missio Dei*: A Missiological Reading of Revelation." In *Christian Mission, Contextual Theology, Prophetic Dialogue: Essays in Honor of Stephen B. Bevans, SVD*, edited by Dale T. Irvin and Peter C. Phan, 3–16. Maryknoll, NY: Orbis Books, 2018.

———. "Revelation from the Margins: A Vietnamese American Perspective." In *T&T Clark Handbook of Asian American Biblical Hermeneutics*, edited by Uriah Y. Kim and Seung Ai Yang, 439–49. New York: Bloomsbury, 2019.

Waddell, Robby. "Revelation and the (New) Creation: A Prolegomenon on the Apocalypse, Science, and Creation." In *The Spirit Renews the Face of the Earth: Pentecostal Forays into Science and Theology of Creation*, edited by Amos Yong, 30–50. Eugene, OR: Pickwick, 2009.

———. *The Spirit of the Book of Revelation*. Journal of Pentecostal Theology Supplement Series 30. Blandford Forum, UK: Deo, 2006.

Wainwright, Arthur W. *Mysterious Apocalypse: Interpreting the Book of Revelation*. 1993; reprint, Eugene, OR: Wipf & Stock, 2001.

Wall, Robert W. "A Pneumatic Discernment of the Spirit-Beast of Revelation 13:11–17." In Charette and Waddell, *Spirit and Story: Pentecostal Readings of Scripture—Essays in Honor of John Christopher Thomas*, 101–16.

———. *Revelation*. New International Biblical Commentary. Peabody, MA: Hendrickson, 1991.

Whitaker, Robyn J. *Ekphrasis, Vision, and Persuasion in the Book of Revelation*. Wissenschaftliche Untersuchungen zum Neuen Testament 2.410. Tübingen: Mohr Siebeck, 2015.

Wilson, Mark. *Charts on the Book of Revelation: Literary, Historical, and Theological Perspectives*. Grand Rapids: Kregel Academic & Professional, 2007.

———. *The Victor Sayings in the Book of Revelation*. Eugene, OR: Wipf & Stock, 2007.

Wong, Daniel K. "The Two Witnesses in Revelation 11." *Bibliotheca Sacra* 154 (1997): 344–54.

Wood, Shane J. *The Alter-Imperial Paradigm: Empire Studies and the Book of Revelation*. Biblical Interpretation 140. Leiden and Boston: Brill, 2016.

Woodman, Simon. *The Book of Revelation*. SCM Core Texts. London: SCM Press, 2008.

Worth, Roland H., Jr. *The Seven Cities of the Apocalypse and Greco-Asian Culture*. Mahwah, NJ: Paulist, 1999.

Wu, Frank H. *Yellow: Race in America beyond Black and White*. New York: Basic Books, 2003.

Yong, Aizaiah G., and Amos Yong. "The Inequitable Silencing of Many Tongues: Political, Economic, and Racialized Dimensions of the Pandemic in American Pentecostal-Charismaticism." In *Response of the Global Spirit-Empowered Church to the COVID-19 Pandemic*, edited by Wonsuk Ma and Opoku Onyinah. Tulsa, OK: ORU Press, forthcoming.

———. "Seeking Healing in an Age of Partisan Division: Reckoning with Theological Education and Resounding the *Evangel* for the 2020s." In *Faith and Reckoning after Trump*, edited by Miguel A. De La Torre, 214–27. Maryknoll, NY: Orbis Books, 2021.

Yong, Amos. "American Political Theology in a Post-al Age: A Perpetual Foreigner and Pentecostal Stance." In *Faith and Resistance in the Age of Trump*, edited by Miguel A. De La Torre, 107–14. Maryknoll, NY: Orbis Books, 2017.

———. "Diasporic Discipleship from West Asia through Southeast Asia and Beyond: A Dialogue with 1 Peter." *Asia Journal of Theology* 32:2 (October 2018): 3–21.

———. "From Every Tribe, Language, People, and Nation: Diaspora, Hybridity, and the Coming Reign of God." In *Global Diasporas and Mission*, edited by Chandler H. Im and Amos Yong, 253–61. Regnum Edinburgh Centenary Series 23. Oxford, UK: Regnum Books International, 2014.

———. "From the Jewish Diaspora to the Indian (Christian) Diaspora: An Autobiographical Look at 1 Peter's Message to West Aisa, edited by John Alex. *New Life Theological Journal* 9:1 (2019): 7–18.

———. *The Future of Evangelical Theology: Soundings from the Asian American Diaspora*. Downers Grove, IL: IVP Academic, 2014.

———. "Glocalization and the Gift-Giving Spirit: Informality and Shalom beyond the Political Economy of Exchange." *Journal of Youngsan Theology* 25 (2012): 7–29.

———. *The Hermeneutical Spirit: Theological Interpretation and the Scriptural Imagination for the 21st Century*. Eugene, OR: Cascade, 2017.

———. *In the Days of Caesar: Pentecostalism and Political Theology*. Grand Rapids and Cambridge, UK: Eerdmans, 2010.

———. "Is There a Future for Evangelical Theology? API Retrospects and Prospects." *Inheritance: Heritage—Culture—Faith* 64 (2019): 42–49.

———. "Kings, Nations, and Cultures on the Way to the New Jerusalem: A Pentecostal Witness to an Apocalyptic Vision." In *The Pastor and the Kingdom: Essays Honoring Jack W. Hayford*, edited by S. David Moore and Jonathan Huntzinger, 231–51. Dallas: TKU Press, 2017.

———. *Learning Theology: Tracking the Spirit of Christian Faith*. Louisville, KY: Westminster John Knox Press, 2018.

———. *Mission after Pentecost: The Witness of the Spirit from Genesis to Revelation*. Mission in Global Community. Grand Rapids: Baker Academic, 2019.

———. "Orality and the Sound of the Spirit: Intoning an Acoustemological Pneumatology." *The Living Pulpit*. May 2015, http://www.pulpit.org/2015/05/.

————. *The Spirit of Creation: Modern Science and Divine Action in the Pentecostal-Charismatic Imagination*. Pentecostal Manifestos 4. Grand Rapids and Cambridge, UK: Eerdmans, 2011.

————. *Spirit of Love: A Trinitarian Theology of Grace*. Waco, TX: Baylor University Press, 2012.

————. "The Spirit Poured Out: A (Pentecostal) Perspective after Pentecost." In *Veni, Sancte Spiritus! Theologische Beiträge zur Sendung des Geistes/Contributions théologiques à la mission de l'Esprit/Theological Contributions to the Mission of the Spirit*, edited by Guido Vergauwen, OP, and Andreas Steinbruber, 198–210. Münster, Germany: Aschendorff Verlag, 2018.

————. "'To Him Who Loves Us and Freed Us from Our Sins by His Blood . . .': A Pentecostal Unveiling of Apocalyptic Love." In Charette and Waddell, *Spirit and Story: Pentecostal Readings of Scripture—Essays in Honor of John Christopher Thomas*, 117–34.

————. "Unveiling Interpretation after Pentecost: Revelation, Pentecostal Reading, and Christian Hermeneutics of Scripture—A Review Essay." *Journal of Theological Interpretation* 11:1 (2017): 139–55.

————. *Who Is the Holy Spirit? A Walk with the Apostles*. Brewster, MA: Paraclete, 2011.

————. "Yin-Yang and the Spirit Poured Out on All Flesh: An Evangelical Egalitarian East-West Dialogue on Gender and Race." *Priscilla Papers* 34:3 (2020): 21–26.

Yong, Amos, with Jonathan Anderson. *Renewing Christian Theology: Systematics for a Global Christianity*. Waco, TX: Baylor University Press, 2014.

Index of Ancient Sources

Index of Subjects

Aaron, 168, 252–53
Abaddon, 127, 207, 230
abominations, 206, 211
  practitioners of, 259–60
action/actions, 145, 176–78, 239
  exhortations to, 239
  good works, 239
  love, acts of, 133
  practitioners of abominations and
    deceptions, 259–60
  single acts vs. practices, 266
  speech-acts, angelic, 139, 153, 178,
    178n1, 181, 183, 192
  See also deeds
Adam and Eve, 157
adultery, 60–61. *See also* sexual
  immorality
affect/the affective, 18, 20, 32, 86
Africa, 3, 7
African American scholars, 5n11
agency, 261
Ahab, Jezebel as queen to. *See* Jezebel
Alexander the Great, 48
allegiance
  to Jesus, 56–57, 277–78
  See also nationalism; patriotism
Almighty, the, 27, 32–33, 149, 199,
  208n5, 219–20, 223, 226
  Lord God, 84–86, 88, 96, 147, 154,
    187, 189–90, 193–95, 215,
    255–56
  silence/reverence before, 116
Alpha and Omega, 27, 32, 244–45, 365

altar/altars, 86, 112, 117–19, 182, 188,
  193–94, 218n1, 233, 251
  golden, 104, 117–18, 130, 186
  heathen, 54
  heavenly, 104–9
  temple and, 141–42, 244
  See also incense
Amen, 91, 111, 194, 219, 272, 274–75
America
  present church in, 41
  See also Latin America; North
    America; United States
amillennialists, 234–35
angel/angels, 157
  of the bottomless pit, 127, 154
  bound, 130
  of the churches, 37–38, 42, 53
  fallen, 126, 230
  interpreting, 207
  with the little scroll, 135–40
  Michael, archangel, 156–57
  mighty, 135–40, 151, 212n2
  seven angelic messages, 178–84
  three, 124, 178–81
  twelve, 251, 253
angels, seven, 25, 35, 38, 69, 116–17,
  187, 200, 220, 249
  with seven plagues, 189–90
  speech-acts, 139, 153, 178, 181, 183,
    192
animals, 126n3
anthropology, 20n43
Antichrist, 93, 171

309